THE I TATTI
RENAISSANCE LIBRARY

James Hankins, General Editor

FRANCESCO FILELFO

ODES

ITRL 41

FRANCESCO FILELFO

• • •

ODES

EDITED AND TRANSLATED BY

DIANA ROBIN

THE I TATTI RENAISSANCE LIBRARY
HARVARD UNIVERSITY PRESS
CAMBRIDGE, MASSACHUSETTS
LONDON, ENGLAND
2009

Series design by Dean Bornstein

Library of Congress Cataloging-in-Publication Data
Filelfo, Francesco, 1398–1481.
[Poems. English & Latin.]
Odes / Francesco Filelfo ; edited and
translated by Diana Robin.
p.   cm. — (The I Tatti Renaissance library ; 41)
Latin text with English translation;
introduction and notes in English.
Includes bibliographical references and index.
ISBN 978-0-674-03563-8 (alk. paper)
1. Filelfo, Francesco, 1398–1481 — Translations into English.
2. Odes, Latin (Medieval and modern) — Translations in English.
I. Robin, Diana Maury.   II. Title.
PA8520.F5A2 2009
874′.03 — dc22   2009030647

Contents

❦❦❦

THALIA: BOOK IV

MELPOMENE: BOOK V

· CONTENTS ·

Introduction

കൈനൈ

Francesco Filelfo was born on July 25, 1398, in Tolentino, a town in the Marche some thirty miles from the Adriatic sea.[1] Among the thousands of autobiographical letters he wrote, Filelfo left no trace of his childhood, nor is anything known of his family history.[2] When he was sixteen he left Tolentino to study law and rhetoric with Gasparino Barzizza at the University of Padua. The friendships he forged at Padua with the sons of Venetian patricians led in 1420 to an invitation to travel with the Venetian delegation to the court of the emperor John VIII Paleologus in Constantinople.[3]

It was this journey to the distant Greek capital that would change Filelfo's life. Once in the city called the New Rome, he embarked on the study of ancient Greek with the famed scholar John Chrysoloras. At the same time he began to buy Greek manuscripts of the storied ancient authors known only by name in the West: the historians Herodotus, Thucydides, Xenophon, and Plutarch; the poets Homer, Theocritus, Callimachus, and the tragedian Euripides; the orators Lysias, Demosthenes and Aeschines; and the philosophers Plato, Aristotle, Proclus and Plotinus, among many others.[4] At the same time, Filelfo's sojourn in Constantinople signaled the beginning of his career as a diplomat. Serving as an envoy to the Byzantine emperor during the years 1422–1424, Filelfo visited the courts of King Sigismund of Hungary, King Ladislaus of Poland, and the Ottoman Turkish ruler Murad II. After seven years in Greece, Filelfo returned to Venice in 1427 to found a humanist school in that city where Greek and Latin would both be taught. He brought with him his Greek wife Teodora Chrysoloras, the emperor's grandniece, and the couple's one-year-old son Gian Mario, who would ultimately follow in his father's footsteps as a writer and scholar.[5] Filelfo and his family remained less than a year in Venice, where they spent a miserable period confined to their lodgings, since the plague was then raging in that city and the surrounding towns and villages.

The following year Filelfo left Venice to teach at the University of Bologna. Fleeing the civil war that broke out in that city, in 1429 he moved on to Florence where he was appointed to the Chair of Greek at the university, a position previously held by Guarino da Verona. He was wildly popular among students and colleagues, and hundreds of Florentines packed the lecture halls to hear the charismatic young chair of Greek studies hold forth on Philostratus' *Imagines* and Aratus' *Phaenomena*.[6] But five years after his arrival in the city, caught up in the crossfire between rival political factions, Filelfo was forced to realize that he and his family would have to pull up stakes again and seek a more secure appointment. When an assassin believed to be in the employ of the Medici ambushed him as he made his way to the university, stabbing him in the face, Filelfo resigned from his post at the Studio and left Florence.[7]

Filelfo taught briefly at the universities of Siena in 1435 and Bologna in 1439. That year he was called to Milan by Filippo Maria Visconti, the lord of the duchy, who named him court poet and professor of rhetoric at the University of Pavia. In 1447, Visconti died, and a coalition of men of all ranks, including the lowest guildsmen, formed a popular government they called the Ambrosian Republic. Within a year of the constitution of the Republic, civil war broke out. Outside the city, Venice and the captains hired by the Ambrosian Republic engaged in a series of wars for control of the duchy and its client cities.

In 1448 Francesco Sforza, husband of Visconti's daughter Bianca Maria and the Republic's most successful general, defected to Venice. Breaking with Venice the following year, Sforza set about to pressure Milan into submitting to him. He cordoned off the city's gates, effectively prohibiting the flow of goods in and out of Milan for thirteen months. In the midst of the famine that ensued, the Milanese overthrew the captains of the Republic in a bloody coup and opened their gates to Sforza. A year later, plague broke out in the city, and some thirty thousand Milanese, survivors of civil war and famine, now died and their corpses lay rotting in the streets. From inside the city, Filelfo wrote,

> Nunc vagor in tenebris; nec quae via certa salutis
> sit capiunda mihi, Karole, nosse queo.
> Pestis cuncta premit, vorat atque ingurgitat horrens
> omnem animam. Perit en vir, puer atque senex. (3.9.19–22)

Now I wander in the darkness, nor, Carlo, am I able to know what road I should take to safety. The plague hangs heavy over everything. Bristling as it goes, it devours and guzzles every soul. Look there, a boy, a man in his prime, and an old man have died.

When Francesco Sforza entered the city and was officially consecrated as its fourth duke in March 1450, Filelfo resumed his duties under the new sovereign as court poet and university professor at Pavia. The first seven years after the restoration of the monarchy in Milan marked Filelfo's most productive period yet. But when the wars between Sforza and Venice and their respective allies continued and Filelfo did not receive the stipend he had been promised, he looked to other courts for support. Having begun to revise his collected Latin letters for publication,[8] in 1453 he traveled to Rome, where he was received by Pope Nicholas V (Tommaso Parentucelli), an old friend from his early years at the University of Bologna.

That summer Filelfo spent the month of August in Naples at the court of King Alfonso I, to whom he brought the gift of a new poetry collection he had composed: a hundred poems set in Latin hexameters, entitled *Satyrae*. At the same time he had begun work on a heroic epic poem, the *Sforziad*. But this was a work that mocked rather than flattered his patron in Milan.[9]

From the 1460s on Filelfo turned increasingly to the Greek studies of his early years, immersing himself again not only in the ancient Greek philosophers, poets and playwrights but also in his friendships with the many scholar refugees who had fled to Italy in the wake of the Turkish occupation of Greece and the fall of Constantinople. After completing a major collection of Latin epigrams, *De iocis et seriis*, in 1465, Filelfo put the finishing touches on his *Psychagogia*, a work of forty-four Greek poems in elegiac and Sapphic meters, dedicated to Cardinal Bessarion, then the émigré dean of Greek studies in Italy.[10] Filelfo next began work on his *De morali disciplina* (On Moral Doctrine), a treatise in which he discussed the ethics and metaphysics of Aristotle, Plato's theory of forms, and the theories of the soul of Pythagoras, Plato, Epicurus, Democritus, and the Stoics.[11] The following year he received an invitation from Pope Sixtus IV to lecture on his new philosophical work at the Studio in Rome.

It was some years after the assassination of the young duke of Milan, Galeazzo Maria Sforza, in December 1476, that Filelfo resolved to leave the city he had called home for over forty years. But life had become increasingly precarious in the Lombard capital. In 1480, Filelfo's longtime friend Cicco Simonetta, the seventy-year-old civil servant and chancellor under Galeazzo Maria Sforza, was condemned to death and decapitated by Lodovico Sforza.[12] Long supported by Lorenzo de' Medici, Filelfo left Milan in July 1481 to occupy the chair of Greek at the Studio in Florence, now the center for Platonic studies in Europe.

On July 31, two weeks after his arrival in Florence, Filelfo died. Only days before his death, he had celebrated his eighty-third birthday in the city where, a half-century earlier, hundreds of students had filled the main lecture hall at the university to hear him.

Patronage and the Odes

The instability of the popular republic that seized power after Visconti's death and the subsequent eruption of civil war in Milan had made it impossible for the poet to support himself and his family after 1448. As Filelfo commented in *Odes* 1.10, with men in power who had no interest in the liberal arts, the Muses were no longer revered. In desperation, Filelfo sent encomiastic poems and letters to a number of heads of state both in Italy and France — men he hoped might offer him a position at court. Among the patrons he approached during the reign of the Ambrosian Republic were King Charles VII of France; King Alfonso I of Naples; Sigismondo Malatesta, lord of Rimini; Malatesta Novello, lord of Cesena; Carlo Gonzaga, the younger brother of the lord of Mantua who aspired to become lord of Milan himself; and Francesco Sforza himself, who after the fall of the Republic became duke of Milan and the poet's primary protector. Still, Filelfo reserved his most florid encomia for King Charles, from whom he hoped to obtain an invitation to the French court and with whose chancellor Guillaume Jouvenel des Ursins and personal physician Thomas Coroneus he exchanged no less than eighteen letters during the years 1454–55.[13] Second among the prospective patrons on whom Filelfo lavished the highest praise in the *Odes* was King Alfonso, in whose cultivated court the poet imagined he might find a safe haven.

Structure and Themes of the Odes

Filelfo would not complete his most challenging work, his *Odae* or *Carmina varia*, an experimental work of fifty poems in all Horace's lyric modes and meters, until late 1455 or early 1456. Filelfo's *Odes* represent his attempt not only to revive but to synthesize the three great poetic traditions inaugurated during the reign of Augustus: first, that of Virgil's *Aeneid,* whose themes were war, exile, and the founding of a just and enduring state; second, that of Horace's *Carmina,* a work of 103 poems in a variety of lyric meters addressed to friends, patrons, and lovers; and third, that of Roman elegy, exemplified by Ovid's *Amores,* the *Ars amatoria,* and the *Heroides* — poems that offered advice, counseling, and cautionary tales for lovers.

Filelfo's *Odes* differ from his classical models in that his large-scale lyric work constitutes a personal epic. These lyric works — some more than two hundred lines in length, others as short as twenty lines — chronicle the poet's experience from the death of Visconti, the founding of the Ambrosian Republic, the civil war, and the postwar famine and plague, to his own attempts after the restoration of the monarchy in Milan to flee to France or Naples, where he hoped to find protection either under Charles VII or King Alfonso I.

Filelfo's *Odes,* like his massive Ciceronian letterbook, constitute a panoramic epistolary memoir. As in his prose *Epistolae familiares,* Filelfo's verse epistles are addressed to a cast of characters we come to know, with the picaresque hero (the poet himself) poised always at the center of the narrative. The autobiographical plotline of the *Odes* — Filelfo's search for both fame and security for himself and his family — is fleshed out with numerous subplots and digressions. The *Odes* are arranged with an eye to thematic balance, repetition, and variation. Ring composition, symmetry, and artistic unity are produced in this sprawling work through the placement of topically related poems at the beginnings and conclusions of each of the five books, which serve as frames or bookends. At the same time variety is maintained in this somewhat repetitive ensemble of lyric poems through the ordering of the pieces for both thematic and metrical contrast.

Book 1: The Program for the Odes

The theme of praise for the model prince is dominant in all five books of the *Odes*. *Odes* 1.1 and 5.1, both encomia for Charles VII of France,[14] stand as a frame for the fifty odes, placed strategically at the opening and close of the collection. Book 1 serves as the program for all five books of the *Odes*. Here the principal themes for the rest of the collection are introduced: the portrait of the *princeps* who will restore peace and the rule of law (1.1; 1.4); the condemnation of war and its horrors, civil war in particular (1.2; 1.10); the incompatibility of poetry and the Muses with mob rule (1.2; 1.10); the conflicting demands of sexual desire, marriage, and the life of the mind (1.9); praises for the generosity of patrons of literature and the arts (1.3); the problem of wealth, which drives men to war and corrupts the republic, yet without which poetry and the arts cannot survive (1.10); criticism of the "false freedom" promised by the Ambrosian Republic (1.10; 1.2; 1.5); the character-ization of the leaders of the Republic and its followers as the dregs of society who are, according to the poet, incompetent, ignorant, easily intimidated and just as easily whipped into a frenzy, insane or chronically drunk (*plebs iners et ignava, vulgus ineptum, populus trepidus, furens, rabidus, insanus, bibulus, ebrius*, 1.3; 1.5; 1.10).

Filelfo does not disapprove either of republican government per se or of the Milanese citizens' decision to constitute the post-Visconti regime as a republic, which he refers to in neutral terms as *haec respublica* (1.10.95). What he does condemn, however, is the specious freedom espoused by the Ambrosian republic (*ficta libertas, libertas simulata*) and the greed of its leaders who pander to the uneducated "plebs." The only key theme in the *Odae* that Filelfo does not introduce in Book 1 explicitly is that of the plague, though the suggestion of pestilence in the city and the portrayal of the Republic as malfunctioning and diseased is ubiquitous even in this first book. In the shortest ode in Book 1, Filelfo describes a pathology that is the product not only of gluttony and sexual excess but political corruption: the man with gout is a "fickle whisperer" who lies to the people and "plays the accomplice to depravity" (1.8.24–25).

Book 2: War and the Tyranny of Plebeian Rule

The figure of Carlo Gonzaga,[15] who is portrayed in *Odes* 2.1, casts a long shadow over Books 3 and 5. Elected captain of the Ambrosian Republic in 1448, Carlo remained one of the city's chief military leaders and political advisors until Sforza's accession to the throne. *Odes* 2.1, which celebrates the mythological origins of the Gonzaga dynasty in Mantua and portrays Carlo Gonzaga as the model prince, makes it clear that Filelfo had at one time championed Gonzaga's ascent to the Milanese signory. Though Filelfo dedicated more odes to the republican captain from Mantua than any other figure in the *Carmina*, this book is informed by Filelfo's commentary on the corruption of the Ambrosian Republic, his condemnation of its leaders, and his celebration of their expulsion and the restoration of the monarchy in Milan (2.1; 2.3; 2.4; 2.10).

Odes 2.6, a poem to King Alfonso's chamberlain Iñigo d'Avalos in Naples, which offers advice on love-making to the king's mistress, Lucrezia d'Alagno, as well as to Iñigo and the aging king himself, recalls Filelfo's dialogue with Venus in *Odes* 1.9. This first of the Naples-oriented poems in the *Odes* also provides a bridge to the several poems addressed to King Alfonso and Iñigo that inform Books 3, 4, and 5, while they pave the way for Filelfo's visit to Alfonso's court in 1453.

In the middle of book two, a trio of very short verse epistles to friends, two of them consolatory, provide relief from Filelfo's constant drumbeat against the political corruption of the Republic and the tragedy of war.

Book 3: Love and Marriage

Beginning *in medias res*, Book 3 of the *Odes* shows Filelfo, as protagonist and narrator, poised in thought between Milan, France, and Naples. In the opening encomium (3.1), addressed to King Charles VII, the Muse Euterpe reprises the narrative from *Odes* 1.1 of the king's expulsion of the English from France at the end of the Hundred Years War. Euterpe's account in *Odes* 3.1 of Charles' ridding France of its "rabid tyrants" (*rabidi tyranni*) and "Gaul's having finally learned to obey the laws of its king" provides a historical analogy with linguistic resonances for the depiction in *Odes* 3.4 of Francesco Sforza's victory over the "rabid tyrants" of the Ambrosian Republic, his ending of the civil war, and his entry into Milan as the city's rightful sovereign and duke.

In a subplot, two poems addressed to Carlo Gonzaga form an inner frame for this book. In *Odes* 3.2, Filelfo eulogizes Carlo as he lies on his deathbed, an apparent victim of the same plague that would soon ravage Milan, while at the book's end the poet bitterly castigates Carlo, who, restored to health, has defected to Venice, a traitor because he has abandoned both Filelfo, his friend and dependent, and his lover Lyda, presumably to face the plague on their own (3.9). Two poems in the center of this book, 3.6 and 3.7, offer short comic epithalamia in which Filelfo urges Sforza Secundo in somewhat crude terms to make love to his new bride, by force if necessary.

Another pair of poems addressed to Iñigo d'Avalos (3.3 and 3.10) suggests yet another inner frame for book three. Both poems set the stage for Filelfo's visit to Naples, and both deal with amatory themes. The first of these poems to Iñigo encloses within it a satirical verse epistle addressed to the king's mistress Lucrezia which advises her in sexually suggestive language how to keep the king interested. The second poem in this framing pair, which is the closing piece in Book 3, ends with questions posed in rustic

terms about Iñigo's and the king's current love affairs, while allud-
ing to Filelfo's own struggle with "the fiery arrows of Venus"
(3.10.164–6). In this final epistle, Filelfo gives Iñigo a detailed ac-
count of the mass deaths and devastation wrought by the plague
in Milan and explains why his journey to Naples must again be
deferred.

Book 4: The Plague, Escape from Milan, and the Problem of Money

The interlocking themes of the plague's ravaging of Milan and
Filelfo's desperate need for money in order to leave the city shape
and darken book four. Yet at the same time the poet's warnings
about the ultimate futility of money and his excoriation of men's
ensorcellment with gold are threaded throughout the book.

The poems in this book, too, are arranged thematically in a
modified ring structure. The opening pair of poems and closing
trio of pieces deal with one theme: Filelfo's efforts to get out of
Milan. In Odes 4.1 and 4.2 Filelfo urgently presses, first, the duke's
wife Bianca Maria Sforza and then his ducal treasurer Cicco
Simonetta for money for his family's flight to a safer port. As if to
counter the poet's petitions to leave Milan, the three poems posi-
tioned at the end of book four, 4.8, 4.9, and 4.10, which address
his future hosts in Naples, King Alfonso and his courtier Iñigo
d'Avalos, argue that the war the king is fighting will not only fail
to bring security either to Naples or Milan but will prevent the
poet from traveling to the Aragonese city.

The five poems inside Filelfo's escape-themed frame offer a var-
ied commentary on money. While the poet targets a character
named Lydus for his all-consuming greed for money and material
things in Odes 4.3, a central block of three poems (4.5, 4.6, 4.7)
demonstrates the futility of money and patronage. Odes 4.5 pres-
ents a kaleidoscopic travel narrative of Filelfo's escape with his
family from Milan by wagon-train and boat to the supposedly safe

port of Cremona—only to find en route that the Cremonese, fearing contagion, will not take their money. Filelfo's commentary on money ends with an odd pair of poems: first, a long-winded, high-minded essay addressed to his longtime friend and fellow humanist Leon Battista Alberti on the futility of wealth (4.6); and second, a twenty-two-line satire in which Filelfo depicts the by-products of what he sees as a modern obsession with easy money: the gaming, whoring, and pimping that thrive in Cremona (4.7).

Book 5: The Peacemakers

The structure of Book 5, whose overriding theme is the hope for peace between the great powers in Italy in the face of the Turkish threat from the east, again suggests a modified ring symmetry. The first four poems of the book reprise the dedicatees, cameo profiles, and themes from the previous four books, while the second half of the book, with the exception of ode 5.9, introduces new characters. The opening encomium to Charles VII (5.1) recalls the inaugural ode in the collection, which summons the French king, now that he has driven the English from the continent, to expel the Turks from the walls of Constantinople, here styled as "Thracian Rome" (5.1.68–69). The next three poems, Odes 5.2, 5.3, and 5.4, import three dedicatees from the earlier books—King Alfonso, Sforza Secondo, and Carlo Gonzaga—into book five, recasting them in new dramatic situations.

The concluding five pieces in the Odae bring six new characters into play. These closing works address the current pope, Nicholas V (5.5); Filelfo's son Gian Mario (5.6); Basinio Basini, court poet of Sigismondo Malatesta, lord of Rimini (5.7); Giovanni Simonetta, secretary of Sforza's privy chancery (5.8); Lodovico Gonzaga, lord of Mantua (5.9); and Malatesta Novello, Lord of Cesena (5.10). This last movement in the Odes looks both retrospectively back upon the courts Filelfo had visited on his journey south — Mantua, Urbino, Cesena, Rome and Naples — and forward to the Peace of Lodi, which Alfonso refused to sign when it was first concluded between Milan, Venice, and Florence in 1454, but which he formally endorsed in 1455. In *Odes* 5.9, a paean of praise for King Alfonso, Lodovico Gonzaga, and Francesco Sforza, Filelfo assigns the principal speaking part to Alfonso, making him the peace-maker and mediator between Lodovico and Sforza. Like many if not most of the poems in the *Carmina*, this piece appears to have been written before Filelfo's journey to Naples and later revised. The final encomium (5.10) in the collection addresses Malatesta Novello and presents a dialogue of the gods in which Mercury, upon receiving his marching orders from Jove, instructs the gods to bring peace to earth.

Poetics in Fifteenth-Century Italy

Filelfo seems never to have advertised himself as a lyric poet until 1455. On July 16, 1456, he wrote King Alfonso's orator in Naples, Antonio Beccadelli (known as "Panormita" from his birthplace, Palermo), announcing that he had just finished composing five books of *Odae*, a collection of poems "set in every possible meter."[16] This was no small claim. It is true that the ancient theorists of Latin prosody, Servius, Porphyrion, and Pseudo-Acron, and the great Latin lyric poets Horace, Martial, Ausonius, Claudian, Prudentius, and Boethius, remained widely known throughout the Middle Ages. Yet the most prominent of the fifteenth-century Latin poets prior to 1470 — Enea Silvio Piccolomini, Giovanni Marrasio, Cristoforo Landino, Basinio Basini, Tito Vespasiano Strozzi, Giovannantonio Campano, Battista Spagnoli, and Beccadelli himself — wrote solely in hexameters and elegiacs, not in lyric meters. Latin lyric poetry appears to have been reborn in the work of Giovanni Pontano, a leading figure in the literary circle around King Alfonso at the time of Filelfo's sojourn in Naples.

Pontano was already composing in Phalaecean hendecasyllables and Sapphic strophes in the early 1450s.[17] That Filelfo first began to experiment with lyric meters soon after his return from Naples was surely the result of his exposure to Pontano's work in the summer of 1453. Filelfo's *Odes* thus represent the first work of Latin poetry in the Renaissance to feature all the lyric meters of Horace's *Carmina*, making Filelfo one of the great poetic innovators in the history of Neo-Latin literature.

I want to thank my first reader for the press, John Grant, for a thorough combing-through and correction of my Latin text and translation; without his profound knowledge of classical Latin literature, grammar, and prosody, my many and varied errors would have slipped under the radar undetected. Next I owe an enormous debt to the Associate Editor of the ITRL, Shane Butler, whose classicist's eagle-eye still spotted errors of translation, punctuation, and accentuation (in the Greek). I also have him to thank for his Sisyphean shaping of the complex of systems contained in this volume — the translation, Latin text, appendices, and apparatus — into a comprehensive whole. I would also like to thank Paul Gehl and Paul Saenger of the Newberry Library for their support of this work and their continued efforts to add to the Library's already prodigious trove of early printed editions of Filelfo's works. I am especially grateful to Paul Gehl for his assistance in my reading of the Newberry's rare fifteenth-century manuscript of the *Odes*. Finally, I would like to express my gratitude to the editor-in-chief of the ITRL, James Hankins, for recruiting this monument of Quattrocento Renaissance literature for Harvard University Press, and for publishing not only the first complete Latin text of Filelfo's *Odes* since 1497, but also the first English translation of the work by a poet who is said, by historians of our own time as well as his own, to have been the cultural dictator of Milan.

Notes

1. Carlo de' Rosmini, *Vita di Francesco Filelfo da Tolentino*, 3 vols. (Milan: Luigi Mussi, 1808); Diana Robin, *Filelfo in Milan: Writings, 1451–1477* (Princeton: Princeton University Press, 1991); Rudolf Georg Adam, *Francesco Filelfo at the Court of Milan: A Contribution to the Study of Humanism in Northern Italy (1439–1481)* (Ph. D. Dissertation, Oxford University, 1974).

2. Francesco Filelfo, *Epistolarum familiarium libri XXXVII* (Venice: De Gregoriis, 1502; hereafter *Epistolae*) is the most complete of the published editions of his Latin letters; 41 early printed editions of the Latin letters are known. Émile Legrand, *Cent-dix lettres grecques de François Filelfe* (Paris: E. Leroux, 1892) published a selection of Filelfo's Greek letters. The most complete manuscript, containing 48 books of Filelfo's Greek and Latin letters, is held in the Biblioteca Trivulziana in Milan, cod. 873.

3. John was emperor of the Eastern Roman Empire, 1425–1448.

4. The list of books Filelfo brought back to Italy from Constantinople is contained in part in Remigio Sabbadini, *Le scoperte dei codici latini e greci ne' secoli XIV e XV*. 2 vols. (Florence: Sansoni, 1905), vol. 1, p. 48; the whole list is given in *Ambrosii Traversarii . . . aliorumque ad ipsum, et ad alios de eodem Ambrosio latinae epistolae*, ed. Petrus Cannetus, 2 vols. (Florence, 1759), p. 1010 (Book 24, Letter 32). Sabbadini, *Le scoperte*, vol. 2, pp. 43–55, notes that the first Italian humanist to sojourn in Constantinople, Giovanni Aurispa, brought back over two hundred Greek codices to Italy in 1423. On his book collection see Aurispa, *Il carteggio di Giovanni Aurispa*, ed. R. Sabbadini (Rome: Istituto Storico Italiano, 1931) and more recently, Adriano Franceschini, *Giovanni Aurispa e la sua biblioteca: notizie e documenti* (Padua: Antenore, 1976).

5. Teodora died on May 3, 1441; she bore him two sons and two daughters. In 1442 Filelfo married the Milanese noblewoman Orsina Osnaga, who bore him one son and three daughters. In 1453 or 1454 he married the Milanese noblewoman Laura Maggiolini, who bore him two daughters and three sons; she died in 1476.

6. These two authors are also included in Filelfo's list of the codices he brought back to Italy from Greece; see his letter to Traversari cited in n. 4 above.

7. On the conflicting accounts Filelfo himself issued on what he believed was an assassination attempt see Robin, *Filelfo in Milan*, pp. 17–22.

8. See Robin, *Filelfo in Milan*, p. 11; and Filelfo, *Epistolae*, letter to Ceba, f. 62v, in which Filelfo requests that Ceba return his letters so that he can include them in his forthcoming *epistolae familiares*.

9. See the detailed analysis of *Sforziad* 3 in *Filelfo in Milan*, pp. 56–81.

10. Diana Robin, "Unknown Greek Poems of Francesco Filelfo," *Renaissance Quarterly* 37 (1984): 173–206, contains synopses of all 44 poems and a translation and commentary on two of the poems.

11. Robin, *Filelfo in Milan*, pp. 138–66, contains an analysis and discussion of Book 1 of the *De morali disciplina*.

12. See Evelyn S. Welch, *Art and Authority in Renaissance Milan* (New Haven: Yale University Press, 1995), pp. 218–19, 221, on Cicco's arrest, torture, and execution. Ludovico Sforza at the time had not yet acceded to the duchy but had arrived in Milan in 1479 and seized the reins of power by fiat.

13. For the location of those letters see Robin, *Filelfo in Milan*, p. 84; Filelfo, *Epistolae*, ff. 85, 89–89v, 93–96v; see also Legrand, *Lettres*, pp. 75–76.

14. A brief bio-bibliography for all the principal characters in the *Odes* is provided in the Biographical Notes at the end of this volume.

15. See the Biographical Notes.

16. Filelfo, *Epistolae*, f. 95: *Scribo etiam odas, quae nostri nominant 'carmina.' Eruntque decemmillia versuum in omni metrorum genere; aeduntur ab me in praesentia libri quinque eius operis, quos ipse ad Karolum Regem Francorum mecum sum advecturus.* . . .

17. Erasmo Percopo, "La vita di Giovanni Pontano," *Archivio storico per le provincie napoletane* 61 (1936): 116–250.

ODES

Praefatio in libros carminum[1]

Franciscus, Francisce, tuus tibi, Sphortia, vates
    principe te digna dona Philelfus agit.
Hic est ille dies quo rex hominumque deumque
    illuxit terris virque deusque simul.
5   Hic est ille dies quo Christus dona salutis
    in genus humanum contulit exoriens.
Hoc igitur, Francisce, die donare poeta
    te tuus iis pergit, quae tibi grata putat.
Non tibi fert aurum, non gemmas, munera nulla,
10   quae Fortuna suo vindicet imperio.
Quicquid habet tempus, perit id cum tempore tandem.
    Hinc fortuna diu nulla manere potest.
Thesauros Croesi tantos brevis abstulit hora.
    Sic et opes Crassi divitiasque Midae.
15   Assyrios Medi fastus ducis ira subegit,
    at Medos Cyrus, Persida rex Macedum.
Romulidas totus dominos quos horruit orbis,
    non gens una probris contudit innumeris.
Munera nulla quidem tibi nunc, dux inclyte, dantur
20   tempore quae ducas interitura brevi.
Sed fidei documenta piae cultique benignus
    collectas fruges accipis ingenii.
Nam quae celsa canunt citharam dum pulsat Apollo
    carmina Pierides, haec tibi dona legis.
25   Iudice nam Phoebo diae celebrare sorores
    res laetantur eas quas fugit interitus
laudibus illustres. Quibus haec extollitur aetas
    per virtutis opus in cumulum referunt.
Laudantur proceres, reges laudantur, et altis
30   ornantur titulis ob bene gesta duces.

Preface to the Odes

Your poet Francesco Filelfo honors you, Francesco Sforza,[1] with gifts worthy of your rank. This is the day when the king of gods and men, himself both god and man, made his light shine on earth; this is the day when Christ was born and brought salvation to mankind. On this day, Francesco, your poet gives to you those 5 gifts he believes will please you. He offers you no gold or gems, nor the prizes that Fortune claims for her empire. For whatever 10 exists in time will die in time: thus good fortune never lasts for long. Croesus lost his great wealth quickly. So too Crassus lost his riches and Midas his gold. The anger of the Median king crushed the Assyrians' pride, but Cyrus subdued the Medes, and the king 15 of the Macedonians conquered Persia.[2] The whole world quaked before the sons of Romulus as its masters, but many a tribe crushed them with countless outrages. Thus you are honored with no worldly prizes, Illustrious Duke, since you know they will soon perish. 20

But since you are kind you will receive the teachings of the sacred lyre and the fruits harvested from a learned mind. For when Apollo strikes his lyre and the Pierian Muses sing their sublime melodies, you gather these gifts for yourself. For with Phoebus as judge, the divine sisters gladly hymn the deeds made famous by 25 their paeans, deeds that will live forever. And they bring to a pinnacle those deeds by which an age is exalted through its practice of virtue. Leading men and kings are praised and princes honored with high titles because of their lofty deeds. Among these men 30

Nobilis hos inter miris tua Sphortia virtus
    emicat auguriis sydera summa petens.
Non Fortuna tui laudem sibi vindicat ullam,
    quae probitate tibi cedit ubique tua.
35   Non aliunde quidem quam ex te, dux optime, pendes,
    hoc externa ratus inferiora bono.
Sola tuum virtus medio tibi nomen in orbe
    fixit, fortunam quae iubet esse suam.
Quis putet exilium nudo doluisse Bianti,
40   qui bona, dum fugeret propria, quaeque tulit?
Num sua quis ducat quaevis non una repente
    auferat invito sollicitumve premat?
Solus es indomitus, vitio qui liber ab omni
    nil pluris facias quam bene facta sequi.
45   Tu bene res gestas bene gestis rebus in omnem
    prosequeris vitam. Nil tibi turpe placet.
Ii tibi sunt mores, qualis in principe summo
    esse decet. Nulla te capit ambitio.
Quoque gradu superas alios magis unius[2] honoris,
50   hoc duce virtute te geris inferius.
Felicem se quisque putat, cui cominus uti
    contigit aspectu colloquioque tuo.
Fronte hilaris, vultuque gravis, verboque modestus
    omnibus unus ades. Quis duce te melior?
55   Non te fastus habet. Facilem maiorque minorque
    sentit, teque nihil mitius esse videt.
Nec tibi grata minus mens est quam iusta, rependens
    qui sua des cuique, qui meruisse velis.
Quantus es in dando, te munificentia carum
60   iucundumque facit regibus et populis.
O nos felices iterumque iterumque beatos,
    qui ductu regimur auspiciisque tuis.

your noble Sforzan virtue gleams and seeks the highest stars in a wondrous prophecy. Nor does Fortune win any of your glory for herself, but everywhere she defers to your goodness. Nor do you depend on anything other than yourself, O best leader, believing 35 that all external things are inferior to this good. Only Virtue plants your name in the middle of the world; it is Virtue who commands Fortune to be her slave. Who would think that exile would sadden naked Bias,[3] who, when he abandoned his own possessions, took with him everything that was good? Should any- 40 one really regard as his own whatever he cannot carry off with him, on short notice and under constraint? Or something that plagues him with worry? You alone are supreme and because you are free of all vice, you value nothing more highly than pursuing the good. You follow up your noble actions with other noble ac- tions for all of your life. Nothing shameful pleases you. These are 45 your customs, as befits the highest prince: you are immune to the struggle for rank; the more you surpass other men in the loftiness of your title, the more humbly do you act, since Virtue is your leader.[4] Whoever is able to enjoy being in your presence and 50 speaking with you considers himself fortunate: with your cheerful brow, serious expression, and modest conversation, you are the same to one and all. Who surpasses you as a prince? No arrogance marks you. You are easy with both greater and inferior men who 55 know no one more gentle than you. You are both generous and fair-minded: you are the kind of man who gives to each his due and who wishes to be just. As great as you are in giving, your mag- nanimity makes you beloved to both kings and people alike. 60

O blessed and fortunate again and again are we who are ruled under your auspices and leadership. Why would any who follow

5

Exemplum, Francisce, tuum quicunque sequuntur,
   hi sibi quid dubitent omnia laeta fore?
65   Flagitium vitam solum mortalibus aegram
   reddit et aeternas mox agit in tenebras.
At pietate homini paritur cum certa voluptas
   luce sub hac fragili: tum fit in astra via.
70   Hinc tu cuncta bono moetitus laeta superno,
   relligione nihil esse putas melius.
Hanc noctesque diesque colis. Tibi semper in ore
   est 'Pater omnipotens,' quo duce cuncta facis.
Hunc unum esse putas ad quem mens omnis et omne
75   debeat humanum tendere consilium.
Non igitur mirum tibi si deus optimus uni
   semper adest, alacer si tua vota fovet.
Hic tibi tam claros tam multos saepe triumphos
   ob pietatis opus imperiumque dedit.
80   Id dedit imperium, quo nullum pulchrius usque
   Delius ex orbe spectat Olympiaco.
Hunc igitur proceres, regesque ducesque secuti
   magna suis rebus emolumenta dabunt.
Non sine mente dei, quem virtus aurea flectit
85   et pietatis honos, Sphortia, tanta geris.
Qui mortalis enim nullis prope viribus omnes
   fudisset vires nobilis Italiae?
Et reges cessere tibi, cessere catervae,
   florentesque urbes colla dedere iugo.
90   Quamquam pulchra tibi laus est quod viceris hostem,
   quisquis sponte furens impia bella tulit,
pulchrior illa tamen longeque illustrior omnes
   quod tibi devinctos iungis amore pio.
Non hominis magis esse reor quam mente carentis
95   immanisque ferae vincere posse alios.

6

your example doubt, Francesco, that all will go well for them-
selves? Wrongdoing alone renders life wretched for humankind
and soon it dispatches us to eternal gloom. But not only does piety   65
bring assured pleasure to mankind in this fragile world: it is the
road to the stars. Thus in measuring all happiness in terms of the
sublime good, you think that nothing is better than worship and   70
you practice it night and day. The words "father omnipotent" are
always on your lips and with him as your guide, you do all things.
You believe he is the only one on whom all minds and human
plans must depend. Thus it is no wonder that the great god is al-   75
ways present with you alone, and that your prayer quickly finds fa-
vor with him: it is because of the work and power of your piety
that he has given you so many brilliant victories.

   He gave you that power, in comparison to which Delian Apollo   80
looks down from the Olympian world on nothing more beautiful.
Therefore when princes, kings, and worldly leaders follow him,
they will earn great profit for their realms. For not without the
mind of god, which golden virtue and glorious piety move, would
you accomplish so many great deeds, O Sforza. For what mortal   85
man could have brought down all the might of noble Italy with al-
most no military strength? Kings have bowed to you, mobs have
bowed to you, and flourishing cities have placed their necks in
your yoke. Although beautiful praise is yours because you have
conquered the enemy, no matter which madman launched unjust   90
wars of his own accord, still more beautiful and brilliant is your
fame for having bound all men to you with chains of pious love. I
believe it is as much in the nature of human beings to be able to
conquer other men as it is in that of wild and irrational beasts to   95

Sed qui se victor cohibet, nec frangitur ira,
　　iure vir egregius ille vocandus erit.
Quin imitaris eum, qui pacis foedera secum
　　attulit exoriens lampade noctifuga.
100　Ut tenebras Christus, quas dira errata parentum
　　intulerant terris, sustulit adveniens
sic pius Italiam ferro flamisque ruentem
　　efficis incolumem iusticiae radiis.
Omnibus ignoscis, cunctos tibi reddis amicos,
105　　devinctosque facis officio vel ope.
Tu solus, Francisce, potes cohibere furorem
　　et revocare citum. Fortis es ac sapiens.
Te duce felici iam pax celebratur ubique:
　　undique bella silent; ferreus ensis hebet.
110　Iam metus omnis abest. Adeunt te, Sphortia, reges,
　　pontificesque tua constituuntur ope.
Quis tibi millenos non exoptaverit annos,
　　cuius sit vita, vita decusque bonis?
O superi, servate virum, quem saecula tantum
115　　nec ventura dabunt, nec genuere prius.
Insubrium regno quam longa in pace fruatur.
　　Sitque diu voto laetitiaeque suis.
Huic flama coniuncta pari expectata senectae
　　tempora longaevae Blanca videre queat.
120　Blanca inter cunctas mulieres floret, ut astra
　　inter luna micat, cum magis orbe nitet.
Haec adeo forma splendet speciosa virago,
　　ut sibi Pandoram cedere cogat Hera.
Namque pudicitia studeat superare Dianam
125　　ingeniique bono praestet, Athena, tibi.
Aspicite, o proceres, faciat qua prole beatum
　　Blanca virum. Pueros aspicite, o proceres.

overcome other animals. But that leader must truly be called a great man whom anger does not corrupt and who restrains himself when he is the victor. But you model yourself on that man who came to us with covenants of peace and who arose with a beacon of light that chased away the darkness. Just as Christ swept away the shadows that the dread sins of the fathers had brought 100 upon us, so you in your piety make Italy, ravished by war and famine, safe with the justice of your rays. You pardon all. You make all men your friends and you bind everyone to you with service and help. You alone, Francesco, restrain and check hasty passions. You 105 are brave and wise. With you as our felicitous duke, peace is celebrated everywhere. On all sides wars are quelled, and swords grow dull. Now all fear is gone. Kings attend you, Sforza. With your 110 help, popes are established on their thrones. What man will not hope for a thousand years for you, who are a source of life and glory to good men? O gods on high, preserve this great man whom future ages will not bestow upon us again, nor did they previously. May he enjoy the kingdom of the Milanese with as long a 115 peace as possible. And may he long be in the prayers of his people and bring them happiness.

And may Bianca, wife of Francesco, who returns equally the love he has for her, enjoy the long life she desires. Radiant among all her women, Bianca is preeminent, as the moon glows among 120 the stars, since its globe emits more light. This is a woman warrior[5] of such dazzling beauty that Hera would have forced Pandora to bow before her. She would endeavor to surpass Diana in chastity, and in the fineness of her intellect, she would outstrip you, O Athena. Look, O princes, see how happy she makes her husband 125 with her offspring. Look at their children, O princes. Does not

Nonne Phaneta oculis Galeacius iste Marias,
    nonne coma Phoebum Mercuriumque refert?
130   Iam fremit indomitum generoso pectore Martem
    enseque fulmineo victor in arma ruit.
Nil sapit abiectum. Laudem studiosior ambit:
    est matris similis estque patris similis.
Hoc deus optato dios haerede parentes
135   saecula post longa muniat omnipotens.
Nam quid in Hyppolyta non est? Quod diva puella
    de se non magnum spondeat et celebre?
Pignora sic deinceps, quae circum cara parentes
    blandiciis ludunt, indole sunt patria.
140   Iure igitur tanti celebremus principis omnes
    muneribus nomen carminibusque novis.
Hic, Francesce, tibi Natalis, Sphortia, felix,
    opto, sit—ut felix primus in orbe fuit.
Hic peperit mundo foelicis gaudia vitae.
145   Hic te det nobis saecula multa frui,
teque tuus cupiat semper cecinisse poeta,
    cui tu solus ades portus et alta quies.

Galeazzo Maria remind you of Phanes with those eyes?[6] Is not his hair like that of Phoebus Apollo and Mercury? Already he roars for mighty Mars with his noble heart, and he rushes forth the vic- 130 tor with his flashing sword. He knows no defeat. Similar to his mother and father, he pursues his glory more eagerly. May almighty God protect his godlike parents with this scion, long-awaited after so many ages. Well, then, is there anything Ippolita 135 is without?[7] What preeminent and brilliant quality does this divine girl not promise? And so, these children who play at the knees of their parents, showered with sweet words, are the beloved pledges of their father's talents.

Therefore, let us all celebrate the great prince's name — and 140 rightly, with new gifts and poems. I hope this Christmas[8] will be as happy for you, Francesco Sforza, as the first on earth. For this day brought glad tidings for a joyous life to the world. May it permit us to enjoy you for many ages to come, and may your poet al- 145 ways wish to hymn you, since you alone are his harbor and his source of deep repose.

APOLLO
LIBER PRIMUS

Otio qui se dederint inerti
nil habent quo sint celebres futuri,
quippe qui temnant decus acris omne
    mentis et usus.
5   Nanque quo ducas numero virorum
quempiam, qui nil acie profunda
spectet excelsum fugiatque pulchrum
    munus agendi?
Languet arescens vigor ille noster
10   intimus, quo quid bene cogitamus
magna facturi, stupidum soporem
    pectus ut hausit.
Ocium vulgi fugimus procacis.
Quicquid a nobis agitur, putamus
15   languida multo potius quiete
    mortis amica.
Me nihil parvum iuvat aut frequentis
voce iactatum populi nec umbra.
Altius quiddam rapidis fatigat
20   pectora flammis.
Ergo quid tandem cupimus referre?
Ducta quem[1] nobis volucris sagitta

APOLLO
BOOK I

: I :

In Praise of Poetry
An Encomium of Charles VII of France

Those men who surrender themselves to idle leisure have nothing
with which they can be celebrated in the future, since they are con-
temptuous of beauty and the uses of a sharp mind. For how in-
deed would you classify someone who sees nothing lofty in intense 5
battle and who avoids the beautiful duty of service? That inner
vigor of ours — though we intend to do great things, whatever it is
that we favor — dries up and withers when our hearts have drained 10
dry the draught of dull slumber. We flee the idleness of the
shameless crowd. Whatever we do, we think that action is better
than languid rest — the friend of death. 15

　　Insubstantial things don't please me — whether I am jostled by
the noise of a thronging crowd or sitting in the shade. Something
higher plagues my heart with raging fires. Therefore, what do I fi- 20
nally wish to say? To what purpose is the swift arrow said to be

fertur ad calcem? Quibus excitamur
    ignibus acti?
25   Quam mihi vellem superi dedissent
res ut illustris gererem virisque
quos alit virtus bene profuturas
    omnibus aeque!
Quod tamen possum facilis libensque
30   praesto. Non vecors celebrator altae
laudis accedo; veniat canendus
    denique quisquam.
Quem virum nobis animus per omnis
optet ad caelum titulos ferendum,
35   tota quem tellus stupeat, nec aetas
    obruat ulla?
Unus in terris viget inter omnes
laudibus praestans: meritis verendus
regibus manans atavis et idem
40   gloria regum.
Franciae quemnam decus atque sydus
splendidum magnae columenque tanta
mole vexati latet ac ruentis
    Karolus orbis?
45   Hunc enim terris hominum redemptor
tradidit regem simul et parentem,
quem truces omnes metuant tyranni,
    horreat Horchus.
Hic erit solus domitor latronis,
50   cuius impuris Arabes scelesti
legibus parent Arabumque tetra
    arma secuti.
Turcus et quisquis domini sepulchrum
servus obscurus premit innocentis

drawn back? By what fires am I aroused and driven? How I wish
the gods had allowed me to do illustrious deeds that would help   25
all those men equally whom virtue nurtures! Still, I will gladly
show what I am capable of doing. I come as no incompetent enco-
miast of glorious acts—let someone finally come forward to be   30
celebrated.

What man does my heart long to see transported to heaven
with every honor so that the whole world will gaze at him in awe
and no age will forget him? One man thrives on earth, surpassing   35
all others in virtue; this man is to be revered for his accomplish-
ments. He comes from ancient kings and he is glorious among
kings themselves. For who does not know Charles—the honor   40
and splendid star of great France and the pillar of this world that
labors under a great weight and is ready to collapse? The redeemer
of men on earth made this man king and father at one and the   45
same time. All cruel tyrants fear him and even Orcus trembles.

This man alone will subdue the thief,[1] whose foul laws are
obeyed by the accursed Arabs and by those who follow their loath-   50
some armies. The Turk and every low-born slave who tramples the
tomb of our innocent Lord will submit under a yoke of shame to

55 heu iugo turpi tibi cedet uni
    Karole regi.
Tu piae cunctos fidei rebelles
punies hostes pariesque sanctis
omnibus miram populis salutem
60   inclytus ultor.
Haec erunt olim referenda celsis
vocibus vati, quibus orbis omnis
gestiat laetus pietate regis
    paceque tanti.
65 Ne dies frustra tamen ipsa nobis
inter haec praesens data iudicetur,
laude quod dignum liceat futura
    munus obire?
Lusimus centum satyras protervis
70 cantibus denas decadas peracti
ad decem senis numeris severos
    millia versus.
Nunc libet plectro modulos inire,
usa quis fertur celebranda Sappho,
75 usus Alcaeus, lyricoque vates
    nomine clari.
His iuvat nostro requiem labori
ferre. Pelliden memorant atroci
Marte defessum cithara suesse
80   pellere curas.
Et senem tradunt Samium vicissim
per lyram membris solitum soporem
fundere intentis iterumque certa
    lege fugare.
85 Magna vis cantus resonante nervo,
quo furor citur, requiescit ira.

you alone, King Charles. You alone, our famed avenger, will pun- 55
ish all the enemies who rebelled against their holy faith. And you
alone will bring forth marvelous safety for all the pious peoples.
These stories must be told in the lofty verses of the poet, which 60
the whole world will be eager to hear, rejoicing in the piety of such
a great king and in the peace he has brought. Lest the present day
itself not be thought to have been granted me in vain, what du- 65
tiful task worthy of future praise should I perform? I have com-
posed a hundred satires with bold songs and I have produced ten- 70
thousand stern verses in hexameters.

Now it is pleasing to sing in lyric meters, such as celebrated
Sappho and Alcaeus are said to have cultivated, both poets re- 75
nowned for lyric fame. It is pleasing to bring some tranquility to
our work with such songs. For the poets say that Peleus's son, ex-
hausted from horrid Mars, drove his cares away when he played
the lyre.[2] They say that one old man from Samos, Pythagoras, 80
could pour slumber over tired limbs with his lyre and that he
could chase that sleep away again in accord with certain laws.[3]
Great is the power of song with the melodious lyre: it stirs up 85
frenzy, yet anger is soothed; the mind boils up in three-pronged
flames, and then it grows cold and shivers in turn.

Mensque fervescit facibus trisulcis
   rursus et horret.
Qui dolens patris lachrymas subacti
90   cladis auctorem gladio petebat,
   cessit iratus numeris coactus
      Empedocleis.
Quam sit excellens citharae potestas,
   sensit armatus pariterque inermis
95   ille, qui totum Macedum tyrannus
      terruit orbem.
Cinxit Amphion fidibus canoris,
   Cadme, quam primus posuisse sacram
   diceris Theben pecudesque ponti
100   flexit Arion.
Hic enim quondam gravibus Tarento
   ditior solvens loculis Corinthum
   nave, dum laetus repetit per aequor,
      fata repellit.
105 Nanque vectorem cithara videntes
   navitae grandis cumulasse gazas
   caede crudeles statuunt nefanda
      perdere vatem.
Ille sed postquam precibus lyraque
110   temptat immanes animos inanis,
   ecce delphinas modulis citatos
      lenit Arion.
Quos ubi circum placidis choreis
   despicit captos fidibus sonoris
115   ludere et saltum veluti precari,
      'Credimus!' inquit.
'Credimus longe melius ferorum
   nostrae[2] delphinum fidei prophanis

The anger of a man lamenting the tears of his father who had been brought low, of a man who was pursuing the perpetrator with his sword, was softened by Empedoclean rhythms.[4] The greatness of the power of the lyre was well known to the king of the Macedonians, both when he was armed and unarmed—Alexander, who held the whole world in thrall.[5] With the strings of his lyre Amphion gave walls to sacred Thebes, which you, Cadmus, are said to have founded first.[6] Likewise Arion moved the animals of the sea. For once upon a time, he set sail from Tarentum by ship, rich with heavy coffers, and when he was happily out at sea and heading for Corinth, he escaped death. For after seeing that this passenger had amassed great wealth with his lyre, the cruel sailors decided to murder the bard. But when Arion tried—in vain—to sway their savage minds with prayers and his lyre, he softened the hearts of the dolphins, who were moved by his melodies. When he looked down and saw that the dolphins, enchanted by his sonorous strings, were playing in peaceful circles and that they were begging him, as it were, to leap down, he said, "We believe!" "We believe," he continued, "far more in the loyalty of the wild dolphins than in the evil men who desire our ruin," and down

quam viris nostrae cupidis ruinae':
120   desilit audax.
Quem citus dorso subiens acuto
excipit delphin patriaeque tutum
reddit. Et quisquam stupeat trahentem
      Orphea silvas?
125 Hunc enim Chiron senior iuventa
fervidum nervis citharae superbae
provocat, paret pudibundus hospes
      vincere Chiron.
Nanque testudo Rhodopes ut altum
130 vocibus volvi resonis per antrum
coepit, extemplo volucres feraeque
      agmine plaudunt.
Quin et auritas memorant cupressos
cantibus captas agitasse celsos
135 vertices dulcis cupidas choreae
      monte sub Aemo.
Insuper lapsus fluvios perennis
fertur oblitos novitate cantus,
quo simul ducti stupuere manes,
140   Terror et Horcus.
Nonne cum summus citharae propheta
tangeret nervos, Saulem sinebat
spiritus dirus rabiem remittens
      ferre quietem?
145 Mite quur ergo simili moveri
mirer humanum ratione pectus,
cuius haec virtus eadem prementis
      flectit habaenas?
Rusticos iuxta Siculum Gelona
150 ac ducem, cuius periere Persae

he boldly leapt. And quickly a dolphin took him on its nimble   120
back, and returned him safely to his native land.

Who then, pray tell, would be surprised at Orpheus's moving
the forests? For aged Chiron challenged this passionate young
man to a contest on the strings of his brilliant lyre. His guest   125
obeys, ashamed at defeating Chiron. For when the lyre began to
send melodies echoing through the lofty cave on Mt. Rhodope,[7]
suddenly the birds and animals all applauded together. They also   130
say that the listening cypresses, now enchanted by Orpheus's mu-
sic and desirous of sweet dance, shook their lofty peaks under   135
Mount Haemus.[8] What is more, because of the novelty of his
song, they say, the rivers forgot their perennial courses, while at
the same time Terror, Orcus, and the shades followed him dumb-
struck.   140

When the greatest prophet touched the strings of his lyre, did
not the dread spirit let go of his anger and allow Saul to usher in
peace?[9] Why do I marvel that the gentle human heart is moved by   145
a similar cause, when this same virtue guides its reins? Those who
are helpless as to how to bow the lyre, like simple country people,
believe it was Gelon, the leader of the Sicilians, under whose lead-   150

ductibus, censent inopes quod essent
  ducere plectrum.
Sic graves ipsi studio canendi
ducimur tandem veterem secuti
155 Socratem longe leviore nervo
    plectra terentes.
Nec mihi solum fuerint canenti
quos lyrae tantum numeros amarunt.
Finibus nullis volumus teneri
160   voce nec una.
Doricus nobis gravior Phrygosque
mollior cantus mediusque Lydus
se ferat coram merito vicissim
    munere fungens.
165 Ergo nec cornu litui nec acrem
sperno concentum; renuo nec ipsam
fistulam. Nullis fidibus nec ulli
    parcimus aurae.
Tibiae quantum moduli valerent
170 ille Tyrtaeus docuit iacenti
qui iugo Spartae petulantis hostis
    colla subegit.
Tibia morbos potuit domare
alter infestos penitus sub imis
175 clunibus fixos. Liceat vagari
    latius ergo
quando nec primus citharae magister
tibiam doctae renuit Minervae.
Hac enim iuxta citharaque fertur
180   usus Apollo,
Phoebe, quam frater chelyn ille divum
nuncius dono tibi cessit olim,

ership the Persians perished.[10] Thus we ourselves in somber mood
are brought in the end by love of song to follow old Socrates and
wear out the lyre with lighter modes.[11]   155

But let me not sing only those meters which lyres love; I do not
wish to be confined to any instrument, nor to one mode or voice.
The Doric mode is more serious, the Phrygian mode more gentle;   160
whereas the Lydian mode occupies the middle ground. Each offers
itself directly to us in turn, in accord with its proper function.
And thus I reject neither the horn nor the bitter harmony of the   165
wartime trumpet; nor do I refrain from playing the reed pipe. Nor
do I refuse to play the lute or any sort of flute. For the famous
Tyrtaeus taught how mighty the beat of the flute is when he forced   170
the necks of Sparta's brash enemy to go beneath his yoke.[12] An-
other could cure harmful diseases lodged deep within the hips
with his flute playing.[13] May I be permitted, then, to continue my
rambling at greater length, since even the first teacher of the lyre   175
did not refuse learned Minerva's flute.[14] For they say that Apollo
used the flute alongside the lyre when his brother, the messenger   180
of the gods,[15] long ago presented it to you, O Phoebus, saying:

23

'Tange concentus,' referens, 'Olympi
voce sororum.

185 Dum lyram vates modulis Apollo
dulcibus pulsas, per amica gratis
singulae reddant vicibus puellae
carmina voces.

Fac modo duris placeat Camoena
190 auribus.' Pluris Ateas futuros
scimus hinnitus avidos equestris
carminis hostes.

Nec iuvant[3] lyppos radii micantes;
dulce mel ducit febriens amarum;
195 nec lyram sensus melioris expers
curat asellus.

Hoc libet paulum requiesse prato,
quod nemus cingit variis amoenum
fontium rivis viridi coronans
200 Naiadas umbra.

Karoli post haec referam triumphos
Regis optatos, quibus ipse ductor
omnibus laetam pariet quietem,
vindice Christo.

205 Stravit hic Anglos, genus acre bello,
atque vi captum patriumque regnum
auxit hostili meritaque poena
victor et ultor.

Haec quidem digno memoranda cantu
210 arbitror, verum satyrae labore
nunc mihi tanto minus expetenda
moleque fesso.

Spiritus cum se recrearit aura
redditus leni dederitque poenas

"Touch the harmonies of the sisters of Olympus with your music. And while you, O poet Apollo, play sweet melodies on the lyre, let 185 each of the girls respond with joyous odes sung in pleasing alternation. Only make sure that Camena[16] will please harsh ears." We 190 know that new Ateases, the enemies of poetry, will be delighted with equestrian whinnying.[17] Nor do flashing rays of light please the blind. The fever-ridden man thinks sweet honey bitter. Nor does the ass, who is devoid of higher emotion, care about the lyre. 195 It is pleasing to rest for a little while in this meadow, which surrounds a pleasing grove with various rivulets of springs, wreathing the Naiads with green shade. 200

Later I will relate the longed-for triumphs of Charles the King, in which he himself, the leader, will bring forth lovely peace to all, with Christ our defender. This ruler, this victor and avenger, defeated the English, a people fierce in war, taking them with force 205 and fierce vengeance well deserved; and he has increased his ancestors' kingdom. His deeds, I believe, must be remembered in poetry that is worthy of them. But now that my strength has been ex- 210 hausted by the work of satire, I should not try to say more. When the spirit returns, refreshed by a gentle breeze, and when the perjurious pillager and impious enemy of the holy faith has paid

215   praedo periurus fideique sanctae
        impius hostis,
    vatibus totus celebrabit orbis
    Karolum nobis, pietate quisquis
    principes cunctos, radiis ut astra
220   vincit Apollo.

:   2   :

    Si, Maeme, cupis nosse quid, olim
    postquam satyris manus extrema
    accessit, ago, brevibus dicam.
    Nimius labor et cura perurens
5   solvens hominem penitus tabe
    conficit. Ubi dux ille Philippus
    superas hinc concessit in arces,
    mox terribilis Pluto Gigantas
    quos tartarei tenebras inter
10   Erebi tetras vincula nodis
    millibus arctis ipsa ligarant,
    Furiis, Furiis undique septos
    miseras nostras misit in oras.
    Subito trepidos furor immanis
15   Martis populos omnia vertens
    iuga cum vallibus aequora segetes
    armis facibus spoliis caede
    late invasit. Pietas nulla
    reliqua est. Ipsae Insubribus dirae

the penalty, then, with me as poet, the whole world will sing in   215
praise of Charles, who surpasses all princes in piety, just as Apollo
eclipses the stars with his light.   220

: 2 :

To Maemo
On war and the consolation of the liberal arts

If you want to know what I've been doing since I put the last
touches on the satires, Maemo,[18] I'll quickly tell you. Toil and
seething care break men down, decimating them with a disease
that wastes from within. When Duke Filippo left this city for the   5
lofty citadels, Pluto soon sent the frightful Giants to our wretched
land, whom chains had once bound with a thousand tightly drawn
knots amid the grim darkness of Erebus, hemmed in on all sides   10
by the Furies—yes, Furies. Suddenly a savage lust for war has
seized the city's fearful people, confounding all things—mountain   15
ridges and valleys, cornfields and plains—with arms, fire, plunder,
and bloody slaughter. No piety is left. The Dirae themselves whip

20 stimulant caecis animos flammis.
 Quod ego meditans quid agam dixi?
 Fatuis memet socium tradam?
 Stolidos vulgi comiter sensus?
 Stultus patiar sponte vocari?
25 Sequar insanos mente carentis?
 Faciam nunquam, meque quietis
 gravibusque viris iungere pergam.
 Me restitui penitus Phoebo
 Musisque sacris, quae iuga summi
30 sacra Parnasi latices inter
 laurosque colunt melle fluentes.
 Resonam citharam pulsat Apollo.
 Variis Musae numeris astant
 vicibusque suis carmina fundunt.
35 Nos sic agimus vacui curis
 vitam curas varias inter.
 Quid agas cupimus discere, Maeme,
 etiam, tu qui Nestoris annos
 prope iam vivas inter apricos
40 quibus exurgit Tuscia colles.
 Alii bellis, odiis, caede;
 nos, Maeme, bonis famae studiis
 certemus et officio recto.

the minds of the Milanese with unseen flames, and pondering   20
this, I ask myself, what should I do? Should I surrender to the
fools as their ally? Join gladly in the brutish emotions of the
crowd? Should I allow myself to be called a fool without protest-
ing? Shall I follow the mindless mob? This I will never do.   25

I shall join now the serious men of peace. I have returned to
Apollo and the sacred Muses who inhabit the holy slopes of high-
est Parnassus amid springs and laurels dripping with honey. There   30
Phoebus strums his mellifluous lyre, and while the Muses attend
him with varied rhythms, they pour out poetry in diverse modes.

Thus I live my life—free from care amid untold cares. I also   35
want to learn what you're doing, Maemo, who are almost as old
as Nestor and live in the sunny hills where Tuscany rises. Some   40
men struggle with one another in war, hatred, and killing; but
we, Maemo, strive for fame through just service and honorable
studies.

: 3 :

Si quis non aliis virum
norit te meritis Karole maximum,
   saltem munificentiae
spectet conspicuum laudibus inclytae.
5   Nam quamquam titulis nites
cunctis, quos probitas altius evehit,
   praestas omnibus attamen
illustris specie munificentiae.
     Haud est quae magis excitet
10   virtus hac homines, ut cupiant bene
   his quos promeritos sciant.
Ingratus fuerit semper et impius,
   huic qui noluerit bene,
cuius promeruit grata benignitas.
15   Vates Aeaciden tuba
Smyrnaeus resona tollit in aethera,
   quod nullum metuat metum
Troianosque premat turbine bellico.
     Pelliden etiam refert
20   idem, quem celebrant Pierides sacrae,
   extinctum misero seni
ingenti precio reddere filium.
     Plus auri valuit nitor
in nato Thetidos quam meriti decus.
25   Auri vendiderat sitis
ultro quem dare claementia debuit.
     Pellides igitur fuit

: 3 :

To Carlo Gonzaga

If anyone does not know, Carlo, that you are a very great man because of all your other virtues, he would at least see that you are noted in encomia for your famous generosity. For though you excel with all your honors — and your virtue elevates these to still 5 greater heights — nonetheless you surpass all other men in your extraordinary magnanimity, and there is no virtue more capable than this one of stirring men to want the best for those whom 10 they know are deserving. Whoever does not want the best for this man whose kindness deserves appreciation is lacking in grace and piety. The Smyrnean poet[19] praised Achilles to the skies with his 15 melodious trumpet, because he feared no peril and beat back the Trojans with his weapons whirling. But this same poet said that Peleus's son, whom the sacred Muses hymn, gave back to the 20 wretched old man his dead son's body in recompense for an enormous ransom. The gleam of gold had more power for this son of Thetis than the glory of a virtuous deed, and so the thirst for gold had put up for sale that which clemency should have given for 25 free.

huius laudis inops qua superas viros
    tu dando reliquos bene.
30   Quis non ergo tibi cedere dixerit,
    Gonzaga, Aeaciden ferum,
qui non Martis opus fortiter efferri[4]
    solum[5] noris et agmina?
Sed longe reliquis, quis remicas, bonis
35   adsit grata benignitas.
Tu me quottidie muneribus novis
    ornas praesidio fovens.
Nullius pateris nos inopes rei,
    mittas qui Cereris piae
40 vim tantam, nitido qui studeas togae
    dono me decorarier
ac nummi facias tempore divitem.
    Nullus nunc hyemis metus
terret, nulla fames. Quando minacibus
45   impendet mala dentibus,
cantabunt merito Castalides tibi
    nostrae, quam poterunt magis,
et te munifico cedere nemini
    ostendent vario lyrae
50 cantu multisonae. Non animus quidem
    gratus defuerit mihi,
quando nec tibi deest grata benignitas.

Peleus's son was poor in the praiseworthy act of gracious giving, but in this you surpass all others. Who will not therefore say, Gonzaga, that the cruel son of Aeacus[20] is a lesser man than you? For you are a man who knows that brave soldiers arrayed for war 30 are not the only subjects who should be extolled. But your pleasing generosity should be added to your other virtues which shine from you far and wide. You honor me daily with new rewards; you 35 care for and protect me. You see that I am lacking in no way since you send me such a large quantity of grain and are eager to see me elegantly dressed in the coat you gave me, and you even shower me 40 with money at the perfect time. No winter frightens me now, nor does hunger — and if she ever hangs over me with bared teeth, our 45 Castalian maidens will rightly sing to you to the best of their ability. And they will show with various songs for the melodious lyre that you are second to no one in magnanimity. Nor will I ever fail 50 to be grateful to you since your beautiful generosity never fails me.

Rex Karole, regibus verendis
qui cunctis merito antecellis unus
fortunaeque bonis tuisque, nostri
O saecli decus inclytum, priorum
5   heroum species, deum propago,
te verbis quibus efferam, poeta?
Tu cunctos superas probos, nec una
polles laude mera, tibi sed omnis
virtus se comitem fatetur ultro.
10   Mars paret tibi; paret et Minerva.
Quis te iustius arma cepit unquam,
aut victor posuit? Tuas in astra
res gestas populi efferunt superni.
Uno Francia rege te triumphat.
15   Omnis Gallia te veretur unum.
Te solum metuunt tremuntque Turci,
qui tot stragibus impii rebelles
insectantur et obterunt per omne
extremum scelus, heu, genus piorum.

: 4 :

To Charles VII of France

O King Charles, you who alone surpass all other venerable kings both in your virtues and in the goods of fortune, O fabled glory of our time, mirror of ancient heroes, offspring of the gods, with 5 what words shall I, a poet, extol you? You surpass all good men; nor do you merit praise alone, but every virtue claims you as her companion. Mars obeys you, and Minerva too. Who has ever gone 10 to war more justly than you? Or as victor ended war more justly? The greatest peoples extol your deeds to the heavens. France has triumphed with you alone as king. All Gaul reveres you alone. The 15 Turks — an impious and rebellious people, alas, who oppress and crush a race of pious men with every atrocity and so much slaughter — fear you and tremble before you alone.

: 5 :

[POETA]

Nobis quid doleas fare, Bisulcere.
   Dic, Martinio, tandem.
Nec te detineat vel bipatrem pudor
   textoris rabulaeve
5   vel quae te bibulum lustra per omnia
   vulgat fama perennis.
Narra quid doleas, nec retice malum.

[BISULCERUS]

   Heu, quid flaetibus addi
nostris amplius aut durius ultimis
10   possit, nominis auram
si nulla miseri sorte merebimur?
   Dum te, Karole, miris
extollit meritis et titulis virum
   heroas super omnis,
15 collegas alios laudibus erigit
   hic ad sydera nostros
orator, tenebras trudit in abditas
   alios fervidus Horchi,
nullo nos hominum nec numero locans
20   nec sermone vel atro.
   Nequam sum penitus? Non igitur miser
   animi torquear aegri?

: 5 :

To Giorgio Bizzozero, Captain of the Ambrosian Republic
A mock consolation

POET

Tell us why you grieve, Bizzozero, O son of Martinio, pray speak.[21] Let not the shame of having two fathers—a weaver or a brawling advocate—deter you, nor the perennial gossip that makes the rounds about you in every brothel that you are a drunk. Tell 5 me why you grieve—and don't remain silent about the wrong done.

BIZZOZERO

Ah, what harsher or greater wrong could be added to my latest sorrows if I earn a bad reputation on the public's lips, and not by chance? While this orator extols you, Carlo,[22] above all other 10 heroes with wonderful honors and titles, and praises some of our companions to the skies, and eagerly consigns others to the dim 15 shadows of Orcus, he puts me in neither group, and does not even mention me with malicious talk. Am I completely worthless? 20 Should I, who am miserable and sick at heart, be thus tormented?

[POETA]

Non de me quereris iure, Bisulcere.
  Nec Martinio nosti
25   te totum penitus, qui bibulus mices
    cyathos spumeus inter.
Alter nam bibulus vel pater est tibi,
  vel si vera negaris,
rivalis pater est quem simulas tui.
30   Hinc tu stirpe superbus
surgens e duplici tum rabulam refers,
  tum maiore triumpho
illum, cui genetrix nupsit adultera,
  et quem suppositus tu
35   textorem vocitas ridiculus patrem.
    Ut fortissimus ille
Alcides gemino sanguine gloriam
  natus lumine rerum
gestarum peperit percelebrem sibi,
40   sic tu, laude bibendi
mirandus, gemino patre superbiens
  bibulus saecla per alta
vives Insubrium cognitus omnibus
  felix ganeo lustris.

POET

You complain about me unjustly, Bizzozero. You, son of
Martinio—a trembling drunkard, frothy amid your mugs of wine   25
—you do not know yourself completely. For either one father is
the drunkard—or if you deny that this is true, then it is the rival
father whom you emulate. Therefore, because of your double pa-   30
ternity, sometimes you talk proudly about the brawling advocate,
and sometimes you talk with greater exultation about the weaver,
whom your adulterous mother married and whom you, his coun-
terfeit child, absurdly call father. Just as that most powerful hero   35
Alcides, born from a double bloodline, won the greatest glory for
himself with the brilliance of his labors,[23] so you, who win acco-
lades for your drinking and take pride in your dual paternity, will   40
live through all the lofty centuries, known to all the generations of
the Milanese as "Bibulus," the happy debauchee.

: 6 :

Sponte mendaces sumus et protervi
fallimus falsis populos figuris
et piis verbis animum rebelles
    fallimur ipsi.
5   Dicimus Christum genitum superno
rege cui paret mare terra flamae,
quidquid et caelum liquidique cingunt
    aeris aura.
Hunc item famur Mariae pudico
10   ventre mortalem coluisse formam,
inter humanos habitasse fluctus
    turbine multo,
gente quem natum perhibent Hebraea
stirpe fabrili regione tetra
15   oppido nullis titulis nitenti
    paupere tecto.
Hunc nec Actaeae tenuit Minervae
docta quam dicunt schola Nicolae,
non magus Perses, Babylon nec ulli
20   Pythagorei.
Hunc nec Aegyptus docuit, nec Indus,
non Atlas Afer, Dryidesve Gallus.
Nulla gens, nullus puero magister
    tradidit artes.
25   Nec tamen quicquam titulis ferendum
novit, Arcimbolde, hominum verenda

: 6 :

To Nicolò Arcimboldi[24]
On the Christian religion against schismatics

We are deliberate liars and shamelessly we delude the peoples of
the world with false images, and rebellious in spirit ourselves, we
are deluded by pious words.[25]

    We say that Christ was born from a heavenly father whom 5
earth, seas, and fire obey, and whatever the sky and the winds of
bright air encircle. We say he assumed a mortal form in Mary's
chaste womb, that he lived in the midst of human floods and 10
whirlwinds. They say he was born to Hebrew people of craftsman
stock, in a squalid district, under a pauper's roof in a town distin-
guished by no shining titles. 15

    Nor did the learned school of Nicolaus[26] train him, which they
say belongs to Athenian Minerva, nor the Persian Magi, Babylon
or any of the Pythagoreans.[27] Neither did the sages of Egypt or 20
India teach him, nor did Atlas of Africa, nor the Gallic Druid. No
people, no teacher taught the boy occult arts. Nor did the venera-
ble minds of men know anything worthy of glory that was not in 25
some way apparent, my Arcimboldi, in this man's heavy heart.

mens, quod illius grave pectus ulla
    parte lateret.
Praetulit nummis caruisse nummis.
30   Non latus cinxit valida cohorte.
Infimae sortis sibi non superbo
    legit amicos.
Hos sibi fecit socios, sodales,
contubernales, comites et omnis
35   conscios vitae; neque vixit ullis
    solus in oris.
Hos sibi testis habuit per omne
tempus ut gentem statuit docere
quae deum rector placidusque rerum
40   iusserat auctor.
Quin patrem secum et patris atque luce
de sua flantem tenebris dieque
spiritum semper studuit praeesse
    rebus agendis.
45   Trinus atque unus. Sator ac is idem
fit satus iactu revirente nullo
et simul purus fluit ex utroque
    spiritus ortu.
Sic deus verax. Homo sic in omnem
50   vixit aetatem patuitque mundo
qualis et quantus foret, et subesse
    legerat ultro.
Ex hero servum fieri putavit
regum munus; superasse cunctos
55   lege parendi imperiale duxit
    omne per aevum.
Hinc tulit mitis rabidos furores
gentis Hebraeae miserum per omne

He preferred lacking money to money. He did not surround himself with a powerful bodyguard. He was not proud and chose 30 his friends from the lowest orders, and he made them his companions, familiars, and partners who shared in every part of his life. Nor did he live alone in any land, but he kept these men as his 35 witness for all time, since he was resolved to teach the people what the ruler of the gods and the gentle creator of the world had commanded. 40

But rather he was always eager that his father and the holy spirit should preside over him in all that he did, flowing with his father's light both by day and in the darkness. Three in one. And he, the father himself, became the son with no loss but rather with 45 an efflorescence of his power. And at the same time pure spirit flowed from each at the moment of their becoming.

Thus God is the source of truth. He has lived as a man in every age and he has made apparent in the world who he is and how 50 great he is, yet he chose to live in the world of his own free will. He thought it was the duty of kings to become a servant after having been a lord; and he considered that all men in every imperial age had conquered through the rule of obedience. 55

And so, enduring the madness of the Hebrew people, through every wretched dishonor, this gentle man was shamefully forced to

dedecus, tractus crucis ad pudenda
60   vulnera saevae.

Hic enim clavis tribus, heu, tremendis
fixus; et dextrum latus a nefando
cuspidis dirae penetratus ictu
      liquerat auras.

65   Clarus admisit tenebras Apollo.
Vulnerum taelis moriente Christo,
totus, hei, mundus tremuit; profundus
      horruit Horchus.

Quin ferunt priscis animas sepulchris
70   corporum sumptis veterum figuris
isse surgentes patriam per urbem
      plebis in ora.

At ferus Pluton foribus reclusis
flevit ereptum genus omne patris
75   illius primi male rebus usi
      divitis horti.

Tertia fati domitor resurgit
luce non soli Mariae nec uni
agnitus Petro placidis in urbem
80   gressibus actus.

Qui dies postquam decies triumpho
quattuor terram stupidam relato
victor ambisset, populo vidente
      astra petivit.

85   Liquit in terris fidei futuros
nuncios sanctae celebrisque testes,
usque quos secum tenuisset usus
      nocte dieque.

Quos quidem sancto voluit refertos
90   spiritu primis populos, ab Indis

suffer the wounds of the savage cross. For, alas, he hung fixed 60
upon three trembling nails, and when an evil spear was cast and
penetrated his right side, he disappeared into the air, and bright
Apollo sent down darkness. 65

When Christ lay dying, mortally wounded, alas, the whole
world trembled and deepest Orcus shuddered. But they say souls
rose from their ancient tombs and, assuming their old bodies, they 70
went to their native cities before the very eyes of the people. But
savage Pluto, when the doors of Orcus opened, wept that the
whole human race, descended from their first father who had mis-
used the blessings of that rich garden, had been snatched away 75
from him.[28]

On the third day he who had been victorious over death rose
again and, recognized neither by Mary or Peter, he came peace-
fully into the city. After forty days the victor Christ travelled 80
round the land which was awestruck by the story of his triumph.
He then sought the heavens while the people watched. He left
future apostles of the holy faith on earth and well-known wit- 85
nesses, whom he had kept with him constantly day and night.

The people he wanted were filled with the holy spirit, from the
Indians who were first to the slow Spaniards. And both poles 90

ad pigros Gades. Polus hos docentis
   sensit uterque.
Omnis hos vidit stupefactus orbis
audiens dantes nova iura mundo,
95   nulla quos mundi docuisset aetas
   talibus uti.
Nam quis indoctos homines et omnis
artis urbanae putet imperitos
gentium linguis variis locutos
100   iura Tonantis.
Ecce piscator rudis et pudendus
audet ingentem caput orbis urbem
ingredi celsos proceres daturus
   legibus imis.
105   Ille sic Graium sapiens adivit
Pallium nullis sociatus armis,
docta quae dudum schola fabricasset
   Socratis alti.
Sic item cunctos similis petivit
110   vulgus indoctus populos et oras
iura quae nullo didicit Solone
   inclyta monstrans.
Si negas Christum, fidei rebellis,
aurium linguae solvisse visus
115   et pedum nodos pariterque fracta
   membra ligasse,
rursus ut pergas vacuus pudore,
redditos vitae penitus sepultos
illius iussu poteris negare,
120   cognita cunctis?
Nonne Romani genus illud acris
Martis invictum, quibus ipse cessit

heard the teaching of these apostles. Amazed, the whole earth saw and heard these men give new laws to the world—men whom no prior age of the world had taught to use such laws. For who would 95 have thought that men so ignorant and untutored in the urbane arts would speak in a variety of the world's languages and lay down the laws of the Father? 100

But look: a crude and unkempt fisherman dared to enter the great city that was the capital of the world so that he might edify the leading men with the most profound laws.[29] And likewise that wise man took up the Greek pallium,[30] though he shared none of 105 the weapons that the learned school of lofty Socrates had forged. Similarly the whole unschooled group sought out all the common people and every shore, preaching the renowned laws which they 110 had not learned from any Solon.[31]

If you, who are a rebel against the faith, deny—just so that you can continue to live your shameful life—that Christ loosed the knots that cause deafness, loss of speech, blindness, lameness, and that he healed broken bones, can you deny that, at his command, 115 those buried deep in the ground returned to life, miracles of his that have been recognized by everyone? 120

Did not that race unvanquished in savage war—the Romans—to whom the sea and the land themselves bowed down, yield to the

pontus et tellus, subiere Christi
    iura fidemque?
125   Quosque nec Gallus, nec acerbus Afer,
nulla gens unquam valuit tremendis
viribus, sola pietate vicit
    rustica plebes.
Arte qui totum potuit superna,
130   ex eo quidquid fuit ante unquam
cogere ut formam caperet stupendam
    rebus et usu,
hic item puris animis et aequis
fudit aeterni iubaris micantem
135   lampada ut lucem populos per omnis
    fundere possent.
Omnis hinc mundi sapiens potestas
cessit indoctis meliore fraetis
spiritus forma rudibusque truncis
140   arboris almae.
Sic enim summus deus ille divum
clarius cunctis voluit supernum
gentibus regnum superasque vires
    pandere terrae,
145   si nec ingentis validum tulisset
corporis robur nimiosque fastus
sortis externae nitidosque cultus
    orbis et auras.
Plura quid nostris repetam Camoenis?
150   Talibus Christi rudibus ministris
quaeque gens, omnis homines, et omnis
    paruit orbis.
Ergo quis sensus, adeo quis expers
mentis ac prorsus fatuus negarit

laws and protection of Christ? Neither the Gaul nor the fierce African, nor any race on earth, despite their fearful might, was ever 125 powerful enough to overcome the Romans. The crude plebs could do so with their Christian piety alone. With his heavenly skill, this man was able to cause the whole human race to assume a form wondrously different in action and purpose from what it was 130 before. This man, with his pure and just spirit, poured forth a glittering beam of immortal fire that was able to shower its radiance upon all peoples.   135

The sage leadership of the entire world bowed down in deference to these uneducated men, who relied on a better form of spirituality, and who were, as it were, the untutored trunks of a bountiful tree. For thus the supreme god of gods wanted to open his 140 high kingdom and heavenly powers to every nation on earth — if only he had not also brought to the world the mighty strength of a 145 large body, an overweening pride in external things, the shining courts of the world, and the shifting winds of fortune.

What more shall my Muses say? Each nation, all men, and the whole world obeyed such rustic ministers of Christ as these. 150 Therefore what emotion, what absence of mind, what utterly foolish man would deny that he who died on the cross will come again

155   esse venturum, cruce qui pependit,
           rursus in orbem?
       Hic ubi vivos pariterque functos
       luce sublimis solio vocarit
       iudicaturus trutina, rependet
160   praemia cuique.
       Rebus hinc forma varia novatis,
       morte divino imperio subacta,
       Christus aeterne dominator omne
           transiget aevum.
165   Credimus cuncti veneranda quaeque.
       Nunciant nobis fidei probati
       ac pii testes: hominem deumque
           ore fatemur.
       Te deum nobis hominemque, Christe,
170   dicimus. Mixta pariter figura,
       te cibo totum capimusque potu
           corde maligno.
       Fallimus gentes ita Nicolae
       sponte mendaces similique fuco
175   fallimur. Sensus varians voluntas
           mutat inertes.
       Unde sed noster fluat error olim
       ambigo. Nam quid fidei pudicae,
       qua nihil nobis melius fatemur,
180   linquimus usum?
       Quaeque fallaces homines inique
       credimus? Nos si bene crederemus,
       nunquid in diros animi tumultus
           verteret error?
185   Spiritus nobis alacerne vires
       forsitan praestat validas? At illas

to the world? When this sublime man calls both the living and the 155
dead to his throne in the light, sitting in judgment with a pair of
scales, he will mete out rewards to each one. 160

When the world has been renewed in myriad ways and when
death has been vanquished by his divine majesty, then Christ the
Lord will conclude the age for all eternity. We all believe each of
these things should be prayed for. The faithful and pious witnesses 165
announce it to us and we declare that he is both god and man. We
say you are both god and man to us, Christ. With sinful hearts,
we partake of you, both forms united in one, in food and drink. 170

Thus, we who are liars willingly deceive the nations of Nicho-
las[32] and we ourselves are led astray by similar deceit. An unstable
will blows our feckless emotions in every direction. But from 175
where our error first came, I know not. For why do we abandon
the practice of the holy faith when we admit there is nothing
better for ourselves? In what do we deceitful humans so perversely 180
trust? If we were really believers, would error catapult us into such
terrible anguish and turmoil? Does a spirit of enthusiasm perhaps
offer us true strength? But neither the wishes of our weak flesh 185
nor our daring is capable of succeeding to that strength.

carnis infirmae nequeunt subire
vota nec ausus.
An gregis pastor potius supremus
190   ac patres coetus reliqui fidelis
turpis exemplo nocuere vitae?
   Dedecus ingens
nanque quis speret scabie levari
ulceris foedi medicum refertum
195   intuens? Pravum facit imperator
   militis usum.
Qui crucis signum titulumque nuper
gessit antistes referebat ipsum
moribus Christum tuus ille ductor,
200   summe sacerdos.
Praesules si se similis per omnem
illius vitam gererent et acta
caeteri, nunquam variaret ipso
   pectus ab ore.
205   Sic ergo mecum meditans opinor.
Ipse quid tandem gravis et peritus
sentias norim. Tibi noster uni
   plaudit Apollo.
Civium nam te decorant patrumque
210   iura sacrorum refugitque nulla
doctior te laus et amica virtus
   novit alumnum.

Did the supreme shepherd of the flock and the rest of the fathers of the faithful council do harm by living shameful lives 190 themselves?[33] For come, who could hope that the terrible shame of eczema could be cured if we saw our doctor covered with the scab of the foul ulcer? It is the general who causes the evil conduct of the soldier. The bishop who recently wore the title and the sign of 195 the cross, that leader of yours, O highest priest,[34] reflected Christ himself in his life.[35] If religious leaders and others were to lead 200 their whole lives like that man, their hearts would never deviate from their words. And thus, these are my thoughts as I reflect. What you,[36] who are a serious and experienced man, think, I 205 would like to know. Our Apollo applauds you alone. For the laws of the citizens and of the holy fathers honor you. No learned praise eludes you, and kindly virtue knows you as her son. 210

Quo Romana sato gaudet, Broccharde, Cremona,
quur fraudem te laude tua? Qui solus ademptos
restituis nobis geminos quos livor et astus
abstulerat certo rabidi discrimine Martis.

5   Laetor enim nobis. Merito tibi gratulor uni,
flectere qui valeas tigres saevosque leones
viribus eloquii motosque remittere fluctus.
Hos igitur nobis, dulci quos luce carentes
iure putabamus, nulla formidine tactos

10   quod tua reddiderit vis et suavissima fandi
copia, non parvam peperit tibi munere laudem
tam pulchro quod nulla queant nec fata, nec aevum
laedere cuncta vorans, modo tu tibi cautior adsis.
Non semper Fortuna viris temptanda probatis,

15   quae dum blanda suis credentes pellicit ullos
pollicitis, scopulos fallens deducit in altos,
infligitque furens cunctis in rebus honestum.
Emineat: primumque sibi summumque fatiget.
Quod palmam promittit iter currentibus idem,

20   in stadium semper calx proponatur ut ipsa
praemia promeriti contingant pulchra laboris.
Nam quamvis soleat flectentibus ordine cursum
interdum simulata monens Fortuna favere,
fallit atrox tandem medio certamine sese

25   ostendens alio fuerit quam nuper amictu.
Omnibus in rebus praestat prudentia, tempus
quam longum multusque parat servatque peritus

: 7 :

To Persico Brocardo
On greed

Why should I cheat you of the glory that is yours, O Brocardo, in whom Roman Cremona rejoices as her son? For you alone brought the two brothers back to us, whom malice and cunning took away at a critical moment in the bloody war.[37] No, I am glad 5 and rightly offer thanks to you alone, since you can calm fierce lions and tigers and quiet the sea's storms with the power of your eloquence. And so the sweet force and elegance of your speech restored these men to us, untouched by fear—though we thought 10 they had died. This has brought you no small praise and a splendid reward that neither the fates nor all-devouring time can destroy—provided that you are more careful about yourself.

Good men should not always be obliged to put Fortune to the test. For while this charming lady seduces those who believe her 15 promises, she deceitfully leads the man who is honorable in all his endeavors to lofty heights and in a rage she crushes him. Let her loom over us, let her assail both the first and the highest man for her own purposes. Because she promises a prize to those who are running the same course, let a finish line always be put on view at 20 the track, so that the winner may be deservedly rewarded for his efforts. For although Fortune, who sometimes gives deceitful advice, usually favors those who complete the course in order, in the end she is savagely deceitful, showing herself midway through the race wearing a different cloak from the one she recently wore. Pru- 25 dence, which is acquired and preserved by the passage of time and by expert and copious practice and dutiful action, is best in all cir-

usus et officium. Iuvenem turbatio mentis
transversum plaerunque trahit sub imagine recti.
30   Nil ineas igitur quod non tecum ante volutes
et saepe et multum. Nam sic quod denegat aetas
invenit ingenium. Qui se commiserit alto
deceptus facieque maris specieque sereni
aetheris, ignarus lateant quae monstra profundo
35   poenitet interdum, nec habet quam rebus in aspris
possit opem subitis horrens afferre procellis.
Principio semper proin prospexisse futuris
fluctibus in placida vel tempestate decebit.
Turpe gravem dixisse virum nunquam hoc fore duxi.
40   Ipsi etiam pueri quod tandem cunque futurum
duxissent. Animi semper si caeca cupido
pareat hortatu rationis et impetus omnis
serviat imperio, quae celsa praesidet arce
sceptriferae mentis, nunquam nos ceperit error.
45   Utilitatis enim non nunquam fallit imago,
et veris iucunda solent infundere noctis
rebus, honestatis penitus ratione relicta.
Quare iterum atque iterum callentem convenit uti
consilio semper cunctis in rebus agendis.
50   Emendare quidem pulchrum est, sed laudibus ille
dignior errato qui se servarit ab omni
innocuum, ne quid causae quaesisse feratur
quo lateant delicta magis. Non omnibus idem
est sensus. Durum est populum subiisse bilinguem.
55   Quottidie mutare vices, nusquamque manere
haud est constantis. Quare id dare fama suevit
aut vitio aut nullo dignari laudis honore.
Nec famam omnino debet contemnere prudens
quam multi peperere viri. Nam tota perire
60   non solet et rebus nocuit male sana secundis

cumstances. Mental disarray leads many young men astray under
the guise of doing right. Do not, then, embark upon anything you   30
have not considered often and thoroughly beforehand. For what
youth denies one, intelligence attains. Whoever trusts himself to
the sea, fooled by the appearance of the ocean and the look of a
calm sky, and ignorant of what dangers lie hidden in the deep,[38]
is sometimes regretful, nor does he, shuddering at the rough   35
weather, have any help that he can bring to bear against sudden
gales. In the beginning one ought to look out for future storms
even in calm weather. I've never believed that a man of eminence
ever said this would be shameful. Even children should consider   40
what may happen in the future.

If the soul's blind desires always obeyed the exhortations of rea-
son — since she stands guard over the lofty citadel of mind, the
scepter-bearer of the body — and if our every impulse followed the
command of reason, then error would never get the better of us.
The image of utility is sometimes deceptive, for pleasing dreams   45
during the night, when the deep-seated principle of honor is aban-
doned, tend to cloud the truth. For this reason it is always fitting
for a man, even an experienced one, to seek advice repeatedly and
in every sphere of action. It is a beautiful thing to improve, but he   50
who deserves more praise is that man who steers clear of all
wrongdoing, lest he be said to have sought a way that his crimes
might remain more hidden.

The same opinion is not shared by everyone. Yet it is hard to be
the slave of a double-tongued crowd. It is not the mark of the man   55
of principle to play different roles each day and nowhere remain
the same. For this reason public opinion has often condemned
such behavior or deemed it unworthy of honor. Nor should a pru-
dent man dismiss entirely the fame that many men have earned.
For fame generally does not perish completely and a bad reputa-   60

iure vel invidia. Livor benefacta malignis
dentibus invadens, ni sint moderamine certo
recta, ferus lacerat; nam iuris nescius omnem
depravat rerum naturam caecus et amens.

65 Quod reliquum est, Broccharde, meis hortantibus aures
si pergas adhibere, tuae pacique reique
prospicies forsan melius laudique futurae.
Ingenium viget acre tibi. Facundia linguam
servat pulchra tuam. Studium si cominus addis,

70 mox eris in primis hominum quem fama frequentet.
Sic aderit tibi certa quies mercesque labore
digna tuo. Noceas nulli. Prodesse probato
cuique queas pariter gratus terraeque poloque.
Nanque tibi quae vita datur Mavortis in atris

75 fluctibus horrisoni, dum nocte dieque periclis
millibus obiectas caput et vix fata repellis?
Num maior te quaestus agit? Maiore periclo
hunc sequeris? Qui tantus habet tua pectora daemon,
ut cupias animi quaestum praeferre quieti?

80 Praeterea non est te dignus quaestus, amice,
qui sit maior habens mixtam cum crimine culpam.
Qualis militia est? Quo bellum iure movetur?
Relligio quae casta duces? Qui castra tuetur
ordo vel officium? Non omnia fraude geruntur?

85 Iusticiae locus ullus? Laus ulla decoro?
Ille quidem miles solus censetur? Avaras
quisquis flagret opes veneresque, feratur ad omnem.
Quid tanti facias quaestum, Broccharde, rapinae
atque doli, species ut te non tangat honesti?

90 Sunt aliae multae, levior quas culpa ministret,
nummiferaeque artes tibi, quae stipare Penates
aere queant grandi. Sed quid tibi fecerit aurum
maius scire velim? Quid plus tibi copia Crassi

tion, whether earned justly or from envy, harms one even when things are going well. Envy assails good deeds with malignant talk, and unless righteous deeds are accompanied by sure governance, savage envy wreaks havoc. For blind, irrational, and utterly ignorant of justice, envy corrupts the entire nature of things.

As for the rest, my Brocardo: if you listen to my exhortations 65 you will perhaps take more care for your own benefit, your peace of mind, and your future glory. Your keen intellect thrives. Beautiful eloquence adorns your speech. If you seriously engage in study, 70 you will be among the first of those men whom fame visits. Thus you will gain a certain tranquility and rewards worthy of your work. May you harm no one. May you likewise be able to help every good man, and may you be equally beloved on earth and in heaven. For what life have you amid the dark storms of discordant war, when you place yourself in the midst of a thousand perils day 75 and night and barely repel death?

No greater business moves you, does it? Will you pursue this road amid still greater danger? What powerful spirit[39] has taken possession of your heart that you have chosen this life over peace of mind? Besides, it is a business unworthy of you, my friend, 80 since it too much mingles a sense of guilt with crime. What does it mean to serve in the army? Under what law is war started? What holy religion moves your captains? What order or service protects a garrison? Are not all wars waged fraudulently? Is there 85 any place for justice? Any praise for honor? Is only the soldier valued? Whoever burns with greed for money and sex, let him go for it all.

Why, Brocardo, do you consider rapine and treachery so important that the image of honor does not move you? There are so 90 many other ways of making money that committing a less troublesome offense could offer you — things that could pack your house with coins. But what would more gold do for you, I'd like to know? What more would the wealth of Crassus, who was swim-

afferat auriflui? Quid lauti mensa Luculli?
95   Non tibi sat fuerit, veniat si mensa secunda
et mediocris honos vestis famulusque modestus
atque ancilla tacens, tectum quod servet ab imbri
aestivaque siti? Quis pluribus ipsa voluptas
mollis eget? Vives laetus musisque tibique,
100   integer et sanus, nullis obnoxius armis
aut praedae aut veneri quam Mars tibi praemia ponit.

: 8 :

Si te trux adeo podagra torquet,
nec cessat laterum dolor, podarge,
affligitque premens nec exeundi
urinae reperit viam profusus
5   imber, pone modum gulae voraci
et dirae veneri. Quibus per omnis
quando luxurias ruis protervus,
morbum non pateris subactus unum.
Membris te cruciat doloris haerens
10   aestus. Quo penitus furis procellis
excitus rabidis per omne mentis
excussae facinus, trahit volentem
hanc corpus, ratio quod ipsa nullis
fraenis compositum suprema rexit.
15   Hinc fervet vitiis furens et atrae
pestis flammigerum recludit aestum.
Hinc humana simul deumque iura
contemnit penitus nefas in omne

ming in it, get for you? Or the banquets of elegant Lucullus? Will
it not be enough for you if you enjoy a full meal, moderately hon-   95
orable attire, a decent manservant and a quiet maidservant, and a
roof to protect you from the rain and the dry heat of summer?
What more does soft pleasure require? You will live happily with
yourself and the Muses and be healthy and well — and not at the
mercy of the arms, spoils, and women that war offers you as its re-   100
wards.

: 8 :

To a glutton

If that fierce disease of the feet[40] torments you so terribly, O fleet-
footed one, and the pain in your side does not subside, if its pres-
sure afflicts you and the copious flow of urine finds no way out,
then muzzle your gluttonous maw and put the brakes on dire sex.   5
Because of this, when you plunge downward into every excess you
suffer from not just one ailment. A hot wave of pain shoots
through you, clinging to your limbs. Then attacked by storms rag-
ing deep within you, you're off on a rampage through every crime   10
of a mind gone mad; for your body — once ruled by lofty reason it-
self but tempered now by no restraints — drags your willing mind
behind it. Your body seethes and rages with disease and lays bare   15
the fiery heat of this dark pestilence, while your mind rushes head-
long into every crime, and prone to every outrage, it treats the

praceps flagitiisque prona cunctis.
20   Quod si sustuleris nimis, podarge,
    quod praestas veneri gulaeque turgens,
    nec torquebere corporis dolore,
    nec tot nequitiis comes protervus
    accedes populo levis susurrus.

: 9 :

[POETA]

    Cypris, quae placidis fluis
in venas facibus, germina frigido
    trunco fundere gestiens,
noli mi, precor, igni latitans novo
5   fallax raetis tendere.
Novi te gemino militiae parens
    functus munere nubilis.
Quid me tertia nunc emeritum premis
    taedis iura iugalibus
10   iam barba penitus veste subalbica
    tecta, diva, resumere?
Caelebs institui quod reliquum datur
    vitae ducere labilis,
quamvis Nicoleos Quintus, Olympii
15   qui servat solium Iovis,
semper pollicitis spem trahat novis,
    facturus penitus nihil.

laws of gods and men with contempt. But if you will give up, O
fleet-footed one, that which you, swollen to bursting, devote to sex   20
and gluttony, neither will you, O thoughtless partner in so many
crimes, be tortured by physical pain, nor will you be the subject of
the tattle of the frivolous mob.

: 9 :

Dialogue of Venus, Neptune, Vulcan, and Filelfo
On the prospect of a third marriage[41]

POET

You, Cyprian goddess, who flow secretly and stealthily into men's
veins with kindly flames, do not, I beg you, prepare nets to catch
me with new fire, desiring to plant seeds in a cold trunk. I am a fa-   5
ther and have performed my duty twice as a soldier of the nuptial
bed[42] and I know you. Why, goddess, do you press me to take on
the obligations of the wedding torches for the third time now,
though I am already a veteran, my tunic now veiled by a beard   10
grown white? I have resolved to lead what remains of my declining
years as a celibate. However much Nicholas V, who guards the
throne of Olympian Jove, prolongs my hopes with new promises,   15
he will do nothing. So still grieving that I, an old man, have

Saevis me tamen uri facibus dolens,
   quas arcu puer impigro
20 te natus iaculatur feriens senem,
   Neptuni patris ad forum
te, Cypris, voco matrem pueri trucis.
   Te praestare decet tuus
quidquid filius erraverit improbus.
25   Aetas nam puerum rudis
defendit, genitrix qua premeris mala.
   Nam praecepta sequens tua,
intactum sceleris linquit atrox nihil.
   Ah, quid pectora vulneras
30 saeva percutiens nuda Venus face!
   Oro parce fatentibus
erratum, superis numen et inferis
   ingens. Nam dolor opprimens
cogit ne penitus cuncta remetiar.
35   Verum non graviter ferens
paucis quod volumus dicere, pectore
   leni sic facilis tuo
hauri ne teneat me timor eloqui
   quod causae faveat meae.

[VENUS]

40 Quamvis nulla queas iura profarier,
   nostrum quae superent tuis
ius nugis, Venus in ius veniens manus
   tecum conferat ultimas.
Neptunus senior quem petis arbiter
45   esto. Cui paribus quoque
Vulcanus sedeat lancibus additus.
   Nanque sic melius duo

caught fire, struck by the flaming missiles that your son, the boy
with the busy bow, has shot at me, I summon you, Venus, mother   20
of the hostile boy, to father Neptune's court. It is fitting that you
should answer for whatever wrong your wicked son has commit-
ted. For though his youth protects the boy, the same thing indicts   25
you as a bad mother. For following your precepts he has left
no heinous crime untried. Ah, why do you wound unprotected
hearts, Venus, when you shake your cruel brand! I beg you, O   30
great divinity to the gods above and those below, spare those who
confess their wrongs. For heavy sorrow forces me not to retrace all
my steps again. But don't take ill what I want to say quickly. Listen   35
with a gentle heart, so that fear won't keep me from saying what
supports my cause.

VENUS

Although you cannot present legal arguments as to why your triv-
ial complaints should supersede our rights, allow Venus to ap-   40
proach the bench and do decisive battle with you. Let aged Nep-
tune, whom you seek, be the judge. May Vulcan also be seated,   45
weighing in equally on this case. For two will be better at reach-

quod verum fuerit iudicium ferant,
    praesertim similes die
50 et priscis odiis pectora dissoni.

[POETA]

    Recte, diva, mones. Duo
isti quos memoras et graviter simul
    et iuste poterunt dei
quid par sit fieri dicere protinus.
55   Quare tu iubeas rogo
ut litem placidis auribus audiant.

[NEPTUNUS]

Sedemus ecce litis omnes invicem
leges et omne ius et omnem protinus
causam volentes nosse prorsus ac simul
60 pernosse. Quare quid querare grandior
dic tu prior, iuris quod habeas afferens.
Venus vicissim siquid haud fictum velit,
referat. Uterque dicet aequos iudices.

[POETA]

Nos tertium iubet senes haec nubere,
65 qui filios et filias maiusculas
minusculasque dotis absque munere
habemus, iniuste movens inuriam!

[VENUS]

Insanit hic homo. Nec ipse se valet
dignosse. Qui nec quinquies soles decem
70 duosque natus integros, simulat senem

ing a true verdict—especially as they are alike in age and at odds
with the other because of ancient quarrels.   50

POET

You give good advice, goddess. Those two gods whom you name
will be able to speak seriously and at the same time say what is just
without delay. Therefore I ask you to bid them to listen to the dis-   55
pute with equanimity.

NEPTUNE

Look, here we sit wanting to know and understand immediately
and wholly all the disputes, laws, the legal points and arguments
pertaining to the dispute. Since you are an older man, state your   60
complaint first, making clear what right you have to be heard. Let
Venus, in turn, bring forth the truth of her case. Each party will
say that the judges are fair.

POET

She commands us old men to marry for the third time, though I
have sons and older and younger daughters without the means for   65
a dowry—thus she wrongly perpetrates an injustice.

VENUS

This man is mad, nor is he capable of seeing who he really is. For
though he is not yet fifty-two, he pretends he is an old man, while   70

sese, valens membris simulque sensibus.
Natos quid audax memorat aut natas refert?
Natura tanquam ponat invidens modum,
vis donec adsit, ne novus fiat pater.
75   Et vitis uvas et nuces arbor suas,
donec nitor subest et intimus vigor,
quae cessat unquam? Iudices aequissimi,
nolite fiat tanta summi filiae
Iovis benignae vis nefas ac dedecus!
80   Nam se quod inquit pauperem fallit volens,
qui dives unus divites superet viros
plaerosque, vulgi quos levis tollit favor.
Non est is unquam pauper hac vita brevi
censendus aeque quisquis unus omnibus
85   in rebus idem possit esse pectore
infractus alto, quisquis et nullam sui
partem fugaci cedat et fragili bono.

[NEPTUNUS]

Utrique vestrum causa suscipitur pia.
Nam credit alter pluribus se demere
90   curis, quietem quae negant animo gravi.
Et ipsa iure vis genus mortalibus
augescat in dies suum iisdem surculis.
Quare, poeta, non tibi natum modo
sed omnibus quot egregius alit labos
95   meminisse debes. Optimis avibus probae
te coniugi concede rursum, nec time.
Nam nos simul duo favebimus tibi,
aderitque Iuno dextera et praesens Venus.
Quid? Et quod admodum tibi optandum putes:
100   multis levabit uxor et magnis tuum

being equally strong of mind and body. Why does he talk about his sons? Why does he chatter about daughters? Envious nature does not set the limit on becoming a parent again — as long as the power is there. A vine produces grapes and a tree nuts: as long as   75
there is a glow and vigor within, what vine or tree ever ceases to produce? O fairest judges, may the great power of the kindly daughter of loftiest Jupiter not become a byword for impiety and dishonor! For he deliberately lies when he says he is a poor man. For with his wealth alone he surpasses the wealth of many wealthy   80
men, who are lionized by the fickle favor of the mob. No one should ever be counted as poor in this brief life who can remain unbroken and high-hearted no matter what the circumstances, yet   85
surrenders no part of himself for a fleeting and fragile profit.

NEPTUNE

An honorable case has been preselected by each of you. For one of you believes he is removing himself from the numerous cares that ravage the serenity of a serious mind. On the other hand, as is   90
right, may the life force in mortals[43] increase its own kind with like offspring each day. And so, poet, you ought to remember that your son is not yours alone but belongs to all men whom your extraordinary labor nourishes. So when the portents are optimal, give   95
yourself to a good wife again and do not be afraid. For we two will favor you and Venus will be present with Juno on the right. What more is there to say? Regarding what you think you should most hope for, a wife will relieve your troubled heart of your many   100

pectusque et omnem mentis affectum tuae
curis, domum quae curet intus provida,
nec te sinat mulieribus premi virum
ullis, ineptiis sed omnino vaces.
105   Quo liber et tuum colas Apollinem
et eius omnis filias simul novem.

[VULCANUS]

Quantum videre videor, est ovis lupis
commissa nostra. Num vir uxori neget
tandem quod urat iurgiis precibus minis
110   subblandienti? Alumnus an quicquam abnuat?

[POETA]

Me sponte victum dedidi. Poenas luam.
Verum quid est verbis opus? Iudex dolo
est omnis omni deditus. Pensi nihil
fidei nihil prorsus; nec ambit nec colit.
115   At nos idem verbis agamus. Postea
tempus monebit quid mihi praestet magis.
Venus una quae dearum
decus omnium peremne
generi benigna nostro
120   tribuis, mihi severo
facilis precamur adsis.
Fateor, meremur omnem
cruciatum; at ipsa culpam
ignosce mitis omnem,
125   tibi quam pudore solum
admiseram, Dianae
fore qui meam pudicam
vitam tuae sorori

cares, since being prudent, she will attend to the affairs of your home. Nor would she allow you as her husband to be bothered by any women, and you would be entirely free of all trivial matters. And so you would be free to worship your god Apollo and all his nine daughters.

105

VULCAN

To the extent that I seem to see the case, our sheep has been entrusted to the wolves. Would a husband refuse a flattering wife what she is determined to get by quarreling, pleading, and threats? And would the one she cares for deny her anything?

110

POET

Since I'm the loser, I have surrendered willingly. I'll pay the penalty. But what more can I say? Each of the judges has engaged in every sort of fraud. There is no thought and no integrity at all; the judges embrace and cultivate neither. But let us do the same verbally. Afterwards, time will tell what course will be preferable for me. Venus, perennial glory of all goddesses, you who alone confer kindnesses upon our race, I beg you: come to me and be easy, because I am heavy-hearted. I confess that I deserve every torture, but you yourself, gentle one, pardon all my sins against you, which I had committed only out of a sense of shame. For I, having no part in love, had decided that my life would be pure for your sister

115

120

125

statuissem amoris expers.

130 Nam filius Cupido
tuus, O Venus, medullas
fulva meas sagitta
cessaverat ferire.
Nunc te libens per omnis,

135 Citherea diva, cursum
vitae sequar maritus,
facias modo pudica
et moribus modestis
taciturnitatis usum

140 servare quaeque norit,
uxor meas in aedis
veniat bonis decora
avibus tuoque ductu
maioribusque digna

145 dignis suis itemque
pulchrae futura prolis
mater viroque grata
et dives et puella.
At vos, quis annos bene concordantibus omnis

150 innocuo deducimus aevo
pollicitis, servate fidem. Tu rector aquarum,
qui fontes pontumque gubernas,
adsis sponte favens nostri radicibus horti,
qui sine te promittere sucum

155 graminibus nunquam speret temerarius ullum
sed penitus languescere pergat.
Tu quo celesti qui primus fulmine flamas
accipiens mortalibus ignem
tradideras Niloque tuo, fac frigidus imber

160 ne noceat, Vulcane, novali.

Diana, since Cupid, your son, Venus, had ceased to strike my   130
heart with his golden arrow. Now divine Cytherea, I shall gladly
attend you for the rest of my entire life as a husband, provided   135
only that you see to it that the wife who enters my house is a
chaste girl, has modest ways, and knows how to follow the custom
of silence. A graceful girl, she should come with good auspices and   140
be worthy under your tutelage of her honorable forebears; and as   145
the future mother of beautiful offspring, she should be young,
wealthy, and pleasing to me, her husband. But you, Venus, whose
treaties and promises we have spent all our years concluding from
an innocent age on,[44] be loyal to us. And you, ruler of the waters   150
and governor of the seas and the springs, come willingly and tend
the roots of our garden.[45] For these would never have the temerity
to hope to produce any juice from the grass without you but   155
would continue to languish. You also, Vulcan, who, after receiving
your heavenly lightning and thunder first handed down fire to
mortals and to your father the Nile,[46] see that your cold rain never   160
harms the crops. At the same time take care of your fellow gods,

Atque simul curate pares, ne torpeat horti
    custos deditus usque sopori,
sed vigilet ne fur incustodita latenter
    surripiat ridentibus astris.
165 Est etiam optandum in primis delectet Apollo
    ut magis et mea numina Musae
uxorem nimius pressi quam cultus agelli
    et repetiti saeminis hora.

: 10 :

Arcimbolde, gravi me voce hortaris ut alta
bella canam, quaecumque modo Mavorte secundo
Insubrium proceres divi post fata Philippi
gesserunt et iure mones. Nam maxima rerum
5 attulit Italiae populus momenta labanti
hic primum nulli cedens pietate nec armis.
Nam dum bella fugit legis servator et aequi,
tranquilla dum pace cupit fovisse quietem,
haud Bellona sinit. Totum perturbat Erinys
10 effera flagrantem flamis surgentibus orbem.
Illinc funereas Aurelia surgit in iras
elatisque furor Germanus cingitur armis.
Hinc et finitimi cunctas populique ducesque
sollicitant urbes et blandis oppida temptant
15 pollicitis. Venetum tempestas ingruit inde
omnia prosternens ac turbinis instar et ignis
templa domosque una vastansque premensque ruina.

so that the keeper of the garden[47] does not grow tired and fall asleep. He should be watchful so that no thief will steal anything from the untended garden while the stars simply laugh. But this should be my first hope: that Apollo and my deities, the Muses, 165 will delight my wife more than repeated seasons of sowing and cultivation of a little field already over-burdened.[48]

: 10 :

To Nicolò Arcimboldi
On war and writing poetry

Arcimboldi, you urge me to sing in a serious vein of the great wars the leaders of the Milanese fought under the favorable auspices of Mars after divine Filippo's death, and you advise me rightly. For bowing to no nation in piety or arms,[49] this people first brought events of the greatest moment to Italy, when she was on a down- 5 ward course. For though the guardian of the law and justice shuns war and longs to foster peace and tranquility, Bellona does not al- low it. Savage Erinys brings madness to the entire world, setting it ablaze with raging flames. In the north, the Aurelian way seethes 10 with deadly wrath and German rage prepares its arms for war. And here the neighboring peoples and their leaders repeatedly ha- rass all our cities, while they lure the towns to their side with sweet promises. A regiment of Venetians rushes in, leveling every- 15 thing to the ground. A firestorm like a cyclone consumes churches and homes together, engulfing everything in ruin. In hard times

Rebus in adversis animos Fortuna recludit,
quos olim fucata fides simularat amicos.
20 Undique deficiunt socii fiuntque rebelles,
quos decuit servare fidem. Ius omne piumque
una strage perit. Nihil est quod servet honestum.
Celsa quidem Probitas firmis radicibus haerens
vim monstrare suam solidumque ostendere robur
25 tum solet intrepide, cum magnis septa periclis
egregios peperit certa pro laude triumphos.
Insubribus postquam pax atque optata negantur
otia, nec possunt ulla vel lege vel aequo
ius apud hostilis animos mentesque feroces
30 defendisse suum, demum per tristia Martis
bella vel inviti dubio discrimine iniquam
vim prohibere parant. Non multo milite Francos
caede sub horribili fusos docuere furentem
in primis nocuisse suis auctoribus iram.
35 Inde Placentini nimia levitate rebelles
edidicere quibus dementia frangitur armis.
At Venetum classes praedamque necemque minantis
Eridanus sensit flamis ferroque ruentes.
Et ne quaeque loquar, quae plurima longius ultro
40 carmen agant: quali quam multo milite fraeti
iidem etiam Veneti funesta clade subacti,
qua Caravaginos cingebant aggere campos,
humanas res quasque deum curare probarunt.
Ter Venetos vicisse quid est, nisi lumen et ipsum
45 Italiae solem velut obscurasse micantis?
Haec sunt Insubribus bene concordantibus acta,
quae, ni stulta hominum mens et discordia praeceps
impediisset, erant iam nobis parta quietis
otia tranquillae rebusque et laude verendis.

Fortune exposes the hearts of men whom feigned loyalty had once
pretended were friends. Thus our allies betray us on all sides and   20
those who should have remained loyal have turned against us. All
justice and piety perish in a single slaughter and nothing is left to
save honor. But clinging fearlessly to firm roots, lofty Probity not
only flaunts her own might and enduring strength but, even when
she is hemmed in by grave dangers, she produces extraordinary   25
triumphs for sure praise. Thus when the Milanese were denied
peace and long hoped-for security, and they could not defend their
rights with either law or justice amid savage minds and hostile
souls through baneful wars, finally they, perhaps unwillingly since   30
the outcome of the war was uncertain, prepared to put an end to
the unjust violence. With few soldiers they first cut down the
French in a horrible slaughter, teaching them that raging anger
harms its authors first. Next the Piacenzans learned, having re-
belled too easily,[50] how folly is broken in war.   35

It was the Eridanus[51] that saw the Venetian warships, which
threatened slaughter and spoils, fall victim to fire and sword. But
let me not recount the story of every battle, for this would call for
a longer poem: how many and what sort of soldiers those Vene-   40
tians defeated in the disaster at Caravaggio deployed, where they
surrounded the Caravaggian fields with a mound, and about what
human affairs they proved God almighty did care. But what did it
mean to have triumphed over the Venetians three times if not to
have eclipsed the very sun of shining Italy? As long as there was   45
concord among the Milanese, these campaigns of theirs were well
fought and they would have brought us the peace of tranquil re-
pose with praise and honorable deeds — if only the foolish minds
of men and rash discord had not stood in the way. But we drove

50   Expulimus nostros et vires auximus hosti
     infestumque virum bellisque armisque tremendum
     reddimus nobis. Civili caede natamus.
     Moenibus obsessi premimur belloque fameque.
     En stimulat rabies. Intus pugnamus et extra.
55   Nec desunt animi tamen et Mavortia virtus.
     Te ductore, modo defensa Moguntia sensit,
     Karole, quam pauci innumeros prostravimus hostes.
     Mox etiam Venetum tanta obsidione labantem
     tendentemque manus Chremam te, Karole, rursus
60   solvimus, intrepido belli duce. Promptus et acer
     est animus nostris cunctisque in rebus agendis
     callidus et fortis. Civilis turbat Erinys
     omnia, seditio qua ius simul omne piumque
     sustulit e medio, miscens hostesque deosque.
65   Haec postrema quidem vitio mihi danda videntur
     Insubribus, quod se per mutua vulnera caedant,
     laude sed ingenti sunt illa ferenda sub astra,
     quis hostes fregere truces pulchrosque triumphos
     advexere suis. Ea nunc si carmine digno
70   prosequar atque suis bene convenientia rebus
     munera reddidero, cuncti laudentque probentque.
     At mea Musa quidem, tam grandi functa labore,
     praemia quae speret? Nescit ieiuna canoros
     expressisse sonos, dum siccis faucibus horret.
75   Non et enim tanti laudes, quae laudibus ornat,
     Musa facit, perisse fame quo multa canendo
     atque toga caruisse velit. Non tale Maronis
     munus erat magni. Nullus mihi Pollio, nullus
     Maecenas. Augustus opem mihi ferre paratus

our friends from the city and added strength to the enemy — and   50
we caused a man magnificent in war and arms to turn against us.[52]
We are swimming in the blood of our citizens. Barricaded inside
our walls, war and famine weigh heavily on us. Look, madness
rages. We battle the enemy without and within. Still, we do not
lack courage or virtue in battle.   55

With you as leader, Carlo,[53] just now the Moguntian[54] defense
learned how we few demolished the innumerable troops of the en-
emy. Again with you as our intrepid leader, we freed Crema. For
weakened by the siege of the Venetians, she held out her arms to
you, O intrepid leader in war. For Carlo's mind is both ready and   60
quick, and in all our campaigns he has been courageous and
shrewd. But the Fury of civil war throws all things into confusion,
and sedition casts out all law and piety from the world, confound-
ing gods and enemies. The blame for these last things must be-   65
long, it seems to me, to the Milanese, since they have destroyed
one another in mutual slaughter. But other things, by which they
broke the savage enemy and brought back beautiful triumphs to
their own people, must be praised to the skies. If I now pursue
these things so deserving of song and offer eulogies well-suited to   70
their deeds, let all men praise and esteem me. But what gifts can
my Muse hope for, once she has performed so great a labor?
Thirsty, she cannot give voice to melodious strains while she shiv-
ers and her throat is dry. My Muse does not value the exploits
which she adorns with her accolades so highly that she would   75
want to die of hunger after all her singing or be without a cloak.
This was not mighty Virgil's fate. But I have no Pollio and no
Maecenas. Nor is there any Augustus who is ready to help me. I

80   nullus adest. Laudes mihi nullas emero, laudes
vaendere cui liceat. Quod si mihi saeva Philippum
servasset Fortuna ducem, qui Caesare maior
unus et Augusto fuerat praestantior omni,
non equidem tales successus Martis opimi
85   interitum Laethes paterer fative subire.
Nunc autem quoniam nullis est cura Camoenae,
quin periit virtutis honos, nec lingua nec ipsa
temptet arundo aliquid mea, quod sit Apolline dignum.
Sic ingrata mihi turbat sententia pectus
90   plebis et istorum quibus haec respublica servit,
heu, miseranda nimis. Nam quos laudavero? Iustos?
Non licet. Exacti sunt omnes urbe probati
illustresque viri. Gerit en zonaria pulchros
turba magistratus: fartor, licitator, adulter,
95   lenoque. Periurus cum collusore superbit.
Horum ego quid laudem? Quas patravere nefandis
insidiis caedes? Tanta impietate necatos
tot cives? Num facta canam civisque tacebo?
Spes mihi quae tandem fuerit? Num fructus honosve?
100   Quin nec abire licet, nec tuta licentia fandi
mi datur. Assenterne loco? Assentatio non est
pectoris ingenui. Nequeo simulata referre;
nam nec vera licet. Quod si deus ipse favebit,
si proceres victrix repetet respublica primos,
105   inclyta nobilitas si plebem franget inertem,
carmine grandiloquo quantum mea Musa valebit.
Prosequar Insubrium partos ex hoste triumphos,
praemia digna meo ducturus fixa labore,
laude quod extulerim qui digni laude fuissent.
110   Nil cum plebe mihi; procul absit vulgus ineptum.
Quin potius toto mihi pectore Karolus ille,

shall buy no praises for myself, since I am not permitted to sell   80
my songs of praise. But if cruel Fortune had saved my Duke
Filippo, who alone was greater than Caesar and more excellent
than any Augustus, I would not have had to suffer the successes of
wealthy Mars or to submit to the annihilation of the river Lethe or
death.   85

But now, since no one cares about my Camena[55] — but even re-
spect for virtue has died — neither my tongue nor my flute can at-
tempt anything worthy of Apollo. And so the displeasing thought
of the plebs and those men to whom this republic is enslaved —   90
she, alas, so much to be pitied — disturbs me. For whom shall I
praise? The just? It is not permitted. All the good and preeminent
men have been expelled from the city. Look, the rabble, girt with
their moneybelts, have taken over our noble magistracies — the
chicken farmer, the auctioneer, the adulterer, the pimp. The per-
jurer and his accomplice now put on airs. What should I praise of   95
theirs? The murders they have committed along with their un-
speakable plots? The number of citizens they killed so treacher-
ously? Am I supposed to hymn their deeds and remain silent
about our citizens? What hope have I left in the end? For profit or
honor? I can neither leave this place nor have I the freedom to
speak. Should I say flattering things about the place? But this is   100
not possible for an honest heart. I can't speak lies, nor am I al-
lowed to tell the truth. But if God himself supports me, if the vic-
torious republic seeks the foremost leaders, if the illustrious nobil-
ity crushes the incompetent plebs, how strong and eloquent my   105
Muse will make my poems. I shall honor the triumphs of the Mil-
anese won over the enemy in order to receive the gifts decreed
worthy of my work — because I will have eulogized men who were
worthy of praise. With the plebs I'll have nothing to do. The fool-
ish rabble should keep their distance.[56] But rather, my whole heart   110

Francia cui sacro paret fortissima regi,
volvitur exhortans sibi ne praeponere quenquam
ex hominum numero studeam, quos novit Eous,
115   novit et occiduus Titan Boreasque Notusque.
Plura loqui prohibet Clio, quae prima sororum
ecce canit citharam digytis dum pulsat Apollo.

turns on thoughts of that King Charles, the holy prince whom bravest France obeys, and he urges me to prefer to him no one who is known to Eos, western Titan, Boreas or Notus. Clio pro- 115 hibits me from saying more — she, first among her sisters, who sings while Apollo plucks his lyre.

CLIO
LIBER SECUNDUM

Quem mihi primum titulos per omnes
inclytae laudis referas canendum?
Quem virum, Clio, memores superbo
    carmine dignum?
5   Karolum siquis meritis parentum
efferat, laudis precium meretur,
quos tamen cunctos velut astra Phoebus
    lumine lustrat.
Mantua gaudet patria paterna
10   stirpe Gonzagas celebrandus heros,
pacis et belli titulis per omnem
    cognitus orbem.
Mantuam magnus posuit Bianor
Mantoos nomen genetricis urbi
15   inserens natus Tiberi parente
    fortis et acer.
Haec enim, postquam pater ille vates
nobilis cessit moribundus Horcho,
navigans nostras avibus secundis
20   venit in oras.
Coniugi sese Tiberi volentem
iunxit Etrusco peperitque natum

84

CLIO
BOOK II

:   I   :

To Carlo Gonzaga
Encomium

Whom would you say I should celebrate first with all the honors of far-famed praise?[1] Whom, O Clio, would you call worthy of a lofty poem? If anyone praises Carlo with a eulogy of his forebears, he deserves a reward for his paean of praise — for the prince illuminates all those men with his own light, just as Phoebus does the stars. The famous hero rejoices in Mantua, the native land of his paternal forebears, the Gonzaga, though he is known everywhere in the world for the honors he has won in both war and peace.

Great Bianor, son of Manto and father Tiber, brave and strong, founded Mantua, giving the city his mother's name.[2] For after the noble soothsayer who was her father died and departed to Orcus, Manto came to our shores, sailing under favorable omens. There she willingly married the Etruscan Tiber and gave birth to a son,

85

et suo dignum simul et paterni
    sanguinis ortu.
25   Hic ut augescens adolevit aetas,
corde nil secum meditante parvum,
finibus celsas patriis et amplas
    addidit urbes.
Quidquid inferni superique fluctus
30   ambiunt pulchris domitans triumphis
signa Benaci statuit sub imis
    vallibus alti.
Hinc fluens claris taciturnis undis
Mincius vallis ruit in virentes
35   et lacum tuta facit arce multo
    aequore crescens.
Hic ubi multam superis Bianor
victimam supplex meritis litavit,
captus aprici bonitate campi
40   condidit urbem.
Mantuam gratus memori Bianor
filius matris titulo dicavit,
ast avito Tiresiam vocavit
    nomine portam.
45   Siquis ignarus veteris decoris
nosse Gonzagas cupiat verende
principes urbis, modulis Camoenae
    praebeat aures.
Haud enim mendax dea vult videri,
50   sola quae laudem studiosa curat.
Nec potest falli dea, nec probatos
    fallere quaerit.
Hercules, magni Iovis illa proles,
aureo cornu gelidae Dianae

Bianor, a man worthy of both her own and his father's line.[3] And
when this son grew up, pondering great things, he added grand   25
and glorious cities to his father's realm. Conquering with beautiful
triumphs lands that were bounded by rivers both to the north and
the south, Bianor placed his standards deep in the valleys of lofty   30
Lake Benacus,[4] from which the Mincio flows, rushing in quiet and
bright waves into green vales. It also forms a lake with a secure cit-
adel as it grows deeper with bountiful water. Here Bianor, taken   35
with the sunny beauty of the land, sacrificed in supplication many
a victim to the just gods and founded a city. And he gratefully   40
called the place Mantua, a name honoring his mother, and he
named the city gate "Tiresia" after his grandfather.

If anyone is ignorant of the ancient glory of the Gonzaga and   45
wishes to know the princes of this ancient city, he should listen to
the lyric poetry of Camena.[5] For the goddess, whose care it is to
foster paeans of praise, by no means wishes to appear the liar. For   50
neither can she be deceived, nor does she seek to deceive up-
right men.

After the hero Hercules, a scion of mighty Jove, caught the fleet
deer with the golden horns that had belonged to cold-hearted Di-

55   victor ut cervam tenuit volantem,
           vincitur arte.
     Nanque tranquillus tumidi remensus
     terga quem frigus solidarat Istri,
     sensit amissam doluitque cervam
60   fraude Getharum.
     Dumque subreptae studio pererrat
     laudis, Alcides capitur puellae
     igne quam fures Synesin per umbras
          sponte tulerunt.
65   Callidum forti Synesis per astum
     Herculi sese parat obsequentem;
     vincit hunc quisquis superabat omnes
          vafra puella.
     Arte Gonzagas monitus Getharum,
70   qui viae sese comitem dedisset
     Herculi duro satus ipse Marte
          furta recludit.
     Nanque Gonzagas genitus Merimna,
     quam gravem dulci domitam sopore
75   fecerit Mavors, duce matre novit
          gesta dolumque.
     Basiis pulchre fruitur puellae
     ductor Alcides. Comes ille cervam
     nocte clam surgens tacitus sub ipsa
80   castra reducit.
     'Gentis O nostrae decus! O suprema
     lux Achivorum! Gethiae colonos
     linque fallaces. Reducem benignus
          accipe cervam.'
85   Talibus ductor monitis vocantem
     sentit Alcides hilarisque surgit

ana, he himself was taken by trickery.[6] For after walking back 55
across the swollen river Ister, which the winter had frozen solid,
this peaceful man realized and grieved that he had lost his deer
through the deceit of the Getae. Now, while Hercules was wan- 60
dering in search of the prize stolen from him, he was smitten with
love for a girl whom the thieves had brought to him at night — and
the girl was not unwilling.[7] So with cunning artifice, this girl
Synesis[8] readied herself to surrender to powerful Hercules. Thus 65
an artful girl got the better of a man who vanquished all other
men.

But Gonzaga, who had gone with Hercules as his companion
on this expedition and who was a son of Mars himself, learned of 70
the deceit of the Getae and found the stolen deer. For Gonzaga
was the son of Merimna, whom Mars made pregnant when she
was buried in sweet sleep. Now with his mother's teaching, he rec-
ognized the trick and all that had transpired. So while Hercules, 75
the leader of the expedition, was enjoying the kisses of Synesis,
Gonzaga, his companion, secretly rose during the night and qui-
etly brought the deer back. "O glory of our nation! O supreme 80
light of the Achaeans!" he said to Hercules, "You must abandon
the scheming Getae. Kindly take the deer which has been restored
to you." After listening to his counsel, the leader Hercules stood 85

'Hanc tuo,' dicens, 'statuo vocari
　　nomine dudum.'
Inde Gonzagam Venetis in agris
90　Mantuae qua se veneranda tellus
erigit cervam vocitant secutae
　　'Mantoa!' gentes.
Nam deum iussu patriis ab oris
fata post cari lachrymanda patris
95　dum petit terras Latii superbi
　　inclyta Manto,
ducit illustris socium laboris,
quem dedit partu Synesi creata
Iphis, exultans genitoris alti
100　　Herculis ortu.
Patre Gonzaga genitus patritum
nomen et robur referens pudicam
Iphin altricem tulerat secutus
　　Mantoa nantem.
105　Nosse iam sortem cupiens futuram,
fata Cirrhaeo didicit sub antro,
quis foret clarus Venetis in oris
　　stirpe nepotum.
Ergo materna simul et paterna
110　stirpe mirandum celebrare summis
Karolum siquis titulis veretur,
　　nescius errat.
Lege naturae parit ulla nunquam
nec virum tigris mulier nec haedum;
115　hinc sui reddunt similem parentes
　　saemine partum.
Laude maiorum seriem per omnem
Karolus florens proprii decoris

up and smiled. "I hereby proclaim," he said, "that this deer will henceforth be called by your name."

Now, where the venerable land of Mantua rises up in the midst 90 of Venetian territory, the people, who were following the deer named "Gonzaga," again and again cried "Manto!" For when the celebrated Manto left her ancestral shores after the sad death of her beloved father and sought the lands of proud Latium, following the gods' command, she brought with her in this illustri- 95 ous task the companion whom Iphis gave her after her birth to Synesis,[9] for the girl exulted in her descent from her father, mighty Hercules. Gonzaga's son, recalling his own father's fame 100 and strength, had then carried chaste Iphis, following his foster- mother Manto on her voyage. For wanting to know his future and the fate of the Gonzaga at the Cirrhean cave,[10] he learned 105 who among his descendants' stock would be famous on Venetian shores.

Therefore, if anyone is afraid to celebrate Carlo with the high- est honors, a man distinguished by both his maternal and paternal 110 forebears, he is ignorant and he errs. According to the laws of na- ture, a female tiger never gives birth to a man or a goat; likewise parents produce offspring like themselves from their seed. Shining 115 with the glory of his ancestors in each of his lineages, Carlo so re-

gloriae nitens adeo refulget
120   munus ad omne,
ut, suis nulla probitate mancis
omnibus, lucem numeros per omnis
afferat, pollens animo simulque
    corpore magnus.
125 Nam giganteis atavum reducit
Herculem membris veluti pusillos,
quosque pygmaeos homines et ore
    reddit et actis.
Est coma Phoebus facie Minerva
130 et Iovem vultu pariterque Martem
monstrat, acceptus Veneri et Dianae
    pulcher et acer.
Adde virtutes animi probatas
quis viros omnis superat deorum
135 munere ac multo meritus labore
    nomen et auram.
Quam sit humanus facilisque nemo
nescit: in cunctos bonus et benignus
rebus et verbis fugiens protervi
140   nomina fastus.
Otii si quid reliquum ferocis
Martis a dura datur officina,
non id ignavo teritur sopore
    nocte dieve.
145 Omne sed Musis sociis dicatur,
quas habet semper comites sodales
rebus in cunctis celebrandus heros
    omnibus horis.
Gratus hinc dulci fluit ore Nestor,
150 hinc et aurata cithara canorus

flects and abounds in the fame of his own honor in all his service
that he brings his light to every rank among the populace— 120
though his own forebears lacked no probity. He is a man powerful
of mind and mighty in body. For he reincarnates his ancestor Her-
cules with his gigantic arms and legs, while he turns men into 125
puny dwarves with his oratory and his sheer physical prowess. He
has Phoebus's hair and Minerva's face. His looks remind one
equally of Jupiter and Mars; moreover, he pleases both Venus and 130
Diana since he is both beautiful and high-spirited. Add to him the
finest virtues of the mind in which he surpasses all men, earning
fame and good fortune for his devotion to the gods and for his
many labors. Everyone knows how kind and gentle he is: he is hu- 135
mane and clement toward all in both word and deed, taking care
not to acquire a reputation for princely arrogance. 140

If Carlo had any time for leisure after savage Mars' hard work-
shop, it was not wasted on idle sleep either night or day. Indeed,
all his time was devoted to his companions, the Muses, whom this 145
celebrated hero always retained as his attendants everywhere he
went and at all times. The sweet speech of Nestor flows from his
lips; he recalls the melodious Phoebus with his golden lyre, while 150

redditur Phoebus, referens Atlantis
    arte nepotem.
Quidquid et Graeci simul et Latini
rebus inventis memorent superbum,
155   ulla quod felix decorarit aetas,
    Karole, nosti.
Altius tollens oculos in imo
spem solo nullam vir, amice, ponis,
quippe qui frustra statuas harena
160   figere gressus.
Inde contemnens humiles beatae
sortis optatus fragilesque palmas,
praemium quaeris tibi quod favores
    vincat et annos.
165   Nulla te vani capiunt decoris
quaeque decernunt simulachra ficto
ore pellaces populi sequentes
    illud et illud.
Temperas omnis animum moventes
170   fraena quae servat ratione fluctus;
nulla te flagrans agitabat libido,
    nec metus urget.
Laxior nunquam stimulat voluptas;
non dolor pectus gelidum pererrans
175   contrahit; semper stabilis serena
    mente quiescis.
Quo fit ut belli placidique pacis
artibus virtus operosa nunquam
te super celsis gradibus meantem,
180   Karole, linquat.
Fortis occurrens tumidas procellas
pellis adversae; moderas secundae

calling to mind the grandson of Atlas in his patronage.[11] You are
skilled, Carlo, in all the inventions in which both Greeks and
Romans take pride and which any fortunate age would honor.   155

Raising your eyes higher, you place no hope here in the world
below since, my friend, you think it pointless to plant your foot-
steps only in the earthly arena. Next, spurning the shallow and   160
transitory prizes of a prosperous life, you seek a reward for your-
self that will surpass men's acclaim and outlast the years. No
dreams of empty honor seize you, for these are phantoms that sy-   165
cophants propose with lying lips, following now this purpose and
now that one. You control the turbulent emotions that stir the
mind, relying on reason which keeps them all at bay. Neither does   170
burning desire move you, nor does fear agitate you. Never does
loose pleasure seize your cool breast nor does the wandering pain
of love contract it. You are always calm, your mind serene.   175

And so it is, Carlo, that virtue, busy with the arts of tranquil
peace and war, will never abandon you who walk with lofty steps.   180
You drive away the gathering storms of adverse Fortune with cour-
age, and you accept wisely and with moderation every trophy she

omne fortunae sapiens trophaeum
    Pallados armis.
185 Laude non parva mihi dignus esto,
cuius infandum subiens periclum
mansit invictis animus per omnem
    viribus usum.
Nemo vir fortis merito vocari
190 quiverit qui se volucri sagittae
obicit nudus; valet omne robur
    flectere prudens.
Talibus fraetus clipeis et armis
Karolus primas Latii potentis
195 gloriae pulchris volitat per urbes
    inclytus alis.
Mente quod sentit loquitur; quod inquit
efficit; nunquam varians amictum
cogitur verbum novitate sortis
200   reddere falsum.
Attamen rerum simul et locorum
ac virum siquis pariterque legem
temporum nescit tenuisse prudens,
    ducitur infans.
205 Non enim quidquid fatuus putarit
lege servandum populus severa,
iure servetur rationis expers.
    Cuncta moventur.
Nanque terrenis nihil usque rebus
210 constat aeternum; variatur omne,
quiquid humanus variarit usus
    lege vel aeque.
Fortis haec heros animo volutans
Karolus prisca Synesi profectus

brings with the arms of Pallas when she favors you. Be worthy of   185
my great praise, you whose mind, having undergone terrible dan-
ger, has remained steadfast, its strength unconquered through ev-
ery trial.

No man can be deservedly called brave who throws himself un-   190
protected in the way of a speeding arrow: the prudent man is ca-
pable of deflecting every attack. Relying on such shields and arms,
renowned Carlo flies on the gorgeous wings of his glory through   195
the foremost cities of powerful Latium. He says what he thinks;
moreover, he does what he says. He is never coerced to lie or to
change his cloak because of a shift in fortune.   200

But if any intelligent man does not believe that men are equally
constrained by the law of things, places, and times, he is consid-
ered a fool. But even the mindless populace would not think that
whatever is maintained by draconian law should rightly be obeyed
if it is devoid of reason. All things are in motion. For nothing con-
stituted from earthly things lasts forever; everything changes that   210
human use alters, whether by law or right.[12]

Now that the courageous hero Carlo has pondered the ancient
stories, starting with Synesis, he weighs matters in a better way,

215 consultat rebus melius, sub omnem
        callidus usum.
    Sic vel in primis mea diva Clio,
    cui locum primae dedimus sororum
    ad lyram Phoebi modulos citandi,
220   hunc canet unum.
    Hunc enim Clio didicit choreas
    Martis ut victi posuit trophaea
    non secus festis pedibus subire
        quam solet arma.
225 Te meus semper numeris Apollo
    ornet et Clio et reliquae deinceps
    quaeque Parnassi coluere divae
        grande cacumen.
    O decus nostrae nitidum senectae!
230 O iubar splendens super omne sydus!
    Sis meo praesens avibus secundis,
        Karole, voto!
    Quam nimis laudi metuo superbae,
    qua viros unus nimis inter omnes
235 clarior surgis? Furit ipse livor
        semper in altos.
    Sed tamen quo te mage livor atrox
    insequi perget, magis ipse claris
    rebus incumbens superabis omnes
240   nomine terras.

prudent in all practical matters. Thus my goddess Clio, to whom 215
first and foremost of the sisters we have given the place next to
Phoebus's lyre and the task of setting the pace, will celebrate Carlo
alone. For Clio learned that when Carlo had erected the trophies 220
of vanquished Mars, he entered the dance with no less joyous
steps than when he took up arms.

May my Apollo, Clio, and the rest of the holy Muses who dwell 225
high on lofty Parnassos always honor you with poems. O delight
of our old age! O splendid light, gleaming beyond every other star!
May you be present to hear my prayer with favorable omens, O 230
Carlo! How can I fear giving too much lavish praise when you
alone rise brighter than all other men, though jealousy itself al-
ways rages against the mighty. But still, the more cruel jealousy de- 235
cides to pursue you, the more you will surpass all men on earth in
famous deeds. 240

Omnis tyrannis impium nutrit scelus,
sed nulla detestabilis certe magis
quam plebis impotentis et populi trucis.
En Insubres animi furor quantus rapit.
5   Immanitas rabidos in omne tristius
facinus trahit. Necantur insontes palam,
nullo reatus crimine ullius rei.
Libido regnat. Praeda funestos iuvat.
Abest pudor; nefas per omne publice.
10   Dirum nocentes evehuntur altius.
Laudi locus nullus. Vicissim boni[1]
alii exulant, alii relegati probrum
coguntur omne perpeti. Satellitem
pudica coniunx excipit vel lachrymans
15   testansque caelites adulterum thoro.
Stupratur omnis virgo. Divina ac item
humana quaeque iura perditis simul
parent. Nec est in improbis ullus modus.
Tu, tu deorum rector atque hominum parens,
20   cui servit omne quidquid et mundus tegit
et si quid est inane quod mundum ambiat,
tandem potenti dextera miseris opem
affer. Nec ulterius canes rabidos sine
per efferatos impiam rictus necem
25   sitire, Iupiter. Velut tigris furit
in Indiae vitulos et Ethiops ruens
taurus lupusve Maenali greges petit,

: 2 :

To Jupiter
An invective against false liberty

All tyranny nurtures impious crime. But no tyranny is more vile than that of the feckless plebs and the angry rabble. See how much insanity grips the Milanese. Savagery draws the rabid mob into ever more tragic crimes. The innocent are slaughtered in public. A 5 man can be brought up on charges and accused without there being any crime. Lewd desire reigns. Spoils please those mourning the dead. There is no shame; those guilty of every heinous crime in public are given great honor. Those doing harm are more highly exalted. There is no place for true praise. As for the good, some 10 are exiled; others are forced into retirement and must put up with every evil. The chaste wife sleeps with her servant — or weeping and invoking the gods, she takes her lover to bed. Every virgin is 15 raped. Divine and human laws both serve the corrupt. There is no moderation among the bad.

O ruler and father of the gods and men, you who are the mas- 20 ter of everything the world holds and of all the empty space that surrounds it, bring help at last to the wretched with your powerful right hand. O Jupiter, do not allow the ravening dogs to thirst for impious killing any longer, their savage jaws agape. As a tiger vents 25 its fury on young calves in India and the Ethiopian bull or the wolf attacks the sheep on Mount Maenalus,[13] just as swiftly, like a

Ossona sic Apanus et Georgius
Bisulcerus civili haustu sanguinis
30   alacres feruntur instar acti fulminis,
et neminem pestis relinquunt horridae
inopem. Perit nullo vir exemplo pius,
locus nec est ullus refellendi datus.
Obiecta sontes efficit immanitas
35   trium latronum. Dedecus nostrae ultimum
aetatis omnes posteri quod auribus
stupidis in omnes audiant gentes viri
et horreant longe. Simul nec desinant
nostri execrari temporis foedum scelus.
40   Exurgat olim quisquis unus denique
gratissimi Iovi fuerit Olympio,
qui nos tenebris eruat teterrimis.
Unus domum ministrat; unus aequore
navim gubernat; imperator bellicis
45   in rebus unus imperat. Caelum deus
ut unus aeterno regit moderamine,
sic unus urbi praesit huic princeps pius,
qui rebus afferat quietem turbidis.
Satis, O deus, poenae satis sceleri datum
50   si quod profanum perpetravimus nefas,
qui nobilis modo Philippi funera
negleximus ducis, nec ingentem sumus
honore digno prosecuti principem.
Ignosce tandem. Fer benignus flaetibus
55   opem fatentibus quod admissum est scelus.
Audimur? An frustra preces veniam petunt?
Aether ciet tonitrum. Micant radiis faces
en caelitus missae. Quis aures Martius
pulsat fragor? Tumultus en populi furit.

bolt of lightning, Ossona, Appiani, and Giorgio Bizzozero are
swept along by their thirst for the blood of the citizens.[14] And   30
they leave no one free of the horrid plague. An innocent man is
put to death without cause and there is no opportunity to refute
the charges. The cruelty of these three thieves proves them guilty.   35

Let all posterity shudder at the ultimate shame of our age,
which men of every nation far and wide will hear with horror.
May they not cease to curse our era's crimes! Let that one who
was once most pleasing to Olympian Jove stand up, so that he may   40
rescue us from foul darkness.[15] He alone tends the house. He
alone navigates the ship at sea. He alone is the commander in
chief in war. Just as one god alone rules heaven with eternal gover-   45
nance, so may one pious prince who can bring peace to this ruined
state preside over the city.

O God, enough penalty has been paid if we have perpetrated a
profane wrong, we who recently neglected the funeral rites of the   50
noble Duke Filippo. For we did not celebrate the great prince with
proper honors. Pardon us at last and kindly bring help to those
who tearfully confess that a crime has been committed.   55

Is anyone listening? Or do our prayers seek forgiveness in vain?
But look: thunder churns the air. Bolts of fire sent from heaven
flash. What clashing of arms pulses in our ears! Look, the people
are rioting. The repeated cries "Bread! Bread!" strike the very

60 'Panem! Panem!' ingeminans polos clamor ferit.
'Pereant scelesti!' Ficta libertas ruat
omni tyranno dirior, crudelior nece,
immanior qui Tartarum servat cane!
Bene est. Priores vindicat vires sibi
65 animus receptus, qui modo cecidit malis.
Passim latrones dant fugam turpi metu.

: 3 :

Sydus illustrans Latium corusca
luce qua totum remicas per orbem,
quas tibi grates referam merenti,
    Sphortia princeps?
5 O decus summum, numeros per omnis
quod means virtus peperit suprema,
tu mihi solus superis secundis
    consulis urbi.
Impii coetus miseram latronum
10 sparserant fusi fluviis cruoris
civium, quos vis furor atque habendi
    perdidit ignis.
Hinc ferus Mavors populatur agrum;
hinc fames cunctos perimit subactos.
15 Nulla spes vitae recreat cadentes;
    cuncta minantur.
Hadriae vires simulant salutem;

poles of the earth: "Death to the scoundrels!" Away with false lib- 60
erty, which is more evil than any tyrant, more cruel than death,
and more savage than the dog who guards Orcus.

All is well. Reason, which had lately fallen victim to the wicked,
regains its former vigor and is back. Everywhere the thieves are 65
fleeing in shameful fear.

: 3 :

To Francesco Sforza
The city of Milan narrates the fall of the Republic
and the triumph of Sforza

O star that shines over all Latium with shimmering luster — for
you shed your light across the entire world — what thanks, princely
Sforza, shall I convey to you? O highest glory, which your sublime
virtue brings to every rank, you alone look after me, the city, with 5
the gods' approval. Impious bands of robbers had spattered the
wretched city with rivers of blood of our citizens — the victims 10
of violence, madness and the passion for plunder. After this, sav-
age war despoiled the land; and famine overcame those it sub-
dued. No hope for life can restore the fallen. All things menace us. 15
The Venetians[16] pretend to offer salvation. They cross the rapidly

Adduam multa rapidum phalange
numine adverso superant et altis
20   collibus errant.
Ipse Franciscus probitate pollens
viribus nullis tremefactus hosti
fortis occurris medioque ponis
        castra sub agro.
25 Nanque Mercatus, tibi Vicus, omni
nudus et fossa vacuusque vallo
cinctus et nulla lapidum corona
        castra recepit.
Octo vix tecum fuerant cohortes
30 militum. Sed quas variis periclis
saepe victrices habuisse summo
        te duce nosses!
Hinc lacessebas trepidos maniplos
hostis infesti per iniqua Barrhi
35   montis errantes iuga, quosque terror
        sterneret ingens.
Hinc item nostras celer et tremendus
copias nullo duce se tuentis,
sed quibus demens furor esset auctor,
40   eminus arces.
Nam quis auderet tibi signa contra
ferre, quem cuncti populi tremiscunt
et pavent reges, Latium veretur,
        orbis honorat.
45 Si tibi soli polus est uterque
rebus in cunctis pius et benignus,
si deus tecum tua semper unus
        signa tuetur,
quae tibi adversae valeant phalanges
50 arma tam caro superis movere?

106

flowing Adda with many a phalanx and no help from heaven, and
they wander in the high hills.   20

You yourself, Francesco, mighty in modesty and unshaken by
the power of the enemy, bravely go to meet them. You set up your
camp in the middle of open land. For the village of Vimercate, de-   25
void of any ditch, without a rampart, and ringed with no circle of
stones received your camp. You had scarcely eight companies of
soldiers with you. But what victorious regiments would you have
seen often standing firm in the face of changing dangers when   30
you were their commander in chief! From here you attacked the
restless troops of the enemy as they wandered over the difficult
slopes of Mount Barrhus and would soon be seized by monstrous   35
terror. After this, from a distance, swiftly and inspiring awe, you
kept at bay our troops, who had to look after themselves since
they had no leader — though mad rage would have been their cap-
tain.   40

For who would dare make war against you, when all peoples
tremble and kings stand in awe of you? Latium reveres you, and
the world honors you. If both poles are kind and just to you alone 45
in all matters, if god alone is always with you and protects your
army, what enemy phalanxes can take up arms against you who are
so favored by the gods? What wicked enemy's powers could harm   50

Quae tibi possint nocuisse vires
    hostis iniqui?
Qualis alternas tolerat procellas
Isthmos immotus geminique cunctos
55   aequoris fluctus reprimit nec iras
    curat inanes,
aut leo qualis medius fugaces
separans cervas vitulasque tardas,
has modo saltu modo terret illas,
60   ludit et arcet,
talis et nostras Venetumque vires
inde contemnis, nihilique ducis;
hinc ferox constans vigil et peritus
    fersque premisque.
65   Quae quidem mecum meditans diuque
cogitans dixi? Quid amica demens
fata contemno? Superos benignos
    odero semper?
Ecce libertas simulata quantam
70   civibus cladem tulit et ruinam.
Publicae nemo studuit saluti,
    nemo decori.
Hinc dolus manat furor et rapina;
hinc caput velat rabidis Megaera
75   anguibus cunctos pariter veneno
    impia fundens.
Phoebus ut solus radiat per orbem,
ut deus mundum moderatur unus,
sic meas unus gerat et gubernet
80   ductor habenas.
Qui meus primus bonus atque fortis
audeat civis tenebras fugare

you? For you are like the Isthmus, which is unmoved by the storms assailing it from both sides and which holds in check all the swelling tides of both seas, caring nothing for their pointless 55 wrath. Just as the lion, once he has separated the fleet deer from the slow heifers and stands between them, frightens now the deer with a pounce and then the heifers, toying with them and hem- 60 ming them in, so you spurn and consider worthless both our own military power and that of the Venetians.[17] And now fierce, constantly vigilant and experienced, you stand your ground and attack.

But what have I said and what have I pondered and considered 65 for so long a time? Why, demented, have I disdained the friendly fates? Why do I continue to hate the kindly gods? Look! What ruin and disaster pretended liberty[18] has visited upon our citizens! 70 No one has been interested in the safety of the state or in its glory. And so deceit, madness, and pillaging flow through the city, while impious Megaera, her head swarming with hissing snakes, 75 pours poison over all the people equally. Just as only Phoebus shines over the earth, and just as God alone governs the world, so one leader alone manages and guides my reins. 80

What good and brave citizen of mine would first dare to expel the darkness and restore the shining day to our lives? Let the

et diem rebus nitidum referre?
    Surgat alumnus.

85 Ecce vir fortis micat inter omnes:
Gaspar ignavo trepidos timore
excitat cives. Rabidos tyrannos
    obsidet aula.

Inde plebii validis latrones
90 viribus surgunt. Volitant utrique
taela ceu nimbus celeri citatus
    turbine praeceps.

Clarus affatu socios diserto
Gaspar hortatur gravibusque vires
95 acer incendens animosque dictis
    pugnat et urget.

'Nobiles,' inquit, 'generosa cives
arma quid tardis manibus moventes
parcitis ferro? Pavidas latronum
100   fundite turmas.

'Hic dies vobis patriam, parentes,
coniuges, natos, decus et quietem
reddet. Adversos alacri tumultus
    pellite Marte.

105 'Quisque Franciscum validos videntem
Sphortiam secum meditetur ictus
principem nostrum, iubar et salutem.
    Sternite fures!'

Praelium noctem trahitur sub atram
110 caede non una; cecidere sordes
terga vertentes. Foribus reclusis
    panditur aula.

Gaspar irrumpit. Sequitur caterva
civium, qui me trucibus tyrannis

young man stand up. Look, a brave man shines above the fray:
Gaspar,[19] who wakes the trembling citizens from their cowardly   85
fear. He lays siege to the mad tyrants in the assembly. Then the
plebian robbers rise up with their mighty forces. Weapons fly on
both sides like a cloud kicked up by a raging whirlwind. The bril-   90
liant Gaspar exhorts his companions with an eloquent speech.
The statesman fights and urges his men on, forcefully mobilizing   95
their strength and rousing their minds with powerful words. He
says, "Honorable citizens, why do you hesitate to take up your no-
ble arms? Why do you spare your swords? Rout the cowardly
bands of marauders! This day will return to you your city, your   100
parents, wives, and children, your honor and peace! End the terri-
ble uprisings in swift battle. Let each man imagine that our prince,   105
our star and salvation, Francesco Sforza, sees these mighty blows.
Kill the thieves!" The battle continues on through the dark night,
and is not over with one rampage; the rabble are cut down even   110
while they flee. The doors are flung wide and the royal court is
thrown open. Gaspar bursts in, followed by a throng of citizens

115 liberam tandem, Veneti cadentis
    sanguine, reddunt.
Sic dies unus famis atque saevi
Martis optatam tulit ille finem,
nulla quem praeceps abolebit ira,
120   nulla vetustas.
Nanque cum primum populi vocantis
accipis dextram veniensque lustras
tecta tam longo miseranda flaetu
    urbe receptus,
125 moenia ingressus pater ipse tecum
Liber et laetae Cereris choreae
Ludus et Comus Iocus et Voluptas
    omnia complent.
Quique tam multas acies agebat
130 terror hostilis, pavefacta vertit
terga. Sic cervus trepidus leonem
    effugit acrem.
Pace nunc cives hilari fruuntur;
nunc meus tecum populus triumphat;
135 nunc suas hostes timidi ruinas
    funditus horrent.
Mente quae mecum repetens profunda
gratias summas tibi sic merenti
debeo; me nam miseram levasti
140   ore luporum.
Restat eversam redigas ut arcem
ad decus primum, monumenta magni
principis nulli procerum secundi
    pulchra Philippi.
145 Inde, quod noster populus rogare
omnis et tellus Latii superbi

who, with the blood of a dying Venetian,[20] have set me free at last
from the hostile tyrants.   115

Thus one day, long awaited, has brought an end to famine and
savage war, which neither precipitous anger nor time will efface.
For as soon as you are welcomed into the city, Francesco, you take   120
the hands of the people calling to you and when you go inside the
walls, you observe the homes long wretched with weeping, and fa-
ther Liber himself enters with you and the happy dancing bands   125
of Ceres and Ludus, Comus, Jocus, and Voluptas fill every place.[21]
Whatever terror led to so many of the enemy's battles now causes
trembling flight. Thus the fearful deer flees the savage lion. Now   130
the happy citizens enjoy peace. Now my people triumph with you,
and now our timid enemies shudder at their own utter destruc-
tion. Reflecting on all this, from the bottom of my heart I owe and   135
offer you the greatest thanks. For you lifted me in my misery from
the jaws of wolves. It remains for you to restore the ruined citadel   140
to its original glory: the beautiful monuments of the great Duke
Filippo, second to none among princes.

Next, since our people and the whole land of proud Latium   145
continue to ask it, be quick to punish the enemy's madness. For
though he has been driven out, the Venetian does not want peace

pergit, hostiles propera furores
    solvere poenas.
Non enim pulsus cupiat quietem,
150   maior insurget Venetus; parabit
fortius robur; socios pericli
    undique fundet.
Quisquis iniusto Furias secutus
Marte temptavit tibi sic amico
155   nuper infestus nocuisse censes
    ferre quietem?
Additur saevo metui cupido:
urit haec pectus, glacie sed ille
urget et, nusquam patiens manere,
160   undique vexat.
Insuper fidos lateri sodales
iunge fucatos fugiens amicos.
Quos viros monstrat probitas verendos,
    utere semper.
165   Nec tibi quenquam reputes amicum
quem socer duxit sibi non fidelem.
Is necem dudum tibi nil nocenti
    fraude tetendit.
Semper ulcisci muliebre censent,
170   ast idem nunquam fatui putatur.
Qui tenet prudens medium supremis
    laudibus ornant.
Si caves vitae insidias serenae,
res geres magnas meliusque natis
175   consules et me super alta vectus
    sydera tolles.
Sis diu mecum superes et annos
Nestoris totos Mariaeque Blancae

and will rise up all the stronger. He will prepare a tougher force   150
and he will dispatch his allies in terror everywhere. Do you think
the hostile Venetian, who follows the Furies in an unjust war
and who recently tried to harm you, a friend, brings peace? In him   155
desire is added to savage fear; the one thing inflames his breast,
but the other moves him with its icy chill, agitating him every-
where; and he is impatient of remaining in any one place. Keep   160
loyal companions at your side and avoid false friends. Always em-
ploy those men whom righteousness proves worthy of respect. You
should not assume anyone is your friend whom your father-in-law   165
thought was disloyal to him. For a long time now this one man[22]
deceitfully prepared death for you, though you did him no harm.
People always think that vengeance is women's work—but never
the province of a fool. Whoever holds his course to the middle   170
road, men honor with the highest praise. If you are wary of the
snares of a peaceful life you will achieve great things, you will
better look after the interests of your sons, and, carried high above
the stars, you will elevate me too.   175

May you be with me for a long time to come. May you live
longer than all the years of Nestor and may that godly ancient

cedat aetati vetus illa vates
180   dia Sibylla.
Si novam te vix subeunte portam
cessit extemplo ferus ille Mavors
et fames diro sociata luctu
       moenia liquit,
185   quid putes, mi dux, fore si seniles
videris annos? Veteres triumphos
Italis reddes super orbe toto
       clarus et ingens.

⁝ 4 ⁝

Humanas quicunque regi res mente negarit
       divina, sensu fallitur ipse suo.
Astra regunt terras; deus astra orbemque profundum
       mundanasque plagas unicus ipse regit.
5   Quae quamquam ratione queunt, Francisce, doceri,
       Sphortia, non dubia, testis es ipse satis.
Nonne vides quantum nullis es viribus aptus
       imperium nullis divitiis nec ope?
Hostis erat Venetus, nec Florentinus amicus.
10   Hostis et Alphonsus, Insuber hostis erat.
Nemo tuas Italus partis, Francisce, fovebat,
       non Italis quisquis adiacet ullus agris.
Ipse tamen nudo statuens tentoria campo,
       milite cum parvo solus eras metui.

priestess Sibyl yield to Bianca Maria in age. If savage Mars and   180
dire sorrow's companion, Famine, immediately abandoned the city
when you had scarcely entered the Porta Nova, what do you
think will happen, my Duke, if you live to see old age? Famous   185
and magnificent over the whole world, you will restore the Italians
to their ancient glory.

: 4 :

To Francesco Sforza
In praise of piety

Whoever denies that human affairs are ruled by the mind of god
is deceived by his own senses. The stars regulate the earth, but
god alone rules the stars, the globe, the ocean, and every region of
the world.

Although all this can be demonstrated with irrefutable rea-
son, you yourself, Francesco Sforza, are witness enough. Do you   5
not see what great authority you have acquired without military
power, wealth, and assistance? The Venetian was your enemy and
the Florentine no friend. Even Alfonso and the Milanese were en-
emies too. No Italian took your part, Francesco, nor anyone in the   10
lands near Italy. Still, though you set up your camp in a bare field
and were alone with a small number of soldiers, you caused great

15 Inde Briantinis Venetorum exercitus errans
    collibus haud audet te propius petere.
Insuber hinc trepidas acuit perterritus iras
    ipse quidem frustra, cui deus hostis adest.
Omnibus iis unus metui, quemcunque cohortes
20   vix octo in pugnam te sequerentur, eras,
nec potuere virum tot millia in arma ruentum
    vel nocuisse tibi vel satis esse sibi.
Aptus es imperium, quo gens habet Itala nullum
    clarius aut melius. At quibus auxiliis?
25 Nempe dei illius qui nutu concutit orbem,
    cui paret quidquid est, erit atque fuit.
Et miramur adhuc modo quod post fata Philippi
    non subiit Venetum Gallia tota iugum.
Quid minus Insubrium Veneti sint urbe potiti,
30   qui iam vicissent omnia Martis ope?
Est occulta dei sententia; punit iniquos
    mitius ut repetant qua cecidere viam.
Iis etiam quandoque favet quos norit abusos
    munere divino per scelus omne citos,
35 scilicet iis maius debetur in impia trusis
    Tartara supplicium quod meruere pati;
affligitque bonos, quo vel certamine tali
    luctantes valeant promeruisse magis
sontibus. Errantes ulciscitur; impia rursus
40   corda premit quibus est usus ad obsequium.
Unum scire quidem videor nil denique cuique
    conduxisse nefas nec nocuisse pium.
Saepe fit ut iustus felici munere vitae
    fungatur moxque sydera laeta petat.
45 Mens iniusta autem contra patiatur; ut olim
    passus es, Antioche, passus es et Pharao.

fear. The Venetian army, wandering in the Briantine hills, scarcely 15
dared to approach you at too close quarters. After this, the fearful
Milanese himself sharpened his trembling wrath in vain. For god,
his enemy, was at hand. You, whom scarcely eight cohorts would
follow into battle, were feared by every army. Neither could so 20
many thousands rushing to take up arms harm you, nor were they
sufficient to protect their own. You acquired power over a realm
that is the best and most distinguished in all Italy. But with what
auxiliary troops? With the help of that god, of course, who shakes
the earth with a nod and is obeyed by whatever now is, will be, 25
and ever has been. And we are still amazed that after the death of
Filippo all Gaul did not succumb to the yoke of the Venetians.
And why was it that the Venetians, who had already conquered
everything else with the help of Mars, did not take possession of
the city of the Milanese? 30

The mind of God is inscrutable. He punishes the guilty less
harshly so that they may return to the road from which they had
strayed. And as often as he favors even those whom he knows have
abused his divine munificence and have been incited to every
crime, surely to those thrust down into godless Tartarus is owed a 35
still greater punishment, because they deserved to suffer. And yet
God afflicts the good, so that even by struggling in such a great
contest these men can become more deserving. He takes ven-
geance on those who have sinned; on the other hand, he crushes
the impious hearts of those whom he uses for their service. 40

Indeed, finally I seem to understand that only the pious man
neither wrongs nor brings harm to anyone. It does happen often
that a just man leads a good life and soon seeks fame and fortune.
May an unjust mind, however, meet the opposite fate — as you 45
once did, O Antiochus, and you, O Pharaoh.[23] But when there is

Quando igitur nihil est hominum quod inania possint
  consilia aut vires, quur adeo efferimur?
Praestat nosse deum; praestat pietatis amore
50   muniri. Deus est omnia qui moderat.
Karole, tu Francis uno rex crimine cunctis
  es prius adversis usus in arma tibi.
Patritoque omni regno spoliatus et auro
  solus eras. Soli spes erat una deus.
55 Nam tibi relligio, pietas quam recta tuetur,
  se comitem semper, se sociam tulerat.
Haec tibi fiduciae tantum dedit omnia prorsus
  ut tibi non dubio pectore susciperes.
Hinc deus omnipotens bene, qui sperantibus usque
60   est praesens, rebus coepit adesse tuis.
Mox pudor invadit Francos Gallosque rebelles,
  submittuntque pio colla superba iugo.
Continuo rabies Anglorum lassa furorem
  ponit et avertens terque quaterque cadit.
65 En sibi de patriis laribus qui nuper Olympo
  bella minabantur, arma tremenda vident.
Ergo quid efferimur stulti? Quo tendimus iras
  insani? Quae nos tristis Erinys habet?
Curat nostra deus; nihil est quod negligat ille,
70   e nihilo quisquis ordine cuncta creat.
Huic igitur studio si nos adiungimus omni
  per pietatis opus perque decus fidei,
nec nos astra queant vafrae nec subdola mentis
  consilia urgere quos fovet ipse deus.

nothing that the futile counsels and physical strength of mortal men can achieve, why are we so arrogant? It is better to know god; it is better to be fortified by the love of piety. God is the one who governs all things. 50

You, King Charles, took advantage of one crime, after the entire French nation had taken up arms against you first.[24] You were alone, stripped of your father's realm and gold; and since you were alone, God was your only hope. For faith, which righteous piety defends, has always made herself your ally and companion: she has 55 given you so much courage that you undertook all things with no hesitation in your heart. And thus the almighty deity, who is present for all those who have hope, has undertaken to support your position. Shame soon overcame the French and Gallic rebels, and 60 they submitted their proud necks to your pious yoke. And then the mad aggression of the English — who were repeatedly put to flight — lost its fury and perished from exhaustion.[25] Look, those who recently threatened war from Olympus over the household gods of their forefathers now see armies they tremble at. There- 65 fore, what do we fools have to be puffed up about? For what purpose are we insanely showing our wrath? What sad Fury has seized us? Our god takes care: there is nothing that he fails to see, for he created all things in due order from nothing. If we, then, at- 70 tach ourselves to him with all eagerness for the work of piety and the beauty of faith, neither can the stars nor the cunning counsels of a devious mind oppress us, whom god himself protects.

: 5 :

Est laus illustris, Karole, magnis
principibus quenquam posse probari.
Quare dum video me tibi carum,
omnis quem probitas laudibus effert
5   et quem magnanimus Sphortia tanto
unum prosequitur semper honore,
gestio laeticia meque beatum
censeo quem tantus diligat heros.
Tu, Gonzaga, tuis pergito donis
10   in cunctos pariter esse benignus,
quos fulgor lustret laudibus ullus.
Sic vives populos clarus in omnis.
Nam fortuna perit, occidit omnis
splendor corporeus. Aurea virtus
15   tempore perpetua permanet omni.
At mihi quae donas, parcius uti
nunc volo. Non opus est, Sphortia postquam
prospexit nostris, Karole, rebus.
Attamen ipse putes omnibus usum
20   me donis quis tu iusseris uti.
Nunc satis est quod adest: omnia nolim
sumere. Sed mihi tu munera parce;
utar enim quando coget egestas.

: 5 :

To Carlo Gonzaga
In praise of his generosity

It is illustrious praise, Carlo, when someone is capable of winning the approval of great princes. Therefore, as long as I know I am dear to you whom all probity exalts with encomia and whom alone among men the magnanimous Francesco Sforza always accords   5 such honor, I thrill with happiness and I think myself blessed since such a great hero esteems me.

    May you, Gonzaga, continue to be equally generous with your gifts to all those whom any light from your brilliant deeds would   10 make illustrious with praise. Thus will you live on as a great man among all peoples. For fortune perishes and all physical luster fades. Golden virtue alone remains immortal for all time. But   15 what you give to me I want to use more sparingly now. It is not necessary since Sforza has looked out for us, Carlo. Yet you your-self should know that I have used all the gifts that you told me to use. Now what is here is enough: I do not want to use up every-   20 thing. But spare me some gifts for now, for I shall make use of them when poverty calls.

: 6 :

Aenice, quem lateri fidum sibi, Davale, iungit
　　Alphonsus comitem consociumque thoro,
nil est quod teneat dubium miratio pectus
　　ulla tuum, tacuit si mea Musa diu.
5　　Nam nec id ulla quidem vaecors oblivio fecit
　　neglectusve tui qui mihi numen ades.
Sed Bellona furens nostras quae obsederat oras
　　impedit primo, tristis at inde febris.
Cum primum licuit calamis en auribus adsum
10　　sponte tuis cupidus quam bene nosse vales.
Nanque amor et vetus est et mirus Davale quo te
　　prosequor et crescit is magis atque magis.
Quo magis augescis probitatis lumine clarae,
　　hoc magis augescens te meus ardet amor.
15　　Ingenti quamquam permultos laude nitentis
　　rex habet Alphonsus, lux tua clara magis.
Nam te nulla fugit praestans, mi Davale, virtus,
　　nec bello insignis, nec veneranda toga.
Te sensit Neptunus aquis: quo turbine Martem
20　　excires, quantis viribus ingrueres,
consilio quantum polles, quo flumine dulcis
　　affluis eloquii. Novit uterque polus.
Conspicuus forma totam tibi iungis amore
　　Parthenopen, facibus quae perit usta tuis.
25　　Ullane te victrix fruitur quam longa subegit
　　flama vorax, felix quam facis una deam?

: 6 :

To Iñigo d'Avalos[26] *and Lucrezia Alagno*
A double encomium

O Iñigo d'Avalos, whom Alfonso[27] has placed at his side as his
faithful companion and ally in love,[28] you should scarcely be sur-
prised, my faint-hearted friend, that my Muse has been silent for a
long time. For neither senseless forgetfulness nor lack of concern
for you was the cause, since you are always present for me, like a   5
god. But first there was the awful war that lay siege to our shores,
and then came the sad plague.[29] But look, as soon as it was per-
mitted, here I am of my own accord with my writing tools for
your ears to hear, and I am eager to know how you are. For the   10
love I have for you is both longstanding and wonderful, Avalos,
and it grows ever greater. The more you grow in the light of your
renowned goodness, the more my love for you increases. Although
King Alfonso keeps around himself many who are gleaming with
accolades, your light is more brilliant. For no excellent virtue   15
eludes you, my Avalos, neither distinction in war, nor the honor-
able activities of peace. At sea Neptune knows you: he knows how
you stir up war with a whirlwind, with what strength you attack,
how powerful you are in counsel, and he knows how sweet is the   20
river of your eloquence. The whole world knows you. Preeminent
in your beauty, you have won the love of all Parthenope,[30] and
scorched by your fire, she is dying of love for you. Does some one
girl enjoy you now, a girl whom long voracious passion, at last the
victor, has laid low,[31] a girl whom you, O happy man, now make   25
your goddess? Why do you avert your face? Are you ashamed to

Quid frontem avertis? Num te pudet ore fateri,
    siqua puella faces sentiat usta tuas?
An tibi turpe putes quandoque cupidinis arcus
30   ferre manu, dum te cura laborque sinit?
Rex et Alexander Caesarque et fortis Achilles
    ac pius Alcides miles amoris erat,
Alphonsusque senex nostri lux fulgida saecli
    post tam multa feri praelia Martis amat.
35   Fama recens nostras etiam pervenit ad aures,
    quantus in Alphonso nunc recalescat amor.
Felix ipsa tuis, O dia Lucretia, flamis,
    quae videas tantum concaluisse virum.
Sed quem forma deum tua non raptarit in ignis,
40   quae superes Helenen et Venerem superes?
Si nondum Pandora suos habuisset in usus
    tam facilis superos morigerosque sibi,
iure quidem Pandora fores, cui munera formae
    singula quisque deus indubitata dedit.
45   Lautos Artemidos mores doctumque Minervae
    ingenium et vitam dia puella refers.
Astra micant oculi, roseo nix candet in ore;
    reddit ebur dentes. Nectare lingua fluit.
Corpore nec brevis es quae suci plena venusti,
50   Incessuque places stansque sedensque places.
O te felicem nimis, O nimium beatam
    si tibi contingant pignora digna patre.
Interea placidis ulnis complectere regem;
    mixta nec abstineas iungere labra labris.
55   Saxea ne iaceas, sed contra umbone petentem
    excipe, quo vires partus utrinque ferat.
Addito blandicias et dulcia murmura, facque
    condiat ut lepidus seria docta iocus.

confess that some girl might know your torches and might have been burned by them? Or do you think it disgraceful for you to take Cupid's bow in your hands on some occasions when toil and care allow you to do so?   30

King Alexander, Caesar, brave Achilles, and loyal Alcides were all soldiers of love, and now Alfonso, an old man and the shining light of our age, has fallen in love after so many battles fought for savage Mars. A recent report has reached our ears that a very great   35 love has now been rekindled in Alfonso.

Happy are you, O divine Lucretia, in your ardor, for you see a great man glowing with passion.[32] But what god has your beauty not set on fire, since you surpass Helen and Venus too? If Pandora   40 had not so easily charmed the gods for her own purposes, you could justly be a Pandora, to whom each of the gods, obedient to her wishes, gave extraordinary gifts of beauty. You, lovely girl, bring to mind the elegant manners of Artemis and the learned mind and life of Minerva. Your eyes are stars; snow gleams in your   45 rosy face; your teeth are of ivory. Nectar flows from your speech. Stately of body, you are full of charming sweetness. Your step is delightful, and you are lovely, whether you stand or sit. O you who   50 are too happy and too blessed! If you receive pledges worthy of your father, embrace the king with lovely arms and do not refrain from joining your lips to his. And do not lie there like a stone beside him but receive him with the boss of your shield when he comes to you,[33] so that your progeny may bring forth strength from both sides. Add compliments and sweet murmuring. And   55 see that he seasons his serious, learned talk with pleasant humor.

Sic retinetur amans. Sic est cum matre Cupido
60   servandus, saties taedia ne pariat.
Haec tu qui regis thalamo fidissimus astas
        invigilans custos, Aenice, mente loca,
dumque mones prudens cauto sermone puellam,
        dic etiam regi parcat ut ipse sibi.
65 Non et enim nescit quibus olim militat annis
        et quot nocte decet praelia ferre senem.
Quin nimium repetita Venus, dum saemine saemen
        obruitur, nullam prodeat in segetem.
At tu, cui viridis robur dat fortius aetas
70   quam sinit hasta, feri! Nulla puella vacet.
Gigne tui similes, quot pluris, Davale, possis.
        Totam Parthenopen ignibus ure tuis.
Tantum age, Clio! Ne Phoebus iure queratur,
        nec cedat Cypriae fons Heliconis aquae.
75 Si te nocte Cypris fruitur, fac luce canentem
        sentiat ad resonam sobria Musa lyram.
Mens est sola viris pariat quae nomen et annos
        quos nequeant ullis fata domare minis.
Immortalis eris, si mentis luce beatus
80   per virtutis opus excolis ingenium.
Ac tu primus eris quem regis laudibus addam.
        Perque vices lyricas hisce ferare modis.
Nostris, Aenice te Davale, cantibus
dum Clio titulis inserit inclytis,
85 omnis Castalidum coetus et Haelius
        respondet resonas vices.
Tellus Hesperiae nobilis ultimae,
cui nomen dederat lucidus Hesperus,
Atlas quem genuit celsior Aenicum
90   nostrae huic Hesperiae dedit.

This is how a lover is kept. And thus must Cupid and his mother
be retained, so that desire, once sated, does not lead to boredom.   60

You who stand as the most trusted guard over the king's bed
chamber, Iñigo, keep these things in mind, and when you warn
the girl with prudent advice, you should also tell the king to take
care not to injure himself. For he is well aware of the age at which
he goes to war, and he knows how many times an old man should   65
take up arms at night. Moreover, when Venus is pursued too often
and one seed is destroyed by another, she will not produce any
harvest. But for you, Avalos, since your youthful years make you
tougher and firmer than a spear, strike! Let no girl be free of your
attention. Produce offspring similar to you, as many as you can.   70
Burn the whole of Parthenope with your fires.

But come now, Clio, let Phoebus not complain and rightly so,
and let not the Heliconian spring yield to the Cyprian. If Venus
enjoys you at night, see to it that the temperate Muse hears you
singing to the resonant sounds of the lyre by day. May a temperate   75
Muse feel the force of the melodious lyre. Only the mind brings
men glory and a long life that even the fates cannot threaten in any
way. You will be immortal, Avalos, if you cultivate your genius
through exercising virtue, for you are blessed with the light of the
mind. And you will be the first whom I shall add to my eulogies   80
of the king. May you be exalted by lyric poems in these modes. As
long as Clio introduces you, Iñigo, in our songs with famous hon-
ors, the entire assembly of the Castalian maidens and Helios[34] will   85
respond with resonant melodies.

The noble land of far-away Hesperia, whose name derives from
shining Hesperus, whom lofty Atlas fathered, gave Iñigo to our
Hesperia.[35] Thus rejoicing at having sent down Avalos, shining   90

Sic Atlantiades Hesperus Hespero
laetatus patruo mittere Davalum
illustrat geminas lumine patrias
    splendens unius Aenici.

95   Natus consipicuo patre gravissimus
hic vir mirificis laudibus extulit
virtutes patrias, se similem gerens
    illi rebus in omnibus.

Alphonsum genitor, Davale, maximum
100   regem per fidei coluit tuus[2]
mores non dubios Marte sub aspero
    tranquilloque sub otio.

Et tu qui patriis laudibus aemulus
accedis, sequeris dura per omnia
105   et terrae et pelagi fortis et integer
    Alphonsi varias vices.

Nunc nostris requiem bella tumentia
postquam temporibus numine prospero
cesserunt, placidas excipit Aenicus
110   Musas hospitio libens.

Et Phoebo pariter Davalus hospite
laetatur studium magnanimi sequens
regis, qui superat mentis acumine
    res quas gesserit inclytas.

Sic te Delius et Pieridum soror
115   alternis numeris, Aenice, cantitant
et nostris modulis altius evehi
    quantum vis tulerit iubent.

Verum quis ego te vocibus efferam,
quem virtus decorans omnis in aethera
120   tollit, quem similem numinibus facit
    et summi speculum poli

Hesperus, the son of Atlas, made two lands famous with Iñigo's light alone. This very great son of a remarkable father, resembling him in every way, has promoted with marvelous acclaim his father's virtues. For your father, a man of unimpeachable character and loyalty, my Avalos, supported great King Alfonso both in savage war and tranquil peace. And you, a man of courage and integrity, who emulate and inherit your father's virtues, follow Alfonso in his varied campaigns through every difficult trial over land and sea.

Now that the gods are happy and the swelling wars have ceased in our times, Iñigo gladly welcomes the peaceful Muses. And with Phoebus Apollo as host, Avalos also takes pleasure in following the literary study of the magnanimous king, who exceeds in matters of the intellect even his renown in the wars he has waged. And so the Delian and Clio, sister of the Pierian Muses,[36] celebrate you again and again, Iñigo, in alternate rhythms and they command you to be hymned more loftily in our poems — to the extent that my powers permit. But what words can I use to exalt you when your fame, adorned with every virtue, ascends to the firmament and the illustrious goodness and honor of Iñigo make you like the gods and the mirror of highest heaven? As to how

95

100

105

110

115

120

illustris probitas et decus Aenici?
Quantum aequalibus excelleret omnibus
est Anglus locuples testis et arbiter
125   dux regum pater optimus.
Quantis o titulis extulit Aenicum
splendens ille Philippus, iubar omnium
virtutum, columen Pieridum, pius
    portus nobilium virum!
130 At quantum proceres exuperet viros!
Hispanae segetis rector et aequoris
Alphonsus liquido maximus approbat,
    qui tanti facit Aenicum.
Quid multis opus est? Omnibus Aenicus
135 si sit Davalus obscurus et omnibus
pravis invidiosus, propriis tamen
    virtutis meritis nitet.

: 7 :

Quod, Baptista, doles fata parentis,
qui multa viguit laude per omnem
conspicuus vitam, flaetibus aegris
sic ignosco tuis, finis ut olim
5 quem iussit ratio, luctibus adsit.
Nam neque tu nescis lege potentis
naturae stabili quidquid et ortum
sumpsit ut in nostris viveret oris,
id quoque natura admittere finem.
10 Sola potest virtus vincere fatum.

greatly he surpasses all of his peers, Filippo Maria Visconti, best
father of kings, is a fine witness and judge.[37] O what titles did the   125
brilliant Filippo Maria bestow on you, Iñigo! For that prince was
the radiant light of all the virtues, a pillar of the Pierian Muses,
and a pious haven for all noble men. But how much he would sur-
pass in eminence the leading men of the land! The ruler of the   130
Spanish land and sea, the great Alfonso, esteemed him plainly and
thought so much of Iñigo. But why should I say more? Even if
Iñigo d'Avalos were unknown — or envied by all evil men — he   135
would still gleam with the merits of his virtue.

: 7 :

To Battista Scharas Barocis
A consolation for his father's death

Because, Battista, you grieve the death of your father, who enjoyed
great fame throughout his life, I pardon your weeping — so pitiable
that the end of mourning, which reason once demanded, must be
at hand. For you know that whatever arises from the unchanging   5
law of almighty nature so that it can live in our world, also receives
its end from nature. Only virtue is capable of conquering death.
And since he who begot you was a man pre-eminent in virtue   10

Qua quoniam vita floruit omni
is, qui te genuit, morte solutus,
non totus periit. Mente supernas
nam sedes petiit, debita terrae
15   pulchris cum titulis membra relinquens.
Tot natos adhibe — iunge sorores
non indigna suo germina trunco.
Vivit in his genitor quis dedit artus.
Quare si sapias, perge Baroci
20   luctu iam posito visere Musas,
quae te sollicitis reddere curis
contendant vacuum. Maeror inanis
qui nullam peperit anxius auram.

: 8 :

Gaspar Castaneas, ingenio vigens
faecundo, gemitus et lachrymas gravis,
parcens assiduis fundere questibus,
cum Musis melius prospicies sacris,
5   tum qui te cruciat maeror et opprimit
tolles. Nil et enim nunc stolidum novi
vulgus quod miseris dilaceras modis;
in te sed fatuos aggreditur solens
ludos. Nam vitiis floridior novo
10   virtus est odio. Stulticiam catus
offendit; tenebris displicet Haelius.
Quare tu potius laetior accipe

throughout his entire life, though he has been released by death, he has not perished wholly. For he has sought with his mind his home in heaven, having left his body and its beautiful honors to the earth. Turn your attention to your many children — and to   15
your sisters, the worthy scions of his line. Your father lives on in those whom he brought to the world. Therefore, if you are wise, go now, Barocis, put aside your sorrow and visit the Muses who   20
will rival one another to free you from anxious care. Mourning, sterile and anxious, brings forth no mitigating wind.

: 8 :

To Gaspar Castaneas
A consolation to a poet who has fallen out of favor

Gaspar Castaneas,[38] though sighs and tears weigh heavily upon you, your genius for eloquence thrives. If you can put an end to your constant flood of laments, not only will you look to better prospects in the future with the holy Muses, but you will cast away the sorrow that tortures and oppresses you. Of course, I do   5
not know the brutish crowd you tear to pieces with your wretched verses. In any case, they are accustomed to attacking you with crude jokes. Certainly virtue is more effective than freshly-con-ceived loathing with its viciousness. The clever man gives offense   10
to boorishness; the sun displeases the darkness. Therefore, receive

quos livor stimulos tristior iniicit.
Maius continuo nam tibi commodum
15   reddet lucidior gloria, subsequens
virtus si comites divitias fugit.
Nil est quod fugias pauperiem probus.
Pauper Maeonides, pauper erat Solon;
quorum quottidie nomen in aethera
20   Croeso splendidius divite tollitur.
Optavit Cynicum rex Macedo virum.
Vir regem Cynicus spreverat inclytum:
contentus propriis qui fuerit bonis,
quaestum temnit et auras populi levis.

: 9 :

Ad caelum, Paraclete, laudibus me
effers exuperans modum decori.
Haud est officii novum probatis
si quem praetuleris virum poetis
5   quos tot saecula iudicesque tanti
aequant syderibus. Quid ore clarum
possim rancidulo referre dignis
tandem promeritis? Sed ille fallit
quem caecum veteres vocant Phanes te.
10   Quod si te ratio tibi quietum
verax restituat, secus putabis.
Nam duplex hominum genus videri
suspectum liceat. Nimis colenti
credendum penitus nego, nec illi

in a happier state of mind the barbs that gloomy spite brings you.
For more brilliant glory will bring you greater advantage if virtue,
your companion, spurns wealth. There is no reason why you, an   15
honorable man, should flee poverty. Maeonides was a pauper; so
was Solon,[39] and their names were praised to the skies more splen-
didly than wealthy Croesus'. The Macedonian King Alexander   20
welcomed Diogenes the Cynic.[40] The Cynic was contemptuous of
the famous king: since he was content with the good that was his,
he spurned the race to get rich and the changing winds of the
fickle mob.

: 9 :

To Paracletus
Thanks for his praise and friendship

You praise me to the skies, Paracletus, exceeding the standard for
honor.[41] It is by no means your duty to prefer a new man to the
accepted poets. Many centuries and so many judges have already   5
likened those men to the stars. With what fine words from my
loathsome lips could I match their great accomplishments? But
that Phanes, whom the ancients called blind, has led you astray.[42]
On the other hand, if trustworthy reason restores your serenity,
you will think differently. For the duplicitous sort of man can   10
arouse mistrust: I don't think we should completely trust a man
who praises to excess nor one who hates us too violently either.

quisquis nos fuerit nimis exosus.
15   Nam motus vaehemens utrunque fallit
istorum neque recta iudicare
permittit, Paraclete. Gratiarum
permultum tamen ipse sic amanti
non possum tibi, amice, non habere
20   ne dure patiens quidem quod ultro
erraris, nec enim puto latere
te quantum valeant meae Camoenae.
Res utcunque tamen fuit, valeto
et nos ut facis usque amando serva.
25   Persuadeque simul tibi futurum
ut te semper amem tibique votis
optem Pieridas tuis adesse.

: 10 :

Quem tibi pulchris capias canendum
laudibus dignum meritisque magnum?
Quem virum nobis celebres supremo
    carmine Clio?
5   Non enim tempus datur ut decore
Karolum regem titulos per omnis
splendidum summae probitatis astrum
    promere possis.
Karolus totum volitat per orbem,
10   sol velut miris radiis coruscans,
quos micans fundit pietas per omnes
    undique terras.

For strong emotion leads both these sorts of men astray. Nor does   15
it permit them to judge fairly, Paracletus. Still, I myself can't fail to
give you great thanks, my friend, since you are so loving and I did
not even suffer harm because of your spontaneous error. But I do   20
not think you are unaware of how much my Muses can do. Still,
farewell and protect us by loving us as much as you do. And rest
assured at the same time that I will always love you and ask that   25
the Pierian Muses will be there for you and your prayers.

: 10 :

To Gaspar da Vimercate
Praise for liberating Milan from tyranny

Of what great man worthy of praises, beautiful and well-deserved,
do you think you should sing, O Clio? What man would you
hymn with a lofty poem? For time does not permit you to cele-   5
brate a star of the highest goodness refulgent with every title and
honor — King Charles. For he flies throughout the whole world,
like the sun shimmering with wondrous rays, which shining piety   10
spreads over all the lands. Among high kings, a poem awaits

Karolum reges manet inter altos
carmen, quod cuncti populi frequentent,
15   nulla quod possint abolere saecla,
      fulmina nulla.

Nunc satis fesso facias poetae.
Si virum, Clio, referas canendo,
Insubres qui sit prior inter omnes
20   laudibus unus?

Neminem tanta probitate quenquam
Insubres nostro genuere saeclo,
praeditus quanta proceres refulget
      Gaspar in omnes.

25   Hic puer primos studuit sub annos
rebus iis quarum decus et voluptas
gloriam doctas homini per artes
      portat in aevum.

Quidquid orator simul et poeta
30   monstrat et Graius docet et Latinus
omne sollerti didicit labore
      firmus et acer.

Socratis vidit variis reclusos
partibus rivos; bibit et decorum
35   omne quod suavis daret unda fontis,
      impiger haustu.

Hinc ad ultoris celer arma versus
Martis argutos moderatus ictus
quos det obstanti pariterque vitet,
40   doctus ab arte.

Inde quod nuper didicisset usu
roborans multo, petiit ferocem
Sphortiam magni generum Philippi,
      numine dextro.

45   Sic puer fertur Thetidos secutus

Charles, which all peoples will throng to hear and which neither time nor tempests will efface.   15

But now, O Clio, give satisfaction to a tired poet. If you could celebrate a man in song, who alone would be first in glory among all the Milanese? The Milanese have brought forth no one in our   20 time with as much virtue as Gaspar possesses.[43] For among all the noblemen, he is preeminent. From his earliest years, this young man strove in all those pursuits with which honor and pleasure in   25 the liberal arts bring a man glory all through the ages. Whatever the orator and the poet taught and demonstrated in Greek as well as Latin, Gaspar mastered with skillful study and he was vigilant   30 and steadfast. He saw the streams of Socrates revealed in various ways and he imbibed all the beauty that came from that sweet spring and diligently drained it.   35

After this, quickly turning to the weaponry of avenging Mars, he controlled equally the ringing blows he parried and those he rained on all who opposed him, for he was learned in this art. Then, strengthening with much practice what he had recently   40 learned, he sought out with divine favor courageous Francesco Sforza, great Filippo's son-in-law, just as Thetis's son is said to have followed the Centaur's teachings and far-famed Phoenix's   45

quaeque Centaurus docuit simulque
inclytus Phoenix monuit sub armis
   Troados orae.
Censor et iudex probitatis acer
50   ipse Franciscus generosus heros
illico novit viridis iuventae
   robur et ausum.
Sensit et pectus valido refertum
spiritu nullis stimulis subacto,
55   quem metus nullus premeret, cupido
   nulla moveret.
Noluit quenquam sequeretur alas
tiro visurus per aperta campi
impigras ferri, volucris sagittae
60   instar, in hostes.
Illico, Gaspar, recipis cohortem
ductor ut praesis iubeasque pugnans
quidquid et Mavors velit et Minerva,
   arte vel usu.
65   Quis queat cantu breviore gestas
res tuas, Gaspar, paribus referre
laudibus? Nunquam sine te iuvanti
   Sphortia vicit.
Quae quidem postquam tulit ad Philippum
70   Fama, non fictis agitata ventis,
te vocat princeps patriae periclis
   ultor ut adsis.
Principi pares, genero querente
qui tamen cernens socero futurum
75   usui tete, veniam petenti
   annuit aegre.
Huius adventu Venetum catervas
Chrema tam longo lacerata Marte

counsel in the war on the shores of Troy.[44] The noble hero Fran-
cesco — himself a man of character and a keen judge of virtue — 50
immediately recognized the strength and daring of the stripling
youth before him. He sensed a heart filled with a brave spirit un-
daunted by threats, which neither fear nor avarice could move. 55
Gaspar, though, as a mere novice, did not wish to follow anyone in
his eagerness to see the swift cavalry moving across the open glades
of the battlefield towards the enemy like a speeding arrow. There 60
you, Gaspar, received your cohort so you could preside as their
leader and take command, fighting in whatever way Mars and Mi-
nerva might wish, whether by art or practice.

Who could give an account of your exploits, Gaspar, and praise 65
them enough in so short a poem? Sforza never prevailed without
your help. And when Rumor, agitated but not by false winds, re- 70
ported these things to Filippo, the prince called upon you to be the
avenger of the threats to his land. And you, Gaspar, obeyed the
prince, though his son-in-law complained. Still, Sforza, seeing
that you would be useful to his father-in-law, agreed reluctantly 75
when you asked his pardon.

vidit averti trepidosque cursu
80   terga dedisse.
Pluribus non est opus ipse tempus
nunc teram. Quantis meritis decorus
hic sit ostendit pater ille regum
     duxque Philippus.
85   Hunc enim clarum proceres Philippus
inter illustres habuit Maria.[3]
Sic enim princeps meritis vigentes
     extulit ille:
quidquid huic uni libuit licebat,
90   at sibi nunquam voluit licere,
quod minus prae se decoranda ferret
     nomina laudis.
Non enim virtus petit alta fastum,
quae satis sese putat esse claram,
95   si nihil dicat faciatque rectum
     praeter et aequum.
Hic viris quanto reliquis honore
praestitit magnis, bonitate pollens
omnibus tanto studuit minorem
100   reddere sese.
Norat hoc laudis decus esse primum,
ut bonus mallet et merito probari
quam levis vulgi titulis et aura
     oreque tolli.
105   Unus hic mitis, facilis probusque;
unus humanus, pius ac benignus
semper in cunctos meritis vigentes
     extitit ultro.
Portus afflictis erat et salutis
110   auctor. Hic nulli gravis aut superbus

Crema, torn by the long war, saw throngs of Venetians turn
away and flee in fearful haste at Gaspar's arrival. Nor is it neces- 80
sary for me to waste your time with more anecdotes. For Filippo,
that father and leader among kings, had already displayed the
many honors that distinguished this man. For Filippo Maria con-
sidered Gaspar brilliant among illustrious leaders. For the prince 85
rewarded men who gave him outstanding service in the following
way. Whatever pleased Gaspar was permitted him, yet never did
he desire privileges for himself. Still less did he display honorable 90
titles of praise. For lofty virtue does not seek pride: she deems her-
self renowned enough if she says and does nothing except what is
right and just. 95

To the degree that Gaspar surpassed all other great men in
honor, this great man, who abounded in generosity, strove to pres-
ent himself as inferior to all other men. He knew this was the first 100
order of praise: that the virtuous man should wish to be extolled
on his own merits rather than wafted to fame on the winds and
lips of the fickle mob. This man alone is gentle, mild-mannered, 105
and upright. This man alone is kind, righteous, and ever generous
towards all men who flourish with honor. He has been a harbor
for the afflicted and the author of our safety. Neither proud nor 110
haughty toward anyone, this man should be cherished equally by
all with wondrous love in their hearts. But when Filippo, whom

omnibus miro pariter colendus
        cordis amore.
Ast ubi nostras tenebras relinquens
ille, quem saeclis abolevit aetas
115   nulla venturis, superas Philippus
        ivit in auras,
Insubres idem fuit inter omnis
Gaspar excellens itidemque Chremam
fecit ut frustra premeret tremendis
120   Hadria castris.
Publicae semper studuit saluti
unus in primis. Veneranda cives
usque quo virtus tenuit decoro
        ulla pudore.
125   At furor postquam rapuit rebellis
impudens mentes licuitque cuique
quod per impurum sceleris licebat
        nomen et usum,
cessit et turpi vacuus rapina.
130   Innocens nullis agitatus atrae
ignibus mentis petiit supremum
        laudis honorem.
Nanque Franciscum propriis per omne
tempus et totum meritis in orbem
135   Sphortiam late celebrem futurum
        mente petivit.
Sic enim ferrum lapidem trahentem
expetit; Phoebi radios tonantis
armiger fixis oculis micantes
140   suscipit ales.
Turba sic regem volucrum renatum
post vetus primae positum figurae

no will ever forget in the ages to come, left our darkness and en-   115
tered the heavenly aura, this same Gaspar emerged as preeminent
among all the Milanese. At the same time, he saw to it that the
Venetians would attack Crema in vain from their much-feared gar-
rison.[45]   120

Gaspar alone — and first and foremost — was always devoted to
the welfare of the people; and his revered virtue held the citizens
together because of his graceful modesty. But when corrupt mad-
ness seized hold of rebellious minds and permitted each citizen to   125
do whatever was allowed in the name of crime and its practice,
then he departed, disengaging himself from the shameful plunder.
This innocent man, driven by no passions of a malicious mind,   130
sought the highest honor in praise.

His intention was that Francesco Sforza should be celebrated
for his merits throughout the whole world and for all time. Thus   135
Gaspar sought out the stone that took back his sword, and the
warlike bird of the god of thunder received the flashing rays of
Phoebus Apollo's steady gaze.[46] In the same way a flock of birds   140
flying in high formation followed their king all across the sky when

corpus excelsa sequitur caterva
aere toto.

145 Cogitat Gaspar patriae saluti
consuli nulla ratione posse,
Sphortias ni rem capiat regendam
nobilis heros.

Hunc enim norat superum benignis
150 viribus fraetum studioque summae
gloriae semper solitum labori
cedere nulli.

Huic item norat pietate et armis
pacis et belli pariter verendo
155 inter humanum genus omne pulchras
cedere partes.

Ergo conspirat sociis vocatis
civibus qui se patriae periclis
dederent salvam facerent ut urbem
160 fulmine tactam.

Impetu facto rabidos latrones
qui fame praeda nece peste flamis
patriam diri miseram premebant
denique perdit.

165 Quique Mercatum meus hic tenebat
Sphortias Vicum reprimens ab ira,
ipse Mercatus placidumque Gaspar
invehit urbi.

Te dedit, Gaspar, patriae parentem,
170 o decus nostri specimenque saecli,
cuius invicta probitate ductus
magna rependis.

Excipis mira pietate fidum
quem diu noras per utrinque sortem.

he was reborn from the ancient body of his first shade, buried long ago.[47]

Gaspar thought that the safety of the city could not be looked 145 to unless the noble hero Sforza became the ruler and took the reins of state. For he knew that this man — relying on the kindly powers of the gods above and his own zeal for the greatest glory — 150 would never be deterred by any labor. Likewise he knew that the beautiful regions among the whole human race would bow down before this man who is equally venerable in piety and the arms of war and peace. 155

Therefore Gaspar conspired with his friends and called on the citizens to commit themselves to their native city and to secure it from danger, though lightning had already struck it. Finally, in an 160 attack on the mad thieves, who now had afflicted the sad city of the Milanese with famine, looting, slaughter, plague and fire, he destroyed them. Then Gaspar led my Sforza, calm in demeanor, 165 into the city, for he had been holding the town of Vimercate, cordoning it off it from the rage. He made you, Gaspar, the father of your city and, guided by his unvanquished probity, O ornament and glory of our century, you have repaid us well. You welcomed 170 with wondrous piety the trusted man whom you have long known and seen through every change of fortune, and afterwards you es-

175 Et gradu post te statuis secundo
    rebus agendis.
    Qui satis digne numerare tantas
    quiverint laudes quibus antecellis
    fama quos omnes celebrat vetusta,
180   Sphortia princeps?
    Inter immensos titulos et amplos
    hic nitet. Quod te duce tam benigno
    gratior nemo, merito probetur
        munus utrinque.
185 Hic enim nullum fugiat periclum,
    dum tuis possit bene rebus uti.
    Ipse nec vinci patiaris unquam
        munere gratus.
    Clio iam satis est. Locum canendi
190 Euterpe dare convenit sorori.
    Nam iussu Iovis haec locum secundum
    exposcit sibi. Gaspari merenti
    ut tempus tulit est satis repensum.
    Si quid defuerit, benignus addet
195 vel gratus potius chori magister,
    ni Gaspar bene desinat mereri.

tablished yourself, administering affairs of state at a favorable
pace.   175

But who could enumerate enough the glorious deeds in which
you, Prince Sforza, surpass all those whom time-honored fame
celebrates? Surrounded by every immense and ample honor, this   180
man shines brilliantly. Because no one is more obliging than you,
kindly duke, let duty deservedly be commended on both sides. For
this man[48] would avoid no danger as long as he can usefully em-   185
ploy your assistance. Nor will you who indeed enjoy favor ever al-
low yourself to be surpassed in your service to him.

Now Clio is satisfied. Now it is fitting to give her sister Euterpe   190
a chance to sing. For this girl demands a favorable place in accord
with Jove's command. Since time has brought Gaspar the reward
he merits, it is enough. If anything is lacking, the kindly and pleas-
ing master of the chorus will supply it, so that Gaspar will not   195
cease to be rewarded.

EUTERPE
LIBER TERTIUS

: I :

Karole Francorum rex praestantissime, nomen
cuius ad extremas, qua terram circuit ingens
Oceanus, moetas tulit invictissima virtus,
inclyta quam rerum delectat fama tuarum,
5   Euterpe me dulcis adit lenique silentem
corripit alloquio, 'Quae te vaecordia,' dicens
'tanta premit? Quo more taces? Age tolle soporem
ac sensus excire para. Me Phoebus Apollo,
quo laetor genitore, tibi[1] demittit ab alto
10   vertice quem volitans de sanguine Pegasus atrae
Gorgonos illustrem sacro fecisse liquore
dicitur. Ah, propera citharam moderare sonoram
et numeros ad verba refer quibus aequor et omnis
terra sonet summumque vehat super aethera regem.
15   Karolus armipotens hic est quem nulla silebunt
saecula, quem populi meritis et laudibus omnes
extollent, quem fata sui livore furoris
interiment nunquam, quem fors casusque sequetur.
Karolus armipotens, postquam pater optimus ille
20   quem natura potens finem superique dederunt
excepit moriens, non se per inertia voluit
otia, lascivis nec se commisit alumnis,
indole sed fretus quam Solque Cyprisque dedisset

EUTERPE
BOOK III

:   I   :

To Charles VII
Encomium, and an appeal to launch a Crusade

O Charles, most excellent king of France, whose name invinci-
ble Virtue, happy with the fame of your deeds, has carried to the
farthest shores where great Oceanus encircles the earth, sweet
Euterpe approaches and chides me for my silence with gentle   5
words. "What great folly overwhelms you?" she says, "Why do
you not speak? Come, put away sleep and prepare to rouse our
hearts and minds. Phoebus Apollo, the father in whom I rejoice,
has sent me to you from the mountaintop that winged Pegasus is   10
said to have made famous with a sacred spring when he emerged
from the blood of the dark Gorgon.[1] Ah, hurry to temper your
sweet-sounding lyre and set words to rhythm, so that the whole
world and the sea will resound with music and will carry this
greatest of kings to heaven.

"This king is Charles, mighty in arms, whom all posterity will   15
hymn, all peoples will praise to the skies, the fates with their mad
envy will never bury, and fortune will always follow. After his great
father[2] died, having met the end that all-powerful nature and the
heavenly gods allotted him, Charles, mighty in arms, neither set   20
himself to idle pursuits nor spent his days with lascivious young
companions. Instead, relying on the nature that the Sun-god, the
Cyprian goddess,[3] and Jupiter, the father almighty, had given him,

ac pater omnipotens, animo meditatus et orbem
25   terrarum caelique vias se finxit agendo
inferior quidquid probitas iubet. Inde superas
contemplatus opes, caput altius extulit oras
vectus in aethereas mentis ratione supremae.
Sic et in humanis rebus multumque diuque
30   per virtutis opus se rex exercuit omne.
Et caeli quoscunque adiit viditque recessus
ac novit sensitque nihil ratione petendum
quod virtute vacet, quod caeli nesciat arces
qui colit et mundi solus moderatur habaenas.
35   Non igitur mirum si tantis stragibus actos
Karolus e regno patrio rex expulit Anglos.
Forte hominum genus est et formidabile cunctis.
Anglus in arma ruens, patria[2] qui sede Britanos
eiiciens veteres, alias sibi quaerere terras
40   impulit et tanta peperit sibi laude triumphos.
Nam si vera loqui liceat, quas vidit et ortus
solis et occasus gentes in bella feroces
laudibus eae cunctae priscis cessere Britannis.
Hos timuit Liber, totum qui terruit orbem.
45   Hos ferus Alcides veritus dedit horrida turpi
terga fugae. Solus, qui Caesaris aemulus armis,
aggressus fuditque truces domuitque Britannos.
Est Anglus cui victa potens iam cesserat omnis
Gallia, ab extremae spumosis Tethyos undis
50   Arctoaeque plagae confinibus usque sub Alpes.
Karolus ingenti virtute deique faventis
praesidio fraetus, tanta iam caede madentes,
quosque explere cruor nullus nec praeda nec ignis
posset, in adversos magna vi percitus Anglos
55   irruit. Utque leo, cui vix dum recta minaces
velant colla iubae, vitulas furit inter et acri

he thought about the world and the paths of heaven, and he de- 25
cided to follow whatever earthly probity might dictate. Then pon-
dering the wealth of the divine kingdom, he lifted his head still
higher toward the heavenly spheres, carried there by the reasoning
of his superb mind. Thus the king trained himself fully and for a
long time in every work of virtue in human life. And whatever re- 30
cesses of heaven he approached and saw, Charles observed and
knew that one ought not to strive for any end that lacked virtue or
that god, who inhabits the citadels of heaven and who alone rules
the universe, would not recognize.

"Therefore it is not surprising that Charles expelled the English 35
from his father's kingdom after so much carnage. Theirs was a
courageous race of men and one feared by all. For rushing to take
up arms, the English drove the ancient Britons from their ances-
tral homes and forced them to seek other lands, while they won 40
triumphs and paeans of praise for themselves. For if one can speak
the truth, every tribe which the sun saw rise and set and which
was praised for its fierceness in war acknowledged the superior-
ity of those ancient Britons. Liber, who terrified the whole world,
feared them. Fierce Alcides turned his back in shameful flight be-
cause he feared them. The English alone, rivaling Caesar in arms, 45
marched forth, subdued and put to flight the fierce Britons. It was
the English to whom all powerful Gaul, now conquered, surren-
dered, from the foaming waters of farthest Tethys and the borders
of the Arctoan lands all the way to the Alps. 50

"Relying on his great virtue and with God as his fortress,
Charles fell upon the savage English with great violence; for these
men, already soaked in blood, could be not satisfied with burn-
ing, killing, or spoils. Charles was like a lion, whose mane scarcely
hides his upright neck, who rages among the heifers, pursuing 55
closely some in a swift attack while he causes others to flee, cruelly

has premit impulsu, fundit furibundus et illas
dilaniatque necatque ferox. Sic Karolus Anglos
prosternit mactatque fugans, qui militis usum
60   atque ducis regisque vices gerit acer et audens
ac prudens, aetate minor, sed laudibus ingens.
Ast ubi certatim iuvenili in corpore virtus
incrementa simul cum robore sumpsit et annis,
non satis esse ratus propriis pollere parentum
65   viribus, Eous quas sensit et Hesperus, addit
externas etiam sibi, quas novisset amicas
Italiae forti conducto milite turmas.
Nam meminit Teucrona olim et Francona potentes
Iliacos venisse duces cum fortibus armis
70   Danubii primum fluvii campique iacentis
Danubium iuxta multa cum laude colonos;
inde autem castris motis felicibus alta
per iuga, Germanos dum sese opponere certant
clade sub ingenti victos fudisse feroces
75   ac Rheni tenuisse solum, Franconia qua nunc
dicitur. Hinc rursus ductu melioris Olympi,
Gallorum populis iusto cum sanguine fusis
belli iure pii campos cepisse feraces
et patrios fecisse Lares nomenque dedisse
80   nobile Francorum, quod nulla aboleverit aetas.
Sic etiam audierat captae post diruta Troiae
moenia quae vario memorant sermone: profectos
Dardanios venisse duces Simoentos ab oris
classe duos gemina terraeque marique tremenda
85   ad fati maioris opus. Quarum altera pulsis
Euganeis Venetum Patavinam condidit urbem
ac Cisalpinos quos Gallos dicimus omnis
imperio tenuit multos dominata per annos.
Altera sed classis Veneris quam natus agebat

butchering and killing still more. Thus Charles destroyed and cut down the English, putting them to flight. And daring, fierce, and prudent, he showed himself by turns a soldier, a leader, and a king. He was young in years but mighty in deeds. 60

"But when virtue grew in the young man to match the increase in his physical strength and years, thinking it was not enough to have his forbears' power, which lands both to the east and west had known, he added the friendly foreign troops he came to know 65 to the brave soldiers he had hired from Italy. For he recalled that two powerful leaders from Troy, Teucro and Franco, had once come as colonists with much praise, accompanied by brave troops from the Danube and the land adjacent to the Danube.[4] Then, 70 however, after successful marches across the high mountain ridges, these two leaders vied with one another in fighting the savage Germans, and after they had vanquished them in a terrible slaughter, they put them to flight and took possession of their land at the base of the Rhine river, which is now called Franconia. After this, 75 following the counsel of a better Olympian god, they routed the peoples of the Gauls in a fair battle and occupied their rich lands in accord with the right of pious war. They adopted the Lares of the Gauls as their own household gods and took the noble name of Franks for themselves, and this no future age has altered. 80

"Charles had also heard the story that was retold in various versions after the destruction of Troy's walls. It was said that with twin fleets feared on land and sea two Dardanian leaders[5] had traveled from the shores of the Simois for a work of great destiny. 85 Of these two armed companies, one founded the city of Padua,[6] and after expelling the Euganii of Venice from the city, they held all the inhabitants (whom we call the Cisalpine Gauls) under their dominion and ruled over them for many years. But the other fleet — which the son of Venus, Trojan Anchises' son, commanded

90 Tros Anchisiades multumque diuque periclis
millibus obiecta ut tandem Laurentis apricos
appraendisset agros, post praelia multa cruore
fusa gravi victrix totam sibi cedere iussit
Italiam. Victae similis nec nomen ademit
95 nec linguam aut mores, sed sese tradidit ultro.
Karolus hinc igitur conducto milite priscae
quem iungebat amor patriae et natalis origo,
fortior insurgens saevos furibundus in hostes,
dum rapitur fulmen veluti quod cuncta ruina
100 sterneret horrisonis caeli de nubibus actum,
urget et imperio cogit parere subactos
quod dudum coluere suo. Sic Gallia demum
iura sui regis didicit servare tyrannis
exactis rabidis per digni praemia luctus.
105 Hunc igitur tibi materiae desume, poeta,
quem dulci cecinisse lyra lauderis in omne
tempus. Musa iubet, quam tanti ducere suesti,
Euterpe parere. Para tibi digna iubenti.
Nec tibi cantanti rex inclytus ille Renatus
110 excidat eximia qui fulgens laude propinquum
regem iure colit comitem sociumque laborum
sese addens huius. Nec frater Karolus heros
ille pius regni decus et tutela potentis
inter honoratos nomen non servet amicos.'
115 Sic ait. Et celeri repetens Helicona volatu
addidit haec abiens: 'Utinam modo Karolus addat
laudibus egregiis Turca de caede triumphos
quos decet, ultus avos et Francae obprobria cladis
nec titulis indigna tuis, rex maxime,' nostra
120 Musa monet, 'Converte oculos et respice quantis
stragibus affecit Turcorum ignobile vulgus
Francos saepe tuos, quam turpi labe serenos

—was long subjected to a thousand perils, with the result that 90
it landed finally in the sunny Laurentine[7] fields. After many bat-
tles with heavy loss of life, this victorious company of Trojans
commanded the whole of Italy to surrender to it. But it abolished
neither the name nor language nor customs of the nation it con-
quered; but like a vanquished people, the Trojans as victors will-
ingly took on their subjects' ways. 95

"Charles therefore, accompanied by the mercenaries whom love
of their ancient homeland and their shared birth had joined to his
cause, rose up still more bravely and raged against the cruel enemy.
Moving quickly, like lightning propelled by thundering clouds in
heaven that levels everything in its wake, he pressed hard upon 100
them, defeated them and compelled them to obey his rule, which
they have now respected for a long time. And, once the rabid ty-
rants had been expelled, Gaul finally learned to keep the laws of
its king with the tribute of proper mourning.[8]

"Therefore, O poet, take this man as your subject, whom you 105
will be praised for all time for having celebrated in song. The
Muse Euterpe, whom you have been accustomed to esteem so
highly, commands you to obey. Prepare worthy songs for your
commander. Nor should you forget, O singer of songs, that fa-
mous king René,[9] who, shining with praises, rightly honors his
kinsman the king, making him a companion and partner in his 110
toils. Nor would his brother, that hero Charles, the pious glory
and protector of the kingdom, fail to keep René's name among his
honored friends."

Thus she spoke, and seeking again the Helicon in swift flight,
she added the following words as she departed: "O that Charles 115
would increase his extraordinary fame with fitting triumphs as rec-
ompense for the Turkish massacre, thus avenging his forefathers
and the dishonor of the French disaster[10]—a mission not unwor-
thy of your honors, O greatest king! Direct your gaze here," our 120
Muse advised, "and consider how many deaths the baseborn horde

foedavit regni vultus, quo tempore dirus
impurusque latro Baisettes omne per atrum
125   dedecus involuit fuerant quicunque secuti
castra Sigismundi comites deformia regis.
Nanque Saladinus Turcorum saevus Amyras
fudit et insidiis Francos regemque Guidonem
et patriam Christi cum sancta sustulit urbe.
130   Nunc tibi perfacile est omnis obtundere vires
Turcorum nuper quas magna ex parte Johannes
ille Vaivodas non una strage peremit.
Unus Amorathus,[3] cuius se Turca salute
speque tuebatur res omnis, vina secutus
135   et venerem obscoenam patrium concessit ad Horchum.
Huius morte iacent Turci nullaque sepulti
spe tolli valeant. Nam quid Mahometus in omni
flagitio natus puer altus ab ubere ductus
polliceatur opis? Satis est si vina frequentet
140   et fomenta gulae, veneri somnoque dicatus.
Quare age, rex ingens, felicibus[4] utere coeptis
ad summum pietatis opus. Tibi gloria victis
magna quidem parta est Anglis. Sed gloria terrae
huic si caelestis multo praestantior uni
145   accedat, nemo fuerit te clarior alter.
Immortale solet nomen regalibus esse
auribus egregie iucundum. Gloria multos
usque adeo iuvit sese ut committere fatis
maluerunt quam luce frui. Sic ille superbus
150   Curtius et Brutus Decii Codrus atque Phileni
atque alii multi ducti dulcedine laudis,
posteritas quam grata viris ingentibus aedit,
sponte sua maestae voluere occurrere morti.
Hos si vana quidem potuit mandare sepulchris
155   gloria, vera tuum quanto perfundere pectus

of Turks has inflicted on your French men and how they have
foully stained and defiled the peaceful appearance of your king-
dom, at a time when the savage and corrupt thief Bayezid had in-
volved King Sigismund's men in every dark infamy, when they   125
came to his horrid camp.[11] Certainly cruel Saladin, the Emir[12] of
the Turks, treacherously routed King Guy and the Franks,[13] and
he sacked the native land of Christ and with it the holy city. It
is now easy for you to crush all the Turkish troops that John   130
Hunyadi[14] destroyed in a number of battles. Murad,[15] in whose
protection the whole Turkish state had placed its hopes, having
lived a profligate life of wine and women, went to his paternal
Orcus. With the death of such a man, the Turks were laid low,   135
and without the hope that the dead man gave them they cannot be
raised up. For what help could his son Mehmed promise when the
boy had been nurtured on, and was schooled in, every shameful
crime? Is it enough for him to drink and eat to excess, addicted to
sex and sloth?   140

"Thus come, O great king, make use of the fortunate cam-
paigns you undertook for the sake of the highest work of piety.
When you vanquished the English, you won great glory. But if
heavenly virtue far surpasses this earthly glory for any one man, no
one will be more celebrated than you. The title "immortal" is espe-   145
cially welcome to royal ears. Glory has pleased many to such an
extent that they preferred to choose death rather than enjoy life.
Such men were proud Curtius and Brutus, the Decii, Codrus and
Philenus, and many others who were seduced by the sweetness of   150
praise which posterity in her gratitude gives great men who were
willing to suffer sorrowful death voluntarily. If vain glory could
send such men to their tombs, with how great a profusion of nec-
tar should true glory fill your heart, O tearful sojourner on this   155
road, who will be a guest at heaven's table forever?"

nectare debuerit, qui flaebilis incola terrae
hoc sis calle poli semper conviva futurus?'
Nec tibi defuerint qui sint tua facta canendo
ingenii per pulchra sui monimenta futuris
160   dicturi populis. Nam me quoque maxima rerum
gloria quas tanta gessisti laude tuarum
reddidit affectum tanti pietatis amore.
Rex invicte, tibi noctes ut flama diesque
urat corda mihi, tu nobis unus in ore
165   semper ades. Nihil est sine te mihi, Karole, dulce.
Quid censes maiora tuae si nomina clarae
addideris laudi, si Christi viceris hostes?
O utinam quandoque mihi te visere coram
affatuque tuo contingat cominus uti!
170   Nam quamvis audita iuvent quae fama benignis
vocibus insonuit, visus tamen acrior omni
est sensu meliusque refert quae vera probarit.
Visere te cupimus, Rex Karole. Tanta locorum
intervalla vetant. Verum te lumine mentis
175   prospiciens merito comitabor carmine vates.

: 2 :

O tu quem Mariae venter ab aethere
susceptum peperit saemine spiritu
Gonzagam placido lumine Karolum
    rerum respice conditor.
5   Hunc febris facibus torrida fervidis

There will be no dearth of poets who will celebrate your deeds, creating beautiful monuments of their talents in song for future generations.[16] The great glory for the wars you have waged with such acclaim has also touched me, filling me with love of your piety.[17] O king invincible, be present always on my lips, so that my light may always burn for you night and day. For nothing is sweet for me without you, Charles. What would you think of adding greater names to your glorious encomia? What if you conquered the enemies of Christ? O that I could visit you and converse with you face to face someday! For although it is pleasing to hear the stories that fame makes resonant with gentle words, still sight is keener than any other sense and better relays the true stories that it finds good. We want to visit you, King Charles. But the great distances between our cities forbids it. But by gazing at you with the eyes of my mind, I shall accompany you as your poet and prophet in song.

160

165

170

175

: 2 :

To Carlo Gonzaga
An elegy written during his last illness

O you, founder of the world, whom Mary's womb brought forth from heaven from the seed of the holy spirit, look with favor on Carlo Gonzaga.[18]

This man, whom a burning fever torments, harrying his senses with red-hot brands, this man, whom no violent force on Mars's

5

torquet sollicitis sensibus opprimens
et, quem nulla feri Martis in agmine
   vis nunquam potuit, domat —
heu — nostrae nimium dura necessitas
10   naturae variis casibus obviae
quos prudens nequeat mente nec artibus
   ullis vincere callidus.
Nam quis, qua Latium nobile maximis
tam multis remicat principibus manu
15   claris ac animo se ferat insolens
   qui tantis vireat bonis?
Mittamus patriam sanguine fulgidam
Mantus. Herculeo saemine floridus
Gonzagas sileat. Nam propriis bonis
20   hic omnes superat suos
heros nae veterum Karolus inclytum
quos iactat proavos urbis et aureae
auctores meritis et titulis domus.
   Excellit decus omnium.
25   Quid formam rutili corporis efferam,
qua vivis adeo fulget in omnibus
ut late pateat caelicolum novum
   mirandum populis iubar?
Vires ac agiles iunge per omnia
30   artus, quae studium Martis et otii
optat, seu studium sive acies iuvet.
   Nil est quod fugiat virum.
Cunctis integritas sensibus additur,
qualis nec melior nec moderatior
35   ulli contigit hoc tempore principi
   nec priscis etiam viris.
O virtus animi lucida maximi,
qua nil splendidius Phoebus Olympius

brutal battle lines could ever conquer, is conquered, alas, by the
harsh necessity of our nature, too often exposed to the varied mis-
fortunes that even a prudent and skillful man could not overcome   10
with all his arts or intellect.

In a land where noble Latium gleams with so many great
princes famous for their gifts of mind and body, who would be ar-
rogant enough to exalt himself for possessing such virtues? But let   15
us not speak of the city shining with the descendants of Manto.[19]
Let the showy orator be silent about the Herculean seed of the
Gonzaga. For he outstrips all his own family members. Truly, the   20
hero Carlo surpasses the ancestors of celebrated men of antiquity,
whom he boasts are the forefathers of both the city and his golden
house with its merits and titles: for he is the glory of all men.

What shall I say of the beauty of his golden body that endows   25
him with a radiance unmatched by any other man alive, so much
so that the rays of a new star seem to be beamed from heaven
to be admired by the people far and wide? Then add his strength
and agile limbs in everything demanded by the pursuits of war
and peace, whether it be study or the battle line that pleases   30
him. There is nothing which eludes the man: to all his senses
there is added a purity, such that no finer or more moderate sort is
found in any prince, neither in this age nor among the ancients. O   35
shining virtue of the greatest mind—for Olympian Phoebus sees
nothing more splendid than this when he looks down in wonder

mirans sydereis spectat ab axibus.
40   Quis te non stupeat videns?
Hic, hic est animus quem ratio potens
disquirens geminis viribus intimae
naturae duplices callibus alteris
        soles numinibus iugat.
45 Nam te non latitat, Karole, caelitus
vis quae magnanimis pectoribus vigens
terrarum fragiles terret inanium
        cultus et varios dolos.
Hinc acris oculos altius erigens
50 unum quem metuas, quem penitus velis,
nosti non levibus sensibus: optimum
        Christum quem colimus deum.
Huc nam te pietas, relligio, fides
mittit non dubio calle per arduos
55 deducens apices multiplicis boni
        quod virtus peperit gravis.
Et quamvis sileas, assequimur tamen
omnem pectoribus quam probus abditis
mentem constituis caelitibus sacram
60   et mortalibus enites.
Nam quid non graviter dicis et efficis?
Quis te iusticiae munere candide
alter vel superet? Vel paribus satis
        aequet lancibus impudens?
65 At quanto valeas robore, Karole,
invicti reliquos quo validos viros
omnis exuperas cordis in asperis
        rebus, promere nesciam.
Ast haec eloquium nectare dulcius
70 condit quod placido flumine laevius

from his starry spheres. Who would not marvel when he gazes at 40
you, Carlo?

You have a mind that fertile reason harnesses to the twin dei-
ties, the forces deep within nature, when you investigate our two
suns on their different paths. For heavenly power is not hidden
from you, Carlo—the power which, flourishing in noble hearts, 45
threatens the shallow beliefs and various deceptions of ignorant
lands.

And so, raising your keen eyes higher, you recognize the one
whom you fear, the one you desire in the deepest part of yourself, 50
the one you know with all your heart—greatest Christ, whom we
worship as God. For to him piety, religion, and faith lead you,
sending you on a clearly marked path and over the steep mountain
peaks of the many-faceted good to which fertile virtue gives birth. 55

And although you may be silent, we will follow nonetheless ev-
ery purpose you decide upon as sacred to the gods, since you
shine, a beacon light, for mortal men. For what do you say or do 60
that is not done with gravity? What other man might surpass you
in the shining administration of justice? What audacious soul
would vie with you in fair judgment?

With what superior strength you surpass all other strong men 65
in difficult affairs of the heart and mind, Carlo—this I cannot
say. But eloquence sweeter than nectar records these things, and
flowing more gently than a quiet river, it outdoes the Muses with 70
the sound of verse that stirs the lyric modes.

manans exuperat Pieridas sono
    vocis quae numeros ciet.
Et belli studiis pacis et artibus
virtus te pariter tollit in aethera.
75   Aeque te sagulum te toga perdecet.
    Te nil egregium latet.
Quid quod belligerae nulla protervitas
sortis te potuit, nulla licentia
fortunae valuit flectere dexterae
80   ad vitae reprobas vices?
Te semper placidum te similem tui
praestas. Et nimium, Karole, temperas
atque id quod medium deseruit viris
    laudatum gravibus parum.
85   Mirandis probitas te decorat bonis
qui caelum titulis nobilibus petis.
Tu vives meritis saecla per omnia,
    livorem superans trucem.
Nam te livor edax insequitur dolis
90   et semper laqueos insidians parat.
At tu vir sapiens fortiter omnia
    fers et dissimulas malum.
Hunc quis non igitur vivere Karolum
optet, quem bonitas efficit improbis
95   cunctis invidiosum et febris ossibus
    haerens urit et opprimit?
Hunc hunc ergo tuis maxime brachiis
natus virginea, Christe, puerpera
amplectens geminis, en, lachrymis, pater,
100   nostris cede precantibus.
Tu cernis, genitor, quam misere premunt
mundanum rapidis turbinibus minae

Your excellence in the knowledge equally of warfare and the peaceful arts raises you to the heavens. Superbly well-suited to both the soldier's cloak and the toga, no great deed is beyond your 75 reach. What of the fact that neither the daring of a soldier's lot in life or the license of good fortune were strong enough to move you to make the wrong changes in your life?[20] You, Carlo, always 80 showed yourself to be a gentle person and true to yourself. Yet you temper excess and actions that have abandoned the middle road, which is too little praised by serious men. Your probity adorns you 85 with admirable advantages, but you seek heaven with noble honors. You will live through all the ages because of your achievements, vanquishing hostile envy. For gluttonous envy pursues you with deceit and is always setting traps and sowing treachery. But 90 you, who are wise, bear all things bravely and ignore the evil.

Who would not hope then that this Carlo will live, for his goodness renders him hateful to all who are evil, and yet a fever consumes him and burns deep within his bones. O Christ, born 95 of virgin birth, embrace this man with both your arms; look upon us, Father, surrender to our tears, our prayers. You see, O Lord, 100 how wretchedly threats press upon this earthly mass with high storm winds, what great battles merciless Tartarus rouses, rushing from the depths.

molem, quanta ruens funditus excitat
    atrox praelia Tartarus.
105   Hic unus clipeo, Christe, bisaureo
omnem vim rabidi Ditis et impetum
non solum ferat, at praeferat impotens
    et lucem tenebris paret.
Hunc febris facibus solve voracibus
110   membris restituens incolumem suis
et nobis pariter iusta rogantibus,
    fusuris lachrymas pias.
Hunc febris penitus, Christe, deum pater,
oramus lachrymis ut fera liberet
115   sed livor levius, perfidus insequi,
    si tolli nequit, urgeat.

⋮ 3 ⋮

[POETA]

Aenice, distuleras nimium mihi, Davale, gratas
    ferre vices. Cupido nam brevis hora nimis.
Iratus Musis deflebam[5] tempus inane
    meque nimis facile rebar amoris opus.
5   Iamque fides odio carmenque et carminis auctor
    fiebat. Totus vitrea bilis[6] eram.

May this one man with his double gold shield, O Christ, not 105
only endure every violence and every blow from raging Dis, but
may he, though he languishes, prefer the light and find it in the
darkness. Release this man from the voracious fires of fever, re-
store him safe and sound to his friends and to us who pray for 110
what is just and will soon weep pious tears. O Christ, father of
the gods, we tearfully pray that the fierce fever may free this man;
but if it cannot be removed, we pray that malice, a treacherous
pursuer, may press upon him more gently. 115

: 3 :

To Iñigo d'Avalos and Lucrezia Alagno
Advice on love

POET

You have delayed too long in giving me a pleasing response, Iñigo;
for even one brief hour is too long for someone eager to hear from
you. Angry with the Muses, I wept at the wasted time and I
thought myself too easy a victim of love. And now my lyre, my
song, and its author have become hateful to me. I've been nothing 5
but glassy bile.[21]

[DAVALUS]

Tempestivus ades. Surdas mihi dulcis in aures
    repis et — O dixti non mihi iure — doles.
Dum canis et nostrum lenis tibi carmine pectus,
10   ipse tibi gratus regia dona paro.
Te meus Alphonsus rex en mitissimus ad se
    ut venias placido sedulus ore monet.
Non et enim frustra regalis videris aedes.
    Aut hic noster eris ditior aut redeas.

[POETA]

15 Haec et plura mones facundo, Davalus, ore
    hortarisque: 'Citus carpat amicus iter.'
Non tua difficilis patietur dicta Philelfus.
    Verba sibi faciet, quidquid, amice, iubes.
Verum nosse velim qua fronte Lucretia nostros
20   diva sales tulerit. Riserit an tumuit?
Nam si dicta ioco non aspernatur amatque
    se celebrem fieri cantibus et cithara,
rebor iter tutum, dextrum mihi numen et astra.
    Parthenopenque celer teque deamque petam.
25 Quod si forte tulit graviter quae lusimus, ipse
    videris an possim carpere tutus iter.
Ulcisci nam semper avet quae canduit ira
    foemina. Num doluit casta puella sales?
At quid te tanto, divina Lucretia, regi
30   vel cessisse doles vel placuisse negas?
Num doluit Semele quod cessit amata tonanti?
    Num doluit Martis basia pulchra Venus?
Magna quidem laus est tantum si mira decorem
    prae se forma tulit ut placeas domino.

D'AVALOS

Your coming is timely. You slip sweetly into my silent ears and—
O, you did not speak rightly to me—you are grieving. While you
sing and soothe my heart with your song, I am readying royal gifts
for you myself in gratitude. My most gentle King Alfonso admon-   10
ishes you in his gentle way to come back to him. For you will not
see the royal palace in vain: either you will be ours here, or you
will return and be richer.

POET

You advise me eloquently, d'Avalos, about these and other matters,
and you also warn me, saying: "A friend should start the trip, as   15
soon as he is called." Nor will Filelfo bear your words with diffi-
culty; he will answer for himself, whatever you command, my
friend. But I want to know in what mood the divine Lucrezia has
received our satires.[22] Did she laugh or did she become angry? For   20
if she does not despise words said in jest, and if she loves becom-
ing famous through my songs and my lyre, then I think the jour-
ney will be safe for me. The heavenly deity and the stars will be
rightly disposed, and I will soon be in Parthenope and I will seek
you and the goddess.[23]   25

But if she takes ill what I wrote in jest, you yourself will know
whether I can embark on the journey safely. For a woman always
longs to avenge that which inflames her anger. Surely the pure girl
does not weep over my satires? But why, divine Lucrezia, are you
either grieving that you've given in to so a great king or denying
that you've pleased him? Did Jupiter's lover Semele regret that she   30
gave in to the Thunderer? Was Venus remorseful over the beauti-
ful kisses of Mars? Indeed, you will win great praise if your mar-
velous beauty displays so much grace that you delight your lord.

35   Quin et si sapias, blandis in raetia verbis
          regis coge animum. Fac tibi totus eat.
       Sic et Francorum regem flagrantibus Agnes
          nuper harundinibus fixerat indomitum.
       Maeonis Alciden sibi sic cautissima dulci
40   obsequio servum subdidit e domino.
       Praeterea quae te prohibet mora labra labellis
          iungere per Veneris dulcia dona deae?
       Num quae pulchra latent prohibet pudor aedere coram
          arma? Patris fulmen num latet usque Iovis?
45   Neptunus saevum num tempestate tridentem
          occulit? Arquitenens num sua taela tegit?
       Non Mars, non Veneris natus premit arma Cupido?
          Harpe Mercurium falxque recludit avum?
       Non hastam Pallas, non hastam supprimit ille
50   Hellespontiacae quem coluere nurus?
       Si rex arma tibi quibus est hastatus in ictum
          intendat, quid non obvia taela[7] pares?
       Nam quid te pudeat, dum rex tam fortiter audet:
          quod liceat regi quur tibi non liceat?
55   Ah, si nosse queas quaenam fluit inde voluptas,
          poeniteat tanta continuisse mora.
       Num fortasse velis uxor, nec amica vocari?
          Nomen amiciciae quur tibi non placeat?
       Uxor saepe viro stomacho fit; semper amica
60   cauta placet. Praestat coniugis esse loco.
       Coniugium secum semper nova iurgia portat.
          Sed quos iungit amor pace tenet solida.
       Hic iocus arridet per mutua dicta. Cupido
          hic auget semper, quod paret obsequium.
65   Furta iuvant dulcesque iuvant in amore susurri.
          Iucundi amplexus, basia grata iuvant.

But if you are wise, you should coax the king into your nets with   35
flattering words. Make him completely your captive. Thus did
Agnes with her fiery arrows make the indomitable king of the
French her prisoner not long ago.[24] And likewise with sweet com-
pliance the very cautious Maeonian woman transformed Alcides
from a master into her servant.[25]   40

Besides, what delay prohibits you from joining your lips to-
gether through the sweet gifts of the goddess Venus? Does shame
prohibit you from displaying publicly the lovely weapons that lie
hidden? Does father Jove's lightning remain so hidden? Does
Neptune conceal his savage trident in a storm? Does bow-bearing   45
Apollo stow his weapons away? Did not Mars and Venus's son
Cupid conceal their arms? Were not a sickle and a curved scimitar
the emblems that identified grandfather Mercury?[26] Did not Pallas
Athena hide her weapon, did not he, whom the brides of the
Hellespont worshipped?[27] If the king were to direct the weapons   50
he possesses toward you, why would you not prepare your weap-
ons to match them? Why should it embarrass you as long as the
king so bravely dares it? Why should you not be permitted to do
what is permitted to the king? Ah, if you could know what plea-
sure flows from this, you'd be sorry to continue this delay.   55

Do you perhaps want to be his wife and not be called his girl-
friend? Why does the term "friendship" not please you? A wife of-
ten angers a man; a girlfriend is always careful to please. It's better
than being in the position of a wife. A marriage always generates   60
new quarrels within itself. But those whom love joins, she keeps
together in a lasting peace. Here both parties enjoy a joke. Here
desire, since it produces compliance, always increases. Stolen de-
lights and the sweet whisperings of love are pleasing. Sweet em-   65
braces, welcome kisses delight. There is no conversation unless
pleasure itself prompts it. There are sweet games, dancing and
music.

Nullus inest sermo, nisi quem ferat ipsa voluptas.
    Sunt dulces ludi, sunt choreae atque soni.
Illa viri querulis obtundit vocibus aures.
70   Invehit in servas. Insimulat famulos.
Villicus in fundum sero deducit aratrum;
    horrea fracta refert atque merum fugiens.
Nunquam certa quies. Hinc murmurat; inde soporem
    dat vitio. Damnat quae benefacta videt.
75 Nec factum esse satis quicquam putat. Omnis avara
    est uxor. Nummis vult cumulare domum.
Haec mala coniugium secum fert omnia, nanque
    cura domus debet coniugis esse probae.
Quo fit ut ante diem viridis matrona senescat
80   et passis rugis os tegat omne suum.
Num patiare tuam faciem cui candida cedat[8]
    Cypris arent rugae destituatque nitor?
Num malis odio coniunx quam taeda phanetis
    esse piis facibus quis recalescit amor?
85 Eia, age ne desis tibi tu. Sed pande secundis
    vela notis. Portus, i, cape fausta tuos.
Nec solum tecum quam sit iucunda voluptas
    versa animo, fructus sed meditare novos.
Ascanium Aeneas Italas advexit in oras,
90   heredem regni quem statuit moriens.
Ascanius regno potitur; nec parvus Iulus
    successit patrio filius imperio.
Silvius Ascanium natus de matre Latina
    excepit fratrem. Sic voluit Latium.
95 Iulia progenies, quae magnum dicit Iulum
    auctorem generis, hoc fuit orta patre.
Silvius Ascanii regno successit. Iulum
    Ascanio natum pontificem statuunt.

A wife, on the contrary, wears out her husband's ears with quarrelsome words. She inveighs against her maidservants. She falsely accuses her serving men:[28] the estate manager brings the   70
plough to the ground too late; the barn is broken and the wine is going bad, she reports. Never is there a moment of peace. First she grumbles and then she complains about her servants' sleeping. She condemns as bad those things which she knows are good. Nor does she think anything is enough. A wife is greedy in every way.   75
She wants to fill her home with money. Marriage brings all these evils with it, and the care of the house should be the duty of a good wife. Thus it happens that a married woman grows old before her time, and wrinkles spread, covering her whole face. Would   80
you allow wrinkles to furrow your face and the glow to leave it, before which even shining Cypris bows? Would you rather be a hated wife than a torch of Eros with the sacred firebrands that can rekindle love?

Ah, come, do not fail yourself. Spread your sails to favorable winds. Go, take possession of your harbor, fortunate one. Ponder   85
not only how you can have delightful pleasure, but think about new benefits. Aeneas brought Ascanius to the shores of Italy, the heir to his kingdom whom he named when he died. Ascanius took   90
possession of the realm, and little Iulus, his son, did not succeed to his father's empire. Silvius, born to his Latin mother, succeeded his brother Ascanius. This is what Latium wanted. The Julian lineage, which claims great Iulus as its founder, is sprung from this   95
ancestor. Silvius succeeded Ascanius on the throne and they established Iulus, the son of Ascanius, as pontifex maximus. Would

Num dubites igitur te tanto iungere regi,
100 quae regis matrem te fore posse scias?
Tu quoque rex ingens, quid longa in verba precesque
  tempus inane teris? Vim cupit illa sibi.
Nanque magis quo quaeque velit sibi foedera iungi
  optatae Veneris, vim cupit illa magis.
105 Obstat enim prohibetque pudor quod mente volutat
  foemina quae nondum stulta iugum tulerit.
Quae tot missa capit fulgentis dona metalli,
  se tibi sat Veneris pignore constituit.
Non igitur frustra precibus vim mollibus addas.
110 Munere fungatur lingua manusque suo.
Verum ego qui metuo te, diva Lucretia, nostros
  offendisse sales utor item salibus.
Parce precor, si forte tuas offenderit auris
  Euterpe, tecum ludere quod monuit.
115 At tu qui nostras tanto colis igne Camoenas,
  Aenice, fac vatem nunc tueare tuum.
Davale, curandum est vel me non vana iocatum
  vel tutum sit iter pignora per fidei.

     ⁝ 4 ⁝

Ambrosi, tandem ferus ille Mavors
ac Fames, duros etiam Gigantas
quae ferox tetris potuisset umbris
tradere et dirum domitare Ditem,
5 hinc ad extremos abiit Trionas.
Nanque Franciscus venerandus heros

you hesitate therefore to join yourself to such a great king, when
you know that you can be the mother of a king?   100

But also, mighty king, why do you waste empty time in long
speeches and prayers? Lucrezia wants passionate lovemaking. And
the more she wants all the treaties of Venus to be concluded in her
favor,[29] the more she wants passionate love. Yet modesty prohibits
and stands in the way of what a foolish girl imagines, who knows   105
nothing as yet of the marriage yoke. A girl who receives the many
gifts of shining plate sent to her has shown herself sufficiently
pledged to you in love. Therefore you would not be adding passion
to soft entreaties to no effect. Let hand and tongue each perform
their own offices. But I who fear, divine Lucrezia, that my satires   110
have displeased you, am using satire again. Forbear, therefore, if
perchance Euterpe has offended your ears because she has advised
me to joke with you.

But you who worship our Muses with such fire, Iñigo, see that   115
you now protect your poet. You must take care, my d'Avalos, that
either I have not joked in vain or that the journey is made safe
with pledges of loyalty.

: 4 :

To Ambrogio[30]
A hymn for Sforza's triumphal entry into Milan

Fierce Mars and savage Famine, who could send even the hard
giants to dark Hades and subdue grim Dis,[31] have finally gone
from our land, Ambrogio, to the remote Triones.[32] For the venera-   5
ble hero, Francesco Sforza, who was sent to us from heaven with

Sphortias nobis avibus secundis
celitus missus rabidos tyrannos
sustulit pacem requiemque fessis
10   attulit. Nunc est populo statuta
vera libertas. Periere fastus
plebis ignavae scelerumque terror,
stupra, vis atrox, furor et rapinae.
Heu, quis infracto meminisse fortis
15   corde vir possit rabidas et omni
peste faerali magis extimendas
beluas, quae nos penitus vorabant
ferreo rictu rigidisque rostris.
Vir bonus nemo poterat tueri
20   nomen invictae probitatis insons.
Nanque suspecti fuerant et hostes
quos pios nosset Rabias et ille
rusticus potu cerebrum diurno
laesus et nunquam Cicerus per umbras
25   sobrius. Cui se comitem Decembris
Candidus semper misere cinaedis
laevibus septus vitiisque mille
scriba pollutus dederat per omnem
criminis culpam. Bibulis cruorem
30   civium suadens ferus innocentum
latro, qui mulcens malesanus aures
plebis impurae nebulo profanis
solus exemplis, ea commonebat
quae nec immanis Phalaris patrasset.
35   Inde quos saevus gladius vel ignis
visque liquisset taciti veneni,
hos fame solus rabida peremit
Candidus; foeno paleaque tritis
posse qui victum solidum parari

favorable omens, has destroyed the mad tyrants and brought peace
and relief to the weary.

    Now true liberty has been instituted for the people. Gone is the   10
arrogance of the cowardly plebs and the reign of terror and crime:
the rape, the wretched violence, the madness and the plunder.
Alas, what brave man could remember with unbroken heart the
rabid beasts with iron jaws and rigid beaks, more frightening than   15
any lethal plague, who fed on us. No good man could keep his
reputation for untarnished probity, even though free of any guilt;
even those who were known to be honorable men were suspected   20
as enemies by Rabias and the rustic Cicerus, whose brain was
damaged from day-long drink and who was never sober after dark.

    His devoted companion in the shades and every crime is the   25
secretary Candido Decembrio,[33] a man polluted by a thousand
vices and forever surrounded by a crowd of effeminate catamites.[34]
Offering the blood of innocent citizens to drunkards, this savage   30
thief—this crazy good-for-nothing who stroked the ears of the
corrupt plebs with impious examples—this man alone urged them
to do things that not even cruel Phalaris would have perpetrated.[35]
Candido alone murdered by cruel starvation those whom fire or
the savage sword and the violence of silent poison had left alive—   35
Candido, who said that solid food could be prepared from the

40 diceret, dum se tamen ipse fallax
rebus expleret per iniqua partis
cuncta quae suadet furor et libido.
Videris passim populum iacentem
perditum loeto, Cereris quod expers
45 annus omnino peperit secundus.
   Quid mihi frustra memores Saguntum?
Aut fame pressos referas Hebraeos?
Nulla gens unquam similem Megaeram
passa narretur! Stomachus tumenti
50 nausea nobis vomitum minatur,
mente dum sortem miseram revolvo.
Nam nihil foedi, nihil impudici
liquit afflictus populus quod esse
posset intactum. Meminisse diri
55 horreo fati merito silendi.
   Tabe tam tetra generosus heros
nostra Franciscus penitus levavit
corda cum membris docuitque quantus
error humanas penetrare mentes
60 assolet. Phoebus nebulae decoros
dum tegunt crines, nequit intuentes
qua micat semper facie iuvare.
   Ambrosi, nobis radios Apollo
noster en coram rutilos suosque
65 pandit et cunctis animi solutis
nubibus nostri, nitidos ocellos
lustrat infusus recreatque dulci
luce deiectos reficitque lassos.
   Ambrosi, laetos agimus canenti
70 voce saltatus, numeris nec unis.
Et novos plectro modulos ciente
versibus miris decus omne vatum

milling of chaff and hay. Meanwhile this liar bloated himself with 40
things he had gotten through every evil that madness and lust
could incite.

You could have seen the dead lying everywhere, for this a sec-
ond year wholly bereft of grain had wrought. Why should you re- 45
mind me in vain of Saguntum?[36] Why speak of the Jews who were
plagued by famine? May no people ever again be said to have
suffered a similar Fury! My stomach turns with rising nausea
when I think of our wretched lot. For there was nothing shameful, 50
nothing corrupt the afflicted people did not attempt if they could.
I shudder to think of the dire end, which deserves to be passed
over in silence. 55

Our hero, the noble Francesco Sforza, lifted our hearts and
bodies from the foul disease deep within the city, and he taught
how much wrongdoing often burrows within human minds. As
long as clouds conceal his beautiful hair, Phoebus Apollo cannot 60
please those who look for his ever-shining face. Look, Ambrogio,
our Apollo now openly spreads his ruddy rays, and now that the
clouds have been dispelled from our minds, he looks down on us 65
with shining eyes. He restores the downcast with his sweet light
and refreshes the weary.

Ambrogio, we perform joyous dances to the accompaniment of
melodious song, and not just in a single meter. With our plectrum 70
beating out new rhythms in concert with wondrous poetry, we call
on all the most glorious of the poets to come to the sacred waters

fontis ad sacros latices vocamus,
quem Medusaeus sonipes sub alto
75   monte defodit. Resonat Cithaeron
ad resurgentis numeros sororum,
quos regit multa pater arte Paean,
pulchra cui Clio meritas secuta
reddidit voces referens superbas
80   Sphortiae laudes ducis et parentis
huius invicti populi, triumphis
cuius Euterpe redimita celsis
gestit et cantus movet ipsa miros,
praeferens cunctis merito laborum
Sphortiam nostris simul et vetustis
85   sola quos virtus dederit verendos.
Si qua te sollers igitur voluptas
capta, ad nostras propera choreas,
quas agit laetam placida per urbem
fronte dux noster populo sequente
90   et simul suavi referente cantu,
quidquid aerumnis gelidis levatus
iusserit cordis renovatus ignis
    sorte secunda.

: 5 :

Andrea, dum placida nobis munuscula mittis
grata manu, noster te magis ardet amor.

184

of the spring, which the Medusa-born steed dug up from beneath
the lofty mountaintop. Now Mt. Cytheron resounds with the   75
soaring music of the sisters, which father Paean artfully conducts.
Obeying him, lovely Clio sings for Sforza lyrics well deserved, pre-
senting superb encomia for the leader and father of his victorious   80
people. And lovely Euterpe, wearing flowers in her hair, rejoices
too in his lofty triumphs, and she herself sings wondrous melo-
dies.

For because of his accomplishments, she prefers Sforza to all
the heroes whom virtue alone has given us to revere — all those of
our own time and antiquity as well. If ever some ingenious plea-   85
sure beguiles you, then hurry to join the dancing bands our duke
leads through the joyous city with peaceful brow, as the people fol-
low him, proclaiming in sweet song whatever the fire in their   90
breasts commands, rekindled and relieved of gelid toil — now that
Fortune smiles.[37]

: 5 :

To Andrea Alamanni
That he not serve the Cyprian goddess
at the expense of the Muses[38]

Andrea, when you send me delightful gifts with a welcoming
hand, my love burns all the more for you. Presents don't move us,

Nec nos dona movent quae sunt pulcherrima, sed tu
    qui mittis nobis talia dona libens.
5   Non minimi virtus ea fit quaecunque benignam
    declarat mentem per bonitatis opus.
Servasti quidquid dandi lex ipsa requirit
    qui dederis dignus munera digna viro.
Hinc nimis, inde parum vitans mediocriter, omni
10   functus es officio temporis atque loci.
Causa fuit dandi tua quod fore dona sciebas
    grata mihi, cui te mutuus addit amor.
Defuit at dandi solum modus. Omnia recte
    caetera gesta tibi, ni modo mutueris.
15   Debuerat nobis tua dulcis epistola ferre
    munera qua nossem quanta mihi grata dares.
Nescio quis venit nullo sermone locutus.
    Reddidit et dixit quod nihil ipse putes.
Num tibi forte senex Samius praecepta silendi
20   tradidit aut Helicon aruit haustus aquis?
Eloquio qui multa vales quae dira tacendi
    te nunc flama tenet? At tibi lingua bona est;
doctus es et Musae tecum noctesque diesque
    invigilant. Dulcem pulsat Apollo chelyn.
25   Huc divas, Helicon, Castalidas sacer
    tantisper sine pergere,
dum causam modulis in medium suis
    miranti referant mihi.
Quaenam tanta tenet nunc taciturnitas
30   dicendi decus Andream?
Andreas semper metuit susurrum,
quem malus livor solet improborum
spargere in vulgus bonitatis expers
    ore maligno.
35   Es bonis carus simul et probatus,

though they are very beautiful, but rather you do yourself, since
you so generously send these gifts to me. A virtue that reveals a
kind heart through good deeds is highly valued. You have vouch- 5
safed whatever the law of giving itself requires. You have given
gifts worthy both for you to give and me to accept. By avoiding
too big a gift here and too little a one there, you have performed
every duty with prudent regard to time and place. It has been a 10
cause of your giving that you know your gifts will please me, for
our shared love also brings you to me. Only missing in your gift
giving is moderation. All the rest you do rightly, except that you
are indebted to me. Your sweet letter ought to have brought me
gifts so I would know how many pleasing things you have given 15
me. Someone came, but he said nothing. He made the delivery
and said what you yourself would regard as nothing.

Has the ancient philosopher from Samos perchance handed
down to you his doctrine about silence?[39] Or has the Helicon
spring dried up and been drained of its waters? And as for you 20
who are capable of so much, thanks to your eloquence, what terri-
ble flames of silence now engulf you? But you are virtuous in
speech, you are learned, and the Muses watch over you day and
night. Apollo beats his sweet lyre for you. O sacred Helicon, allow
the divine Castalian maidens to come here into our midst with 25
their music, as long as they tell me, their admirer, the cause of
your silence. For what momentous reticence grips you, Andrea—
you who are the glory of orators? 30

Andrea has always feared the whispering that the envy of evil
men maliciously sows among a populace devoid of goodness. And
yet you are beloved and regarded with approval among the good.
But satires with their abrasive tone are troubling to evil men. The 35

sed malis reddunt satyrae molestum
voce non grata. Fluit omnis inde
   pestis origo.
Nam tibi livor minus obfuisset
40   si tacens fraudum laqueos tulisses.
Quisquis exertus furit ac tremendo
   fulminat igni
non potest enses, Alamannus, in te
ferre livoris nimium prementis,
45   et tuae semper cupidi ruinae
   otia curat.
Est item molis gravius volenti
additum pondus, quod oportet acri
perferat nisu subeatque victor
50   nocte dieque.
Duxit uxorem Veneris decorem
quae refert, castae similis Dianae.
Huic studet soli cupiens parentis
   nomen inire.
55   Quin ait nobis pudibundus hospes:
'Vos rogo paulum lepidae sorores
hinc ad Insubres properate. Nostrum
   linquite tectum
donec hunc fontem penitus recludo,
60   cuius est vestro melior liquore
unda quae pisces parit et subactos
   reddit alumnos.'
Hinc tacet dulcis placido labori
deditus tantum Cypridos, Cupido
65   quam puer invictam tenet et Voluptas
   omnibus horis.
Novi: tacendi causa quae te non sinit
loqui maritum. Sed velim mediocriter

source of every plague emanates from their envy. To be sure, envy
would have stood less in your way if you had borne the traps of
deceit silently. Whoever rages openly and thunders like a raging 40
fire is not able to endure the swords of the envy that weighs
heavily upon you, Alamanni; instead he concerns himself for the
safety of a man who has always desired your ruin. 45

It is the same when a man willingly carries a weight given him
which is too heavy: he must bear it with fierce straining — and
he must continue to tackle it victoriously night and day. This 50
man has taken a wife who mirrors the beauty of Venus. She is
like chaste Diana. Wanting to become a father, he is devoted
to her alone. But he, the bashful host, speaks to us: "You and 55
the charming Castalian sisters, I beg you, hurry back to Milan.
Leave our house until I release completely the spring within me,
whose streams — superior to yours — will produce fish and plant 60
offspring." After this he is silent, having surrendered to the pleas-
ing work of the Cyprian goddess, whom the boy Cupid and Plea-
sure hold as their invincible lady for all seasons. 65

I know: the rule of silence prohibits you as a husband from
speaking. But I do want you to indulge with moderation in this
work, lest, while you are cultivating the ground too frequently, it

operam labori indulgeas, ne, dum nimis
70   fundum colis, quod ieceris saemen neget.
Segetem vomis nam saepius scindens facit
glebam carere fructibus sterilem suis.
Intercapedo rebus in multis valet.
In hac sed in primis perutilem scias.
75   Quos tu meos si pergis hortatus sequi,
et liberis et coniugi et Musis simul
melius cavebis. Nec silebis munera
mittens amicis, Andreas, pulcherrima.
Nam quod times livoris impias vices,
80   sane tibi ignosco. Malum est livor viri
deique quod simul nimis graviter ferunt.
Sed est opus probitatis ingens pellere
inuriam, nec improbos homines pati.
Ius omne fasque prorsus humanum premant.
85   Inuriam qui cum potest prohibet minus,
non est is admodum minoris noxiae
reus putandus quam auctor ipse criminis.
Metuas tamen nolim. Sed aude scribere,
nam nullus omnino sciat quod scripseris.
90   Num forsitan livor magis te litteras
misisse damnet quam dedisse munera?
Nescire tu quidem videris in bonam
nos gratiam rediisse cum invidiae grege.
Quare tacendi cum tibi causas vides
95   nullas adesse, vel loqui posthac stude,
vel deprecatorem para qui te sua
possit tueri dignitate et gratia,
ne desidis nomen reus subeas viri.

may reject the seed you scatter. For the ploughshare that splits the   70
earth too often renders the field sterile, causing it not to produce
fruit. A rest from work is salubrious in many circumstances; but
in this case, be aware that it is especially useful. If you proceed to
follow my counsel, you will take better care of your wife, children,   75
and the Muses—all at the same time. Nor will you, Andrea, be si-
lent when you send very beautiful gifts to friends.

Now, because you fear impious instances of envy, I surely par-
don you. Envy is an evil that both gods and men bear with very   80
great difficulty. But it is a huge task of probity to drive out wrong-
doing and to refuse to tolerate criminals. For they would suppress
all justice and human right. And so, whoever does not stop a
crime when he is capable of doing so, should himself be thought   85
of as the perpetrator of a crime rather than as a man accused of a
lesser failing.

Still, I don't want you to be afraid. But dare to write—for no
one will know you have written. And would spite cause them to
condemn you more for sending letters than for giving gifts? You   90
seem not to know that we have come back into the good graces of
envy's devoted flock. And so, when you see that there are no rea-
sons for you to remain silent, either make an effort after this to
speak or find an advocate who can protect you with dignity and   95
grace, so that you won't be accused of—or acquire a bad name
for—being a slothful man.

: 6 :

Postera lux aderit quae te ieiuna cogat
   dura quaterdenos, Sphortia, ferre dies.
Nam totidem mundi servator monte tulisse
   exuriens luces traditur innocuas.
5   Est tibi connubio felici iuncta puella,
   dulcia cui nondum munera soluit amor.
Ingratus fueris si lux haec sobria prorsus
   transierit, dum te nesciat illa virum.
Fac Venus[9] arridens quantum valet hasta tremendis
10   ictibus ingeminans sentiat ipsa tibi.
Fac videat quanto te robore sustinet umbo,
   quo decus ipsa suum casta puella tegit.
Fac ne te imbellem vulgus vocet. Arma capesse,
   irrue. Fac redeas victor in ora virum.

: 7 :

Dum pares monitis equo citato,
   Sphortia clare puer, obvius ire meis
adversatur anus procax et ipsis
   tristior Euripi fluctibus instabilis.
5   'Prosternis pavidam tuis puellam
   viribus in nuda, Sphortia, nixus humo!'

: 6 :

To Sforza Secondo
Epithalamium[40]

Tomorrow will come and you will be forced, Sforza, to endure hard fasting for forty days. For the savior of the world is said to have endured as many days on the mountain, suffering hunger through guiltless days. A girl, for whom love has not yet released its sweet rewards, has been given to you in happy matrimony. You will be unhappy if this day is spent in abstinence, without her knowing you as her husband. Take care that smiling Venus knows how strong your spear is, when you redouble your fearful blows. Take care that the pure girl sees how powerfully her shield sustains you,[41] for with it she conceals her glory. And take care that the people not call you averse to war. Take up arms, make a charge. Take care to return a victor in the eyes of men.

: 7 :

To Sforza Secondo
Another epithalamium[42]

Just as you, Sforza, are following my advice and are making a charge on your horse, O illustrious boy, an old lady, bold and more forbidding than the stormy waters of the perilous Euripus,[43] steps in to oppose you. Look, the old lady screams, "You're killing the poor frightened girl with your violence — and on the bare ground!"

En exclamat anus. Socrus tumescit.
  Tignum clamor adit, omnia tecta fremunt.
Quam perdant superi! Replens quieta
10 vocibus ehululans omnia miscet anus.
At tu si saperes, caput dedisses
  dirum, tristis anus, Tartareis canibus
Num plus possit anus mero soluta
  quam tu magnanimo principe patre satus?

: 8 :

Nostra Sigismundi laetatur Pieris alto
  hinc Malatestei nomine multisona.
Diligit hic musas, hunc musae carmine tollant
  inter se variis ad citharam modulis.
5 Euterpe, quid muta siles? Dedit ipse choregus
  quem vario procerem carmine ferre queas.
Fac tua delectent quantum potes ore canoro
  cum numeris tantum consona verba virum.
At quibus primum super astra tollam
10 laudibus clarum, nequeo referre.
Principem sic se meritis canendum
  omnibus offert.
Nam Sigismundi memorare laudes
inclytas si quis velit, ante Phoebus,
15 qui modo Gangen oriens reliquit,
  lustret Iberum.

The aged mother is up in arms. The noise rises to the rafters
and — may the gods destroy her! — the whole palace echoes with it.
Wailing, she fills all the silent halls with her cries. But if you were   10
wise, sad old woman, you would surrender your dire head to the
hounds of Hades. Now could an old woman emboldened by wine
be more potent than you, the son of your father, the magnanimous
prince?

: 8 :

To Sigismondo Malatesta
Encomium[44]

Our melodious Pierian delights in the high name of Sigismondo
Malatesta. This man loves the Muses. Let them exalt him then in
songs in a variety of rhythms accompanied by the lyre. Euterpe,
why are you silent? You should celebrate the prince whom the pro-   5
ducer of the chorus himself has given us to hymn in various lyric
modes.[45] Do your utmost to see that your harmonious words de-
light this great man with verses from your melodious lips.

But as to what praises I'll use first to send this brilliant man
into the firmament, I cannot say. He presents himself thus to   10
be hymned — a prince endowed with every merit. For if anyone
wishes to call to mind the famous deeds of Sigismondo, Phoebus,
who has just left the Ganges river on his ascent, would shine on   15
the Ebro before he finished.[46] This one man gleams with complete

Hic unus probitate fulget omni,
praestans ingenio, gravis, modestus,
pollens eloquio deisque iuxta
20   cunctis atque bonis viris amandus.
Hic omnis decorat fovetque rebus
doctos omnibus. Ergo dignus unus
quem nemo sileat sed huius omnes
certatim studeant referre nomen.

25   Gestis hic nitidum rebus in aethera
fertur quas Latium Marte sub effero
sensit. Per varias dum trahitur vices,
    hic omnes acie domat.

Qui nondum pueri dum superat tener
30   annos, insidias fortis et impiger
quas sollers tenebris eruit opprimit,
    diris horribilis viris.

Hunc Flaminii fortiter armis
pugnantem et Flaminiis quisquis
35   se stulticia socium iunxit,
violataeque obnoxia fidei
manus omnis, populi omnes pariter
experti stulticiae poenas
ubi soluissent, Sphortia, virtus
40   generum tibi, Francisce, dicavit.
Hunc Nicolaus, Martis horrendum fulmen,
Perusinus ille, cuius Itali res gestas[10]
omnes in ore simul habent et mirandis
tollunt in astra laudibus, semel ac rursus
45   expertus horruit. Hunc et Alphonsus pugna
vidit superbum, dum ferocibus oppugnat
terra marique militibus Ethruscorum
rex nobile oppidum tremendus Plumbinum.

probity. His mind is superb: he is serious, modest, and he has the
power of eloquence. He is beloved by all the gods and men alike.
This man honors and cherishes all men who are learned in all   20
things. This is a man, therefore, about whom one cannot be silent.
Rather, all men rival one another to extol his fame. This man is
carried to the shining heavens because of his deeds, which Latium   25
has seen in savage war. Though he has endured various changes of
fortune, he triumphs over all in war. While still a tender lad, spir-
ited and brave, he crushed an ambush which he skillfully un-   30
covered — a frightening sight to terrible men. And this man's vir-
tue commended him to you as a son-in-law, O Sforza,[47] after
he bravely fought against the armed forces of Rimini and against
all those who had foolishly allied themselves with the citizens   35
of Rimini, and when every people and every company guilty of
treachery had paid the penalty for such folly. This man made   40
Niccolò Piccinino of Perugia shudder more than once — Niccolò,
Mars's own bristling lightning bolt, whose exploits are on every-
one's lips and whom all men extol to the stars with wondrous
praise. Alfonso too witnessed this proud man in battle, when the   45
formidable king, accompanied by the fierce soldiers of the Etrus-
cans, laid siege by land and sea to the noble town of Piombino.

Quid pluribus tempus terere verbis velim?
50 Veneti Sigismundum legunt,
qui rebus in dubiis probus dux imperet
  exercitibus unus suis.
Heros Fluentinis bis imperitat bene
  hic militibus ac vincit item.
55 Franciscus huic quas copias mittit socer
  Florentiam ut regat iubet.
Hostilis acies trucemque Martis
  intrepidus rabiem ruentis
hic semper reprimit. Patique cogit
60 quam meruit furor et libido
poenam. Nec tamen ipse victor unquam
  se subicit tibi blandienti.
O quam mens hominum colit malorum
  non secus atque deam verendam.
65 Nihil est quod anteponi
animi boni quieti
queat. Hic enim fugacem
minimi facit nitorem.
Solidum decus secutus
70 sibi servit et pudori.
Nihil est quod efferamus,
probitas nisi quod aedit.
Corporis omnis abit vigor uti
nox ab Apollinea face perit.
75 Extera quid cupiam bona mihi
quae famulos faciunt sibi quibus
se mage dediderint? Habet opes
ille Midae famulatur opibus.
Quoque minus caruit, magis eget.
80 Quisque sub imperio iacet herus.

But why should I waste more time with words? The Venetians chose Sigismondo alone so that he, a righteous captain, would 50 take command of their own armies in difficult campaigns. Twice this hero led the Florentine soldiers and twice he conquered. His father-in-law Francesco ordered him to command the troops he 55 sent to Florence. This intrepid man has always repelled the forces of an advancing enemy and has held in check the mad fury of Mars; and he has forced rage and lust to endure the punishment they deserve. Nor does he, as victor, ever subject himself to your 60 flattery, Francesco.

Ah, evil men's minds cherish nothing but the fearsome goddess,[48] but to the good man nothing can be preferred to peace of 65 mind, for such a man thinks little of ephemeral glitter. Pursuing true glory instead, he is subject to himself and his honor. There is 70 nothing we should praise unless it is the product of goodness. As the night perishes with Apollo's first flames, all the body's strength soon vanishes also.

Why should I want external goods[49] for myself, which make 75 men slaves to the things to which they have devoted themselves? The man who has the wealth of Midas is a slave to that wealth; the less he lacks, the more he craves. Every king is oppressed by his power. For me, that praise would be sure which true goodness 80

Certa mihi laus ea sit quam bonitas pararit
    vera animi. Nec ulla
vulnera formidet, honorem nec amet malorum
    iudicio tributum.
85   Qui vacuum se stimulis praestiterit, nec ardet
    corde nefas malignus,
iure meretur celebrari populi frequentis
    vocibus ut probatus.
Igitur merito celebraverimus Lyricorum
90   Malatestigenam modulis
citharaque tubaque virum meritis superantem
    animi bona corporis et
speciem illius instabilisque trucisque ferae quam
    hominum ruditas fatua
95   colit ac veneratur ut egregium illius almae
    decus aethereae patriae.
Nanque Sigismundus vir bello clarus et armis
fortunam putat esse nihil ratione carentem.
Hunc virtutis opus, mens hunc sibi conscia recti
100   semper habet comitem. Quisquis Virtute sodali
utitur et socia, nunquam vereatur inanem,
quam sibi finxerunt dementis somnia vulgi,
Fortunam. Virtute nihil praestantius una est,
qua Malateus princeps ad sydera fertur.

of the soul begets: it neither fears any wounds, nor does it love honor that is conferred by the judgment of evil men. The man who renders himself free from such goads and, who, not being 85 wicked at heart, does not burn to do wrong, justly deserves to be acclaimed by the shouts of the people.

Thus have we worthily celebrated the scion of the Malatesta with the honorable rhythms of lyric poetry, the lyre, and the trum- 90 pet. For he surpasses with the virtues of his mind the physical advantages and appearance of that unstable and hostile creature which the fatuous and boorish among humankind worship and revere as though she[50] were the superb glory of the heavenly city. For 95 Sigismondo, a man famous in arms and war, thinks that Fortune without reason is nothing. For the exercise of virtue and a mind conscious of justice always keep this man as its companion. Whoever looks to Virtue as a partner and friend never fears empty 100 Fortune, whom the dreams of the foolish mob fashion for themselves. Nothing is more excellent than Virtue, for she alone carries the Malatestian prince to the stars.

Quam mihi nunc opus es, mea lux Gonzaga, Latinae
    nobilitatis honos Pieridumque decus.
En pestis formido premit nec abire facultas
    ulla mihi. Quid me, Karole, linquis atrox?
5   Duxisses tecum Scythiam seu sive supremos
    Gangaridas peteres Hesperon aut Libyen,
spes mea solus eras tecum. Mea vota Camoenae
    semper erant. Quid me, Karole, linquis atrox?
Nil mihi dulce queat sine te contingere. Vitae
10   O spes, O requies dimidiumque meae,
si te livor edax profugum mi, Karole, fecit,
    fecisset profugum me quoque livor edax.
Non minimi laudem faciundam censeo livor
    quam premat insanus, exitiosa lues.
15   Invidit Fortuna meae teterrima sorti,
    qua me felicem fecerat illa prius.
Haec mihi te dederat lena virtute, probatos
    quae pia conciliat. Quo duce tutus eram.
Nunc vagor in tenebris, nec quae via certa salutis
20   sit capiunda mihi, Karole, nosse queo.
Pestis cuncta premit, vorat atque ingurgitat horrens
    omnem animam. Perit en vir, puer atque senex.
Rerum humanarum quam spes incerta suique
    nescia sit monstrat Insubriensis ager.
25   Haud urbem invenias qua sol circumspicit omnes
    terrarum tractus et maris omne salum,

: 9 :

To Carlo Gonzaga
Lamenting his abandonment of his mistress Lyda and his friend Filelfo

How necessary you are to me now, Gonzaga, O honor of the Latin nobility, O glory of the Muses, and my light! Look, fear of the plague bears down on us, and I have no power to leave.

Why, cruel Carlo, are you leaving me?[51] Whether you had pondered setting out for Scythia, or the most easterly people of the Ganges, or the Hesperus, or Libya, still you were my only hope. My prayers to Camena[52] were always with you. Why, cruel Carlo, are you leaving me? There can be nothing sweet for me without you. O hope, O repose and my life's other half, if grasping envy made you a fugitive from me, Carlo, that same envy could have made me a fugitive as well. Nor do I believe that praise should be valued as worthless, though mad envy, a deadly pestilence, can crush it. Foul Fortune now begrudges me the lot with which she gratified me before, when she had given you to me with Virtue as her procuress. For holy Virtue brings honorable men together, and with you as my leader, I was safe.

Now I wander in the darkness, nor, Carlo, am I able to know what road I should take to safety. The plague hangs heavy over everything. Bristling as it goes, it devours and guzzles every soul. Look there, a boy, a man in his prime, and an old man have died. The land of the Milanese shows how unreliable hope is in human affairs and how ignorant it is of itself. Where the sun looks down on all the tracts of land and the entire salt sea, you would not find a single city to which fertile nature has given everything more than

cui natura potens magis omnia cesserit uni
    Insubrium quam gens quam colit ut dominam.
Nanque ferax et amoenus ager collesque virentes
30   multifluique amnes huic bona cuncta ferunt.
Temperies caeli talis fuit ante per omnem
    temporis aetatem qualis in Elysio.
Id probat ipse frequens populus quo nullus in omnis
    est alius terras plenior ipse suis.
35 Sed nunc dira febris sic omnes peste voraci
    interimit subito quosque fragore premens,
ut fas esse putet nemo sperare salutem,
    sed sua quoque die funera quisque paret.
Num fortasse merens quod plebs admisit iniqua
40   in te grande nefas, Angle Philippe, luit?
Te, decus heroum, plebs ingratissima nullo
    cum moreris sequitur funeris officio.
Hinc fortasse deus qui cuique[11] digna rependit
    praemia, in Insubres saevius intumuit.
45 Plebeii sceleris poenas patiuntur et ipsi
    qui nihil insontes promeruere pati.
Nunc ego quid faciam? Nam nec licet aeminus ire.
    Nec scio qui vitem tristia taela necis.
Ah, quam crudelem mihi te, Gonzaga, dedisti,
50   qui mihi nolueris, dum tibi consuleres.
Verum ego quid mirer si nostri oblivio mentem
    cepit tanta tuam, cum tibi Lyda perit?
Haec tibi qui potuit quae tanto arderet amore,
    hinc dum maestus abis, vilius excidere?
55 Non igitur nequeo tibi succensere tabellis
    quod te tam durum gesseris atque geras.
Quae tibi cura mei, cui nec vel epistola verbis
    obsignata tribus obstrepat ulla tua?

to the city the Milanese people honor as their mistress. For the fruitful and pleasant land, the green hills and criss-crossing rivers have brought all good things to this land. And such a mild climate 30 prevailed all through the summer that we might have been in Elysium. This is proved by the great numbers of people; no other place on earth is more populous than their own land.

But now an awful fever is destroying all the people in the city, suddenly crashing down on all, in such a voracious pestilence that 35 no one thinks he can rightly hope for safety; but each person prepares each day for his own funeral. Is now the evil plebs deservedly expiating the great crime they committed against you, Filippo Maria Visconti? For the ungrateful plebs honored you with no fu- 40 neral mass, when you — the jewel among heroes — died. After that, perhaps god, who pays out to each his just deserts, became violently angry with the Milanese. For they are suffering the punishment for the crimes of the plebs and the innocent citizens too, 45 who in no way deserved to suffer.

What shall I do now? For neither am I permitted to go far away from here, nor do I know how I can avoid the sad arrows of death. Ah, how cruelly you have treated me, Gonzaga. While you looked to your own interests, you were unwilling to consider mine. But why should I be surprised that such forgetfulness of me has 50 come over you when your Lyda[53] is dying? How could she, who burned with such great love for you, be so cheaply forgotten now that you are sadly leaving? Therefore I can't fail to bear a grudge against you in my writings for your past and present cruelty. But 55 what do you care about me, for I have not even had a letter with as much as three words from you?

Quamquam laeta, reor, sunt et iucunda beato
60   cuncta tibi, Venetus quem fovet usque leo,
es tamen expertus quam sit mutabile numen
    fortunae quamque se gerat instabilem.
Haec quodcunque manu fallaci prodiga munus
    contulit, eripiat per scelus omne ruens.
65 Sola quidem virtus stabili vestigia firmat
    certa gradu nullis casibus acta loco.
Quos tibi coniunxit virtus studiumque decori,
    hos Fortuna nequit ulla tibi eripere.
Horum ego de numero tibi cum sim iunctus amicus,
70   miror ut exciderim mente, vir magne, tua.
Fac[12] igitur norim: quae sit tibi causa tacendi
    et quur hinc abiens nolueris comitem.
Quod si nosse cupis qua sit tua Lyda salute,
    accipe ne videar immemor esse tui.
75 Tristis agit ruri, lachrymisque miserrima fusis
    non cessat flavam dilacerare comam.
Dilaceratque comam cui tu cum nuda sub istos
    funditur amplexus oscula mille dabas.
Nam nec es oblitus quotiens mihi luce referres,
80   quae tibi nocte Venus gaudia praestiterat.
Saepius ingeminat: 'Quid me mea sola voluptas,
    Karole crudelis, deseris hinc abiens?
O utinam vel me rapiant mea fata repente,
    vel tibi me propere iungat amica Cypris!'
85 Quin praesente viro quem multus soluit Iachus
    clamitat interdum: 'Karole, me crucias.'
Atque iterum multo repetit dum victa dolore,
    'Karole, me crucias! Karole, me crucias!'
Flavius attollens tandem caput oraque dulci
90   consopita mero murmurat in tenebris.

Though, as I believe, everything is happy and pleasant with you, fortunate one, whom the Venetian lion now fosters and supports,[54] still you have seen yourself how mutable the goddess Fortune is and how unstable she shows herself to me. Whatever reward this wasteful goddess confers with her deceitful hands, she snatches away again, rushing into every calamity. Virtue alone plants her feet on stable ground: she is sure of her step and not moved from her position by any misfortunes. Those men who are bound to you by virtue and the desire for honor cannot be seized from you by any change of fortune. Since I am bound to you as a friend, as one of these, I am surprised that I should have been forgotten by you, O great man.

See to it then that I hear why you have been silent and why, when you went away, you did not want a companion. But if you want to know what the state of health of your Lyda is, hear me lest I should seem to forget you. She is sad and she lives in the country. The wretched girl does not cease to tear her golden hair and weep. She to whom you gave a thousand kisses when she lay naked in your arms, now tears her hair. For you have not forgotten how many times you spoke to me during the day of the joys that Venus gave you at night.

"Why do you abandon me, cruel Carlo? Why, my only pleasure, have you gone away from here?" She often repeats, "O that the fates would either suddenly spirit me away or that your friend Venus would quickly unite me with you." But instead, with her husband beside her, whom much wine has lulled to sleep, she sometimes shouts: "Carlo, you are torturing me," and then, overcome with sorrow, she cries out repeatedly, "Carlo, you are torturing me!" Fabio finally raises his head and his eyes, sleepy with wine, murmuring in the darkness. He then heaps threats on Lyda,

Inde minis honerat Lydam, quae cauta soporem
   dum simulat, madidum ludit in ore virum.
Misit et ancillam quae me versuta rogaret
   siqua meae fidei credita furta latent.
95   Huic ego respondi sibi quae se velle putassem
   narrari. Repetit saepius illa vices.
Pascitur illa quidem verbis. Spe pascor at ipse.
   Ipse metu pereo. Lyda perit venere.

: 10 :

Euterpen cithara patris citatam
sperabam fore, gressibus secundis
uti qua duce mi viae liceret
ad vos, Aenice, saepius vocantes.
5   Sed multo secus accidit quod aegre
indigneque fero. Mihi malignus
intercludit iter negatque gressum
aer Insubribus luem voracem
infundens miseris, atrox deorum
10   quam miscet nimio furor veneno.
Hinc loetale malum ruit per omnis
mortales perimens senes et omnem
aetatem pariter. Nec ulla pestis
humanum trucior genus subegit
15   unquam: non ea quae premebat olim
urbem Romulidum dei repressa
flatu Phoebigenae, nec illa Thebis

and while she cautiously pretends to be asleep, she continues to deceive her drunken husband under his very eyes.

She has sent her wily serving girl to ask me whether any secret love messages were stowed away that he had entrusted to my loyal care, to which I told her what I thought she wanted to hear. She 95 often reopens the conversation. She feeds on words. But I feed on hope. Myself? I die of fear, but Lyda dies of love.

: 10 :

To Iñigo d'Avalos
Why he has not yet come to Naples[55]

I was hoping that Euterpe would be roused by her father's lyre so that, with her as my leader on the road, I might be allowed to enjoy an easy journey to you, since you have often summoned me, Iñigo. But events have gone otherwise and I bear it with regret 5 and indignation. Pestilent air pouring a voracious sickness down on the wretched Milanese blocks my way and denies my journey. And the horrible fury of the gods infuses this sickness with excessive venom. 10

And so the deadly disease falls on all mortals equally, striking down the very old and those of every age alike. Never did a worse pestilence afflict the human race: not the plague that once lay siege to the Romulides' city and was expelled by a breeze Aesculapius 15 sent;[56] not the plague that inflicted so many scourges upon doleful

quae tot flaebilibus tulit flagella
ob matris facinus patrisque caedem,
20   non qua Graiugenas, Apollo, bilis
afflixit tua Troiis in oris,
non cui totus ut ipse cessit orbis
misit Cecropiam rogans in urbem
ut pro se precibus deos adiret.
25   Invadit veluti leaena cervos,
quam nati rabida fame coacti
ad pastum stimulant humi profusi,
ut tigris vitulas premit necatque,
quam ieiuna dies in omne ferrum
30   expertem trepidi metus et ira
ardentem rapit ad fluenta Gangis.
Sic mors excita syderum tremendo
fato, quod superi dedere maestis
agris Insubrium, furore cunctos
35   sternit loetifero. Iacent acervi
passim quod nequeant dari sepulchris.
Sic terra premitur frequens cadaver.
Turmatim pereunt et insepulti
spirantes animas odore tetras
40   vivacis etiam trahunt ad Horchum.
Stipatum properat sequi pheretrum
pollinctor simili receptus aura.
Hic fiunt plateae sepulchra fatis
tristes innumeris sub axe nudo.
45   Fiunt et loculi canes relictis
saevi corporibus rapaxque milvus.
Nam quisquis potuit, fugae dedit se,
qua sors se magis obtulit secundam.
Soli nos colimus domi sedentes
50   urbem quam populus frequens reliquit.

Thebes because of a father's murder and a mother's crime;[57] not the plague by which your wrath, O Apollo, afflicted the Greeks on the shores of Troy;[58] and not the plague to which the entire world submitted when Apollo sent a suppliant to the Cecropian city to approach the gods for his own sake.[59]

    Just as the lioness attacks the deer when her cubs, prostrate on the ground yet driven by rabid hunger, rouse her for a feeding; just as the tiger stalks and kills heifers when a day without water causes her to have no fear of any weapon and rage drives her burning to the river Ganges; in just this way, death, roused by the ghastly fate that the stars brought and that the gods had assigned to the sad country of the Milanese, massacres all its people with a lethal fury. Bodies lie in heaps here and there, for they cannot be buried. And so, corpses without number are simply covered with earth. They die in troops and the unburied, releasing a foul stench, draw even the living into Orcus: an undertaker, prey to the same foul air, hurries to follow a crowded funeral procession. Here under an empty sky, the sad broad streets become tombs for the innumerable dead. For the abandoned bodies, savage dogs and the ravening hawk are their coffins.[60]

    Certainly whoever could, fled to wherever the fates offered more favorable odds. I alone sit here at home living in the city that people have abandoned in droves. The bankrupt magistrate, who

Me quaestor fugiens dolo fefellit
decoctor, meriti nec aeris ullam
mi partem minimam dedit nefandus.
Id causae facit ut tuos, amice,
55   postes, Davale, nobilis adire
nobis non liceat. Dolosus, inquam,
mi nummus vetitat tuos penates.
Nec solus nec equi nec aeris expers
me longae poteram viae per aestus
60   tantos tradere. Nam nimis laborum
aetas iam prohibet mihi gravescens.
Membrorum nimii quidem labores
aeque ac desidiae solent inertis
grandaevum penitus vigore laxi
65   langores spoliare. Iamque cani
en velant caput albicante barba.
Num grandis faciat viam poeta
quam vix iunior audeat viator?
Nec Musas deceat, nec ipse laudet
70   Alphonsus decus inclytum Minervae
perpulchre minus ut Philelfus aedes
regalis subeat futurus hospes.
Quare me Dolor angit et minaces
infigens stimulos premensque cordi
75   exprobrans mihi pervicax: 'Quid,' inquit,
'annos tot nihil aureum reponis
qui tot millia sis lucratus aeris?
Quidnam sufficiat tibi tuenti
omnino nihil? Omne temnis aurum?
80   Ac prorsus nihili facis quod ipsum
si non esset apud tuos penates
neglectum, tibi nec lues nec ulla
pestis pernicies metum intulisset?

has now fled, deceived me, nor has this corrupt man given me the smallest part of the pay I earned. This means that I am not free to go to your noble court, dear friend d'Avalos. Stolen money, I say, bars me from your Penates.[61] Nor could I commit myself to a long journey by myself in such heat without a horse or money. For heavy old age already prohibits me from too much toil. One or both—working the legs too hard or the relaxed inactivity of a slothful life—tend generally to rob an old man of his vigor. And now see how the grey hairs veil my head and my beard has grown white. An old poet wouldn't make a journey that even a younger traveler would hardly dare, would he? It would neither be fitting to the Muses, nor would Alfonso himself praise Minerva's famed glory just so that Filelfo, his guest, might enter the royal palace in a shameful state.

Therefore Grief overwhelms me and, harassing me with his menacing spurs, he stubbornly reproves me: "Why," he says, "do you, who have acquired thousands of coins over so many years, put aside no gold? How, pray, can you manage your affairs when you save nothing at all? Do you spurn gold altogether? Do you count as nothing the fact that, if gold had not been neglected by your Penates, neither the plague nor any other pernicious pestilence would have been able to cause you any fear? Therefore why do you alone show contempt for wealth when you see in prospect

55

60

65

70

75

80

Ergo divitias quid unus usque
85   spernis cum videas tibi periclum
loeti propositum quod arcet aurum?'
Talis nunc mihi cura cogitanti
praesentis rabiem die perurit
cor sane requiemque tollit omnem.
90   Et ni Pierides paterque Paean
cantu dulcisono simul levarent
curam qua crucior, necaret altus
qui me vulneribus Dolor medullas
affligit penitus meas recludens.
95   Nunquid si rogites, studebo nummis
posthac, ne patiar quod urit olim?
Num fervens[13] bibulum neget futurum
Hydrops quem sitis aridum fatigat?
Num linguam cohibere Codrus olim
100   optet Karolus unus impudicam?
Num speres fieri licere cuiquam
quod natura fugit, nec usus affert?
An fulvum cupiat Debas metallum
quod coeni pedibus loco subacti
105   contemnit? Locuplesne fiat usus
quem longus docuit nihil cavere
id praeter probitas quod alma suadet?
Virtus divitiaeque prorsus una
nec florere quidem nec esse rursum
110   praestantes pariter queant. Habentes
plus auri bonitatis ii minoris
fiunt participes. Apollo malim
nostras excipiat pius Camoenas,
quam fallax et avarus ille Pluton.
115   Quis nobis igitur deus fovebit
dexter Castalidas pericla pellens?

the danger of your dying, which having gold would prevent?" Such 85
care now burns my heart each day and when I think of the mad-
ness of our times it robs me of all peace. And unless the Pierian
maidens and father Paean[62] lighten with melodious song the care 90
that tortures me, Grief will afflict me profoundly with his blows,
laying bare my very marrow.

But what if you ask whether I'll go after money eagerly in fu- 95
ture so I won't suffer again what hurt me before? Would a man
suffering from dropsy[63] who was dying of thirst deny himself a
drink? Would Karolus Codrus one day hope to curb his shameless
tongue?[64] Would you hope that everyone would be allowed to have 100
what nature forbids and utility refuses? Or would Debas want the
tawny metal which he disdains in place of the dirt he has worked
with his feet? Would that man become wealthy whom long experi- 105
ence has taught to care for nothing except what kindly probity
urges? Virtue and wealth cannot flourish together; nor can they be
equally excellent. For those who have more gold come to live less 110
virtuous lives.

I would prefer that Apollo would welcome my Muses rather
than deceitful and avaricious Pluto. What propitious god will
cherish our Castalian girls while he expels danger from our midst? 115

Idem qui genuit deus sorores,
qui totum radiis comatus orbem
lustrat, qui medicas benignus artes
120 humano generi prior paravit.
Phoebo si patre natus a tenebris
tetris Hippolytum vocat necatum,
quid non commodius parens amicum
a loeto tueatur hunc poetam,
125 cuius se videat pio labore
et noctu fieri dieque clarum?
Haec me spes recreat metuque tactum
magna parte levat. Metus dolorque
qui me non capiat fores videntem
130 a diris iaculis prope obsideri,
quae vis nulla quidem nec ars repellat
humani ingenii? Metus feroces
et fortis etiam solet movere.
De nobis satis haec superque tecum.
135 Nunc tu, Davale, dicito vicissim.
Quid vobis agitur quibus secundae
res sunt et placidae? Datisne Phoebo
et musis operam sacris? An urit
vos flama Cypris et puer Cupido?
140 Quid de te rogitem, virens iuventa
quem pungit stimulis agitque laetae
in ludum Veneris gradu citato?
Aetas te tua reddit innocentem
et rex quem sequeris benignus iste
145 Alphonsus. Quis enim faces seniles
ignorat, quibus ardet iste semper?
Num multas amat, ut solet, puellas
rex Alphonsus? An una pectus urit?
Quot tandem latus ambiunt utrumque?

The same god who fathered the sisters, who with his long golden locks has brought light to the entire world, and who first imparted the arts of healing to the human race. If father Apollo's son could summon the dead Hippolytus back from foul Hades, why should it not be more fitting for the father of his country to protect his friend, the poet, from death, in whose work he would see himself made famous day and night? This hope restores me and raises me up, though I am greatly overcome by fear. But how could I not be overwhelmed with fear and sorrow when I see houses besieged by deadly arrows which no human art or force can repel? Fear is wont to affect even bold and brave men. But this is more than enough about us.

Now you, d'Avalos, tell us all the things, one by one, that are happening there with you. How are you, whose situation is peaceful and pleasant? Are you devoting yourself to Apollo and the sacred Muses? Or do the fires of the Cyprian and the boy Cupid burn you? Why do I need to ask you about this, when green youth stings you with its goads and drives you toward the games of joyous Venus at full speed? Your age and the kindly king you serve, Alfonso, render you blameless. And who does not know the fiery torches of old men with which your king is constantly burning? Does King Alfonso love many girls, as usual? Or does only one fire his breast? How many does he have on each side? Perhaps two? Does he think he protects himself too little with only two?

150   Num fortasse duae? Parumne ducat
       se munire duabus? Adde quinque:
       dum vomis segetem scindat subactum
       recta cuspide, quod seni negatur.
       O quam dulce malum mihi voluptas
155   et quam loetiferum solet videri!
       Qua sensus misere capi protervus
       se postquam patitur, nefas in omne
       fertur praecipiti citus ruina.
       Nam nusquam vitium stetit. Procellis
160   non unis agitatur; omnis urgens
       tempestas id agit scelus per atrum.
       At magnum vitium est premens voluptas,
       qua plures periere quam dolore.
       Quo fit ne dubitem magisne vobis
165   flagrantis Veneris frequens sagitta
       an pestis mihi sit cavendus horror.
       Tu Lucretia nobilis puella,
       regi verba dato senemque pasce
       spe. Nam copia vilior putatur.

Add five, as long as the plough splits the earth with an upright   150
share, a thing denied to an old man.

O what a sweet evil pleasure seems to me and yet, usually, how
disastrous! For once violent emotion wretchedly allows itself to be   155
taken captive, it is swept toward every evil in headlong ruin. For
nowhere does vice stand still, nor is it driven on by just one storm;
every pressing turbulence propels it toward dark misfortune. But   160
seductive pleasure is a great vice, from which more men die than
from grief. And so I have no doubt which danger I should be
more wary of — the repeated arrows of fiery Venus or the perils of   165
the plague.

As for you, Lucrezia, noble girl, beguile the king with words,
feed the old man with hope, for abundance is little prized.

THALIA
LIBER QUARTUS

: I :

Thalia, partes ordine tertia
tuas futurum florida Pieris
vides. Canendi muneris accipe
tibi quod ipse tradidit anxius
5   chori magister. Laeticiam pater
summus deorum turbat et obterit,
augere quam te carmine maxime
decebat unam. Fulminat undique
tonans sagittis qualibus efferos
10   stravit Gigantas montibus arduis
ausos Olympum ascendere fulgidum.
Summum periclum turbida vatibus
minantur astra rursus et omnibus
quos ulla praestans evehit altius
15   doctrina claros, Musa. Moventibus
quem bilis urit fervida vocibus
adi tonantem flectere moliens.
Preces nec absint. Nanque precantibus
vel numen aiunt mitius effici.
20   Nihil quod esset, Iupiter optime,
fecisti ut esset non chaos abditum.
Fuit nec ulla materies tibi
opus, o pater qui cuncta creaveris.

THALIA
BOOK FOUR

To Bianca Maria Visconti Sforza
A request for assistance[1]

Flowery Pierian Thalia, third among our Muses, you know your
role for the coming time. Hear now what themes the restless
leader of the chorus gives you to hymn. The highest father of the   5
gods upsets and tramples the happiness that was yours alone to
magnify with song. Thundering on all sides, he lights up the sky
with the arrows that felled the savage Giants who dared to scale   10
the lofty mountains to shining Olympus. Coming from the turbid
stars, O Muse, the highest danger threatens all the poets and fa-
mous men whose extraordinary learning lifts them to the skies.
Go to the Thunderer who seethes with burning bile and labor to   15
turn aside his anger with moving words. May there be prayers! For
they say even a god's will is softened when men pray.

    O best Jupiter, there is nothing you have created that does not   20
dispel chaos. Nor, O father who created the whole world, did you
need any material from another source. O highest founder of the

Succurre nobis iusta precantibus,
25   O summe rerum conditor omnium.
Quae nostra culpa, quod sceleris nefas
tantum benigni pectora numinis
potuit tui in nos, maxime Iupiter,
excire cunctos ut nece fulminis
30   perdas repente caelitus exciti?
Funus Philippi plectitur inclyti
ingrata plebs quod ferre merentibus
neglexit umbris egregii ducis.
Culpam Philelfus Insubrium ferat—
35   dic, O virorum rector et aetheris!—
qui solus omni munere principem
secutus illum, nullius horruit
odium nec iras, semper et aureis
quem solus ausus laudibus extulit?
40   Tui est cavere vitet ut impetum
vates ruinae fulminis ignei.
Abscedat urbe; fulmina nesciunt
modum tueri missa vagantius.
Franciscus isti Sphortia consulat
45   quem saepe nobis carmine celsius
evectus audax comparat admodum.
Satis monuimus quod foret usui.
Obaudit ille prorsus et auribus
clausis notis dat verba volantibus.
50   At uxor eius Blanca puerpera
virtutis ingens gloria nobilis
surdas nec aures commodat audiens
patique nequeat serius optime
isti merenti ferre quod expedit.
55   Blanca, quam princeps genuit Philippus
ille, qui priscos superavit omnis

universe, help us who pray for justice. What sin of ours, what 25
criminal wrong could turn your kindly heart and will against us,
so that you, O greatest Jupiter, would suddenly kill us all with ce-
lestial lightning? The ungrateful plebs are punished because they 30
failed to honor the deserving shade of the sublime and celebrated
Duke Filippo with funeral rites. But should Filelfo suffer for the
sins of the Milanese — O ruler of men and the heavens, speak! — 35
when he alone followed that prince with every obeisance and he
alone dared to hymn him with golden paeans of praise, fearing the
anger and odium of no man? It is yours to ward off evil so that the 40
poet may avoid death by fiery lightning. Let him depart from the
city since lightning does not know how to check its wandering
missiles. Let bold Francesco Sforza, whom our songs have often
raised to the stars, look well to the interests of this man he sup- 45
ports. We have often told him what would be useful. But he lis-
tens solely with closed ears and responds only with the briefest of
notes.

But his wife, noble Bianca, who will soon give birth and who is 50
great in the glory of her virtue, does not turn deaf ears to our
plight. She listens and would not allow this deserving man of
yours to receive too late his proper due. O Bianca, daughter of
prince Filippo — who alone surpassed in the magnificence of his 55

unus heroas pariterque vivos
  laudis honore,
Blanca, quae divi generum Philippi
60   Sphortiam pulchra probitate clarum
uxor illustris placidis maritum
  moribus ambis,
non opem vati bene promerenti
afferes qui te super astra saepe
65   extulit vitae titulis probatae,
  clara virago?
Unus hic Anglum meritis Mariam
omnibus magnum fuit inter omnes
qui metus expers coleret minasque
70   temneret omnis.
Unus hic idem superas in arces
ille ubi cessit, Mariam Philippo
patre te dignam sequitur canendo
  laudibus altis.
75   Unus hic rursus medios in ignis
plebis infestae populique fluctus
ausus est templo celebri tyrannos
  sternere verbis.
Viribus tandem mage profuerunt
80   quos modo terror dederat silentes.
Fortis hic unus medios in enses
  ora resolvit.
Sphortiam solus populo fremente
syderis fato genitum superni
85   esse testatus. Docuit quis esset
  finis habendus.
Karolum solus monuit poeta
plebis infidae insidias dolosque

legacy all other heroes both of our own time and antiquity—O
Bianca, illustrious wife who most gently entreats her husband
Sforza—Filippo's son-in-law and a man renowned for his glorious   60
probity—O warrior maiden, celebrated with the honors of an un-
blemished life, will you not provide assistance to the deserving
poet who has exalted you to the stars?   65

This poet, alone among men, was one who spurned all threats
and fearlessly honored the great Filippo Maria with every praise.
And when he went to the lofty citadel, this one man followed you,   70
Bianca Maria, with songs and lofty praise, for you are worthy of
your father Filippo. This man of yours alone dared, amid the fiery
passions of an angry plebs in a crowded temple and the flooding   75
fury of the people, to smash the tyrants with his oratory. And his
words were more potent than physical force for those whom terror
had silenced. Amid a sea of swords, this brave man alone began to   80
speak. Amid a roaring populace, this man alone testified that
Sforza had been engendered by fate and a sublime star; he taught
what end the people ought to consider. This poet alone warned   85
Carlo Gonzaga of the treachery and betrayal of the disloyal rabble,
so that, made wary, he would follow your friends with all his

90 ut cavens partes sequeretur omni
    pectore vestras.
Quod quidem si rem liceat fateri,
profuit primum tumidoque bello
attulit finem patriaeque luctum
    sustulit omnem.

95 Ast ubi rerum superis secundis
estis in nulla patriae potiti
caede, spes ingens aluit poetam
    tempore multo.
Praemiis pulchris Latio petitus
100 unus a toto, renuit quod esset
certius vero dubiam secutus
    spemque fidemque.

Pluribus sed quod tero, Blanca, tempus?
Quidquid en princeps statuit benignus
105 Sphortias tandem meritis amici
    transit in auras.
Quaestor illudit, studet et dolosus
verba vaendenti dare verba. Num sit
huic opus verbis? At abundat alto
110   fonte loquendi.

Ergo si quicquam iuvat et parentem,
Sphortiam siquid iuvat et maritum,
siquid et temet iuvat esse cultam,
    consule vati.
115 Pestis hunc horrens pariter famesque
obsidet. Septo geminis periclis
est opus nummis quibus hostis atrox
    utraque cesset.
Blanca, quae nulli veterum decore
120 foeminae cedis titulis pudici

heart. But if I am allowed to confess the truth, Carlo first brought 90
us help; he first put an end to rising war, and he first wiped away
all the city's tears.

But now that you have acquired the gods' favor in affairs of 95
state and bloodshed is gone from the city, great hope has nour-
ished the poet for a long time. Though all Latium pursues him
and promises him every reward, this man alone refuses what is 100
more certain than true in order to follow things that are uncer-
tain—hope and trust. But why should I waste more time with
talk, Bianca? Look, whatever the good Duke Sforza has finally set
aside for the services of a friend is vanishing in thin air. The 105
quaestor laughs and with lying words he strives to cheat someone
whose words are his stock-in-trade. But this man doesn't need
words, does he? For they already overflow from a deep fountain of
eloquence. Therefore if anything I have done is helpful to your fa- 110
ther, if anything pleases your husband Sforza, and if anything
helps you to live a learned and elegant life, look to the interests of
your bard. The bristling plague and famine have equally oppressed 115
him, and hemmed in by these twin dangers, he needs money, so
that those harsh enemies may withdraw on both fronts.

O Bianca, you who yield to no woman among the ancients in
your glory and renown for your virtuous life—you who surpass all 120

moris et vivas superas verendis
   laudibus omnes,
si tibi salvos pius ille servet
liberos caeli dominator alti
125 teque cum dulci tueatur omne
    coniuge tempus,
si brevi fias Itali triumphi
totus compos super orbe toto
signa felicis statuens mariti,
130   inclyta victrix,
da manum vati rapidis procellis,
ne miser fluctu pereat supremo.
Sola tu loetum potes et salutem
   ferre poetae.
135 Sin minus, saltem pateat facultas,
qua solum et sortem meliore mutans
et Iove et fulvi clipeo metalli
   fata repellat.

: 2 :

Spes me dulcis alit quam semper, Cicche, benigno
   affers ore pius. Spes mea corda nutrit.
Aediles nam verba mihi quaestorque dederunt
   saepe adeo bilis ut stomachum cierit.
5 Opportunus ades, cum iam ferveret in iram
   ac furere inciperet mens agitata malis.

living women in venerable deeds — if that holy king of high heaven keeps your children safe and protects you and your consort for all 125 time to come, and if you are soon to share in Italy's triumph over the whole world, displaying the colors and standards of your fortunate husband, O triumphant heroine, then lend a hand to your 130 bard so that he does not, in the awful flood and lethal winds, die miserably. You alone have the power of life and death over the poet. If not, may he be at least allowed, by changing his home and 135 his lot, to repel death under a better sky and with a shield of gold.

: 2 :

To Cicco Simonetta[2]
A request for cash

Sweet hope nourishes me: the hope that you, Cicco, always bring me with kind words feeds my heart. For the aediles and the quaestor have tricked me so often that I cough up bile. You come at a good time, since now my anger has reached a boil and my 5 mind stirred by evil begins to rage. I can't very well put up with

Non equidem perferre queo quae iusque piumque
    ferre vetat. Res est non toleranda fames.
Nam quid loetiferi memorem contagia morbi
10   quae vitare loco non valet aeris inops?
Princeps digna iubet quae dedignantur obire
    hi quos iste suis praeposuit loculis.
'Ique redique,' monent. 'Tibi mox numerentur eruntque
    praemia digna tuis reddita muneribus.'
15 Sic et eo redeoque iterum. Rursusque revertor
    tanquam ridiculus terque quaterque die.
Non decet hoc Musas, vacuas quas semper oportet
    esse labore gravi per gravitatis opus.
Ni mens laeta manet penitusque intacta labore,
20   odimus et carmen odimus et citharam.
Nuncius ecce tuus suavi mihi more salutem
    dicit opem referens quam mihi praestiteris.
Non te vana loqui iam pridem novimus unum.
    Spes nos firma tenet mox fore quod cupimus.
25 Sic tibi non fragilis debetur gratia, Cicche:
    quam tibi dum refero, mente gero memori.
Verus es in cunctis et non fucatus amicus,
    quem rebus norim semper adesse meis.
At facit id virtus, qua praestas omnibus unus
30   quos habet egregios Sphortia dux proceres.
Id doctrina facit (qua nulli cedere suesti)
    eloquiumque potens ingeniumque ferax.
Nam similes mores animos moderantur amore;
    dissimiles odium gignere, Cicche, solent.
35 Perge igitur, coeptis incumbe et perfice munus
    quod iussit princeps rusticitasque negat.
Non ingratus ero. Nam tu per saecula mecum
    multa diu vives nescius interitus.

what justice and piety forbid me from enduring. Starvation is not a thing to be tolerated. Why should I speak of the contagion of the deadly disease that a man without money can't avoid? The prince issues worthy orders which the men he has placed in charge of his treasury refuse to carry out. "Go and come back again," they say. "Your money will soon be paid and a supplement worthy of your services will be paid you." And so I go away and again I return. And again, like a fool, I return again, three or four times a day.

This does not suit the Muses. They should always be free of hard labor because of the gravity of their work. But if the mind does not remain happy, if it is wounded by hardship, we hate to sing and we hate the lyre. But look, your messenger greets me agreeably. He tells me about the help you've offered me. I have known for a long time that you, for one, don't make empty promises. I have real hope that what I want will soon come to be. And no half-hearted gratitude is due you, Cicco, and I keep the memory of it in my heart, even while I'm telling you this. You are a true friend in every way, not a false one, and you have always been with me, I know. But that is due to your virtue, in which you alone surpass all the other excellent men whom Duke Sforza retains as his leaders. This is due to your learning (in which you are second to no one), your forceful oratory and your resourceful nature. For whereas men of similar dispositions have feelings of love for one another, dissimilar ones, O Cicco, tend to engender hatred. Come, therefore, further the things you've begun and complete the task that the prince has ordered and boorishness denies. I will not be ungrateful. For you will live on for many centuries in my work, nor will you ever know death.

Lydo quem vitiis virum supremis
praeponas alium nefas per omne
nemo est. Lydus enim pudoris ipsum
abiecit penitus vir impudicus
5   vultum cum facie. Venus gulosa
famosum celebrat, facitque notum
hunc unum populis vagata turpis
cunctis Enceladi soror furentis.
Num servet petulans fidem sodali
10   et dulci socio suam sororem
qui nuper vitiarit et sororis,
quae nupsit modo, creditam puellam?
Nam quod mollibus unus in cinaedis
excellit scelus omne per nefandum,
15   non[1] Tuscus modo novit Insubres; at
omnes nec vario fatentur ore.
Hunc Bacchus sibi vindicat[2] protervus,
qui laeso penitus miser cerebro
insanit rapida meri procella
20   excitus facinus furens ad omne.
Hinc lites parat improbus dolosas
et fingit reus ore non pudico
crimen vaniloquum, suas recludens
immanes animi faces latentis
25   et diros stimulos ad omne probrum
proclives. Miser, o miser, Megaera
quae te, Lyde, rapit trahens cathaenis

: 3 :

Against Lydus[3]
An invective

You would find no one who surpasses Lydus in outrageous vices of
every unspeakable type. For Lydus, who is utterly shameless, has
wiped even the semblance of shame from his face. Gluttonous Ve-
nus toasts him and Enceladus's shameful sister,[4] wandering among   5
all the peoples of the world, makes him notorious. Would this
lewd fellow keep a promise to a companion and a dear friend
when he recently raped his own sister and his sister's daughter   10
who had newly become a bride, though she was entrusted to his
care?

For among all effeminate men, Lydus alone excels when it
comes to every forbidden crime; not only do the Florentines know
him but all the Milanese know him as well.[5] And they say the   15
same thing. Violent Bacchus claims this man as his own, who —
his brain now damaged by a virulent deluge of wine and roused
to every crime — rages insanely. And afterwards, this evil fellow   20
launches crafty lawsuits and, playing the plaintiff, he brings
trumped-up charges with his lying lips, while exposing the savage
fire in his heart and the cruel passions that goad him to every
abuse.   25

O wretched, wretched Lydus, what Fury seizes you and drags
you off headlong in chains, while denying all peace to your impi-

vinctum praecipitem negans quietem
menti sacrilegae? Deumne censes
30 res nostras oculis videre pressis?
Cui quidquid fuit et futura cuncta
sunt coram. Nihil est quod esse possit
illi, qui peperit polos creator
et mundi reliquos iacentis orbes,
35 occultum. Videt is libido quanta
te cepit, furor ut volutat aegrum
pectus. Nec patitur viam salutis
noris. Sic oculis tibi tenebras
fudit lucifugas. Quod ille docte
40 ac recte studuit monere fratrem
vates Hesiodus secutus erres
nunquam—quin potius gradu secundo
sis laudis quoniam fugis priorem.
Omnes hic bonitate praestat unus
45 qui per se satis est, ut omne quod sit
norit. Sed monitis item probatis
qui paret probus est. At ille nequam
qui neutrum valuit. Secundus ordo
nequaquam tibi cedit. Ergo primus
50 postquam te renuit palam, nec ullus
est ordo reliquus, nisi locari
malis inferior, quod aio nequam.
Nequam te fatearis est necesse;
nam quis flagitiis cares? Fidemne
55 laudarim, fidei sacrum ligamen,
qui tollis violans probris amicum,
his cunctis inimicus ipsa caelo
quos aequat meritis decora virtus?
Nam quos non laceraris innocentes
60 ac sanctos? Etiam malos et omni

ous mind? Do you think that god turns a blind eye to the world? To him all things — whatever has been and will be in future — are   30 known. From him who created the universe and brought forth the heavens and all the celestial bodies in the sky, nothing can be hidden. He sees the extent of the desire that holds you, when mad-   35 ness overturns a heart that is sick. Nor does he allow you to know the path to salvation. Thus he pours unremitting darkness over your eyes.

But were you to follow the advice that the poet Hesiod learnedly and rightly strove to give his brother, you would never err —   40 well, rather, you might be worthy of praise in his second order of men, since you flee the first order.[6] According to the poet, that man surpasses all others in goodness who is complete in himself, with the result that he examines everything that exists. But also   45 good is the man who follows good advice. But he who is capable of neither is worthless. The second order cedes in no way to you. Therefore, since the first order of men would openly reject you, there is no order left for you — unless you would rather be placed   50 in the one still lower, which is for worthless men, I say.

You have to admit you are worthless, Lydus. For what shameful crimes have you not committed? Should I praise you as a man of honor — you, who by shamefully violating a friend, destroy the sa-   55 cred bond of honor, while you are hostile to all those men whose glorious virtue raises them to heaven? For what innocent and pious men have you not maimed? Be aware too, Lydus, that it is a   60

impuros vitio palamque, Lyde,
famosos tibi turpe tam scelesto
castigare puta. Nimis nocebis
vel laudans. Et enim tuorum
65   morum qui fuerit comes malorum
et vitae socius tuae impudentis
laudabis. Tibi nullus ore sermo
manat, quem pudor et Minerva ducat.
Oscoene loqueris: geris Timarchum[3]
70   qui cunctos puer et vir impudicus
probris exuperas inertis oti.
Eructansque gravi fugas odore
omnem quae tibi iungitur coronam —
casu vel studio dati petendi
75   aeris. Quidquid inops ruboris olim
importunus homo fide Pelasga
usus, ceperis usui quod, inquam,
nunquam restituas. Ubique pedis
discumbens etiam simulque ridens
80   trullas ingeminas. Ubi quiescis
illic et matulae loco vetustae
lectus totus olet domum vel omnem
secessum faciens ubique pressam
turgens exhoneras, ut ursus, alvum.
85   Qui foetor Styga possit ullus atram
aeque tristis habere? Totus unus
sic foetes mihi nauseam tumente
ut cites stomacho: nocens utroque
aeque gutture, displicens oleto,
90   offendens oculis mero, trisulcis
et lingua nimium spuens venenum
ac laedens manibus tibi, rapaces
quae sunt egregie, quibus repostum

disgrace for you who are so vile yourself to reproach men who are base, wicked, and notorious perpetrators of every vice. Even if you praise them you will injure them grievously. For whoever joins you 65 in your evil habits and vile life you will praise. Nor does any talk flow from your lips which is guided by modesty or wisdom. You speak obscenities: you play the Timarchus,[7] you who as a boy and degenerate adult surpassed all others in the corrupt nature of your 70 decadent pastimes.

When you belch, your foul breath drives away the entire circle of men that gather around you, whether they're there to ask you for the money they have lent you or just by chance. Whatever you 75 borrow, you'll never return, never, I say, though you beg for it relentlessly and swear a Pelasgian oath without blushing.[8] When reclining at dinner, you break wind, and laughing at the same time, you fill the drinking bowls again. The entire bed where you sleep 80 smells like a country chamber pot, making the whole house a privy where you can relieve your swollen belly like a bear when it's full. Could the sordid Styx have a stench so foul? All of you smells so 85 bad that you make me sick, and my stomach turns. Both ends of you are equally harmful: the one offends us with its filth, the other spews wine in our faces. Your triple-forked tongue spits venom 90 while you do harm with your hands. For these are unusually rapacious, and nothing remains concealed from them.

sic prorsus nihil. Omne quidquid usquam
95   occultum latet est tibi reclusum
et raptum pariter. Quis abdat aurum
furi tam vigili—dolosus uni
cuius cum Sisipho Sinonis ille
quem dicunt avus abditae rapinae
100   cedat? Nanque gulae nihil timere
frangendae didicit. Manus per atras
noctes hinc agitat vigil rapaces.
Nec parcit socio. Premit sodalem,
mortales superosque fallit hostis
105   nocturnus. Nec enim timere caesus
pulsatusve solet. Nec ulla sani
oris verba veretur. At monentem
ducit ridiculo Typhon salutans.
Quare mors nisi curet ipsa Lydum,
110   non est spes reliqua ulla sanitatis.

: 4 :

Quaeris Alexandro quem praelatura per omnes
    sis laudis numeros, nostra Thalia, viro?
Quidquid prima dedit, quidquid nova pertulit aetas,
    unus Alexander laude refert propria.
5   Hunc decorat virtus animi: quancunque suprema
    arx fundit geminis turribus acta polo.
Vis animi interior nihil est quod nescia musset;
    hinc agitat quidquid moribus intus alit.

Whatever has ever been stowed away, you find and purloin for 95
yourself. For who could hide gold from a thief as vigilant as you,
whom even that guileful grandfather of Sinon (with Sisyphus,
they say) would acknowledge as his superior in the hiding of plun-
dered goods?[9] For he learned to have no fear that he would be 100
hanged.[10] And so, on dark nights, this man watches, waits, and
sets his thieving hands to work. He spares no friend and he goes
after his comrade. This nocturnal thief cheats both men and gods.
He has no fear of being stabbed or beaten, nor does he respect ad- 105
vice from salubrious lips. Instead this Typhon greets with ridicule
anyone who warns him.[11] And so, unless death itself takes care of
Lydus, there is no hope of his being cured. 110

: 4 :

To Alessandro Sforza [12]
Encomium

You ask, my Thalia, whom you should prefer to Alessandro as a
subject of praise for all the lyric meters? Whatever antiquity be-
queathed to us, whatever the present age has offered that is praise-
worthy, Alessandro alone embodies. He is ennobled by the virtue
of his mind, which flows from the supreme citadel of heaven and 5
its twin towers. This force deep within the soul is not something
that mumbles ignorant opinions, for it produces in his character
whatever it nourishes within. You, Alessandro, can wage war but

Et conferre manus et Martem flectere fraeno
10   nosti. Tu gladiis eloquioque vales,
mitis es et facilis, tibi nullus pectore fastus.
      Gratus es officio, dulcis es obsequio.
Hinc tibi multa meo caedetur victima cultro
      et canet ad laudes ipsa Thalia tuas.
15   Quod si digna tuis meritis tibi dona referre
      non dabitur, memoris sit mihi mentis opus.
Nec fore desperem nobis ut Phoebus Apollo
      det cytharam dono, quam dedit ales ei.
Sic pulsabo chelyn. Reddent sua carmina Musae
20   teque suis manibus floribus instituent.
Nec sunt parva quidem quae divae reddere suerunt
      praemia Pierides. Nanque mori nequeunt.
Manlius, heu, nati percussit colla securi,
      saevit et in natos Brutus ad usque necem.
25   Alter in horrentem se praecipitavit hyatum.
      Se tulit in gladios et Codrus et Decii.
Quae spes tanta viros hos Loeto tradidit ulla?
      Sperarunt mortem laudibus opprimere.
Stoicidis dum summa boni finitur honesto,
30   quid sibi proponunt? Gloria sola iuvat.
Res age praeclaris titulis gere maxima dignas,
      ductor Alexander, vincere perge tuos.
Sphortia magnanimus res gesserat omne per aevum
      victuras, bello clarus et imperio.
35   Hunc superat natus Franciscus Sphortia rebus
      fortunaque prior per probatitis opus.
Tu quoque perge parem te tantis laudibus heros
      reddere. Nam Musae te super astra ferent.

you also know how to bring peace. You are a master of the sword and also eloquence. You are gentle and easy. There is no arrogance in your heart: you are gracious in service and noble in compliance. 10

Thus while many a victim will be slain by my knife, Thalia will celebrate you herself in verse. But if it is not permitted to me to give you gifts worthy of your merits, at least may my work call 15 those merits to mind. Nor should I abandon hope that Phoebus Apollo will present me with a lute, since the winged god[13] did the same for him. Thus I shall strike the lyre. In return, the Muses will give me their songs and they will celebrate you with flowers in their hands. Nor are the rewards small that the divine Pierian 20 maidens are accustomed to give in return. For they can never die.

Manlius, alas, struck his son in the neck with an ax.[14] Brutus in his rage pursued his sons to their death.[15] Another Roman lept into a hideous, gaping pit.[16] Both Codrus and the Decii 25 threw themselves on the swords of the enemy.[17] What great hope brought these men to their deaths? They hoped to vanquish death with glory. While the Stoic philosophers defined the supreme good as virtue, what did those men imagine for themselves? Glory alone was pleasing. 30

Thus you should attempt deeds worthy of the highest praise and surpass your own ancestors, Prince Alessandro. That most noble Sforza, who was famous both as a warrior and a ruler,[18] performed deeds that will live forever. But his son, Francesco Sforza, surpasses him in his deeds, his fortune and his works of probity. 35 You, Alessandro, hero, go: make yourself equal to such paeans of praise. For the Muses will carry you to the stars.

: 5 :

Tristes Insubrium denique liquimus
terras, quas rapido syderis ignei
vastant horribiles fulmine caelites.
Plaustro dum vehimur cum Laribus piis
5   et quiquid reliquum longa protervitas
Martis vel Cereris saeva Neccessitas
fecit, iam penitus fervor[4] Apollinis
omnes corripuit. Nos sitis ac fames
una dum premeret, quae propior fuit
10   hinc cauponula tendentibus aeminus,
qua nos mox Ticinum suscipit[5] obvia,
illuc numine divertimus horrido
et nummis petimus quod fuit usui.
Turbatus iubet excedere ianua
15   caupo, 'Pestiferae discedite belvae!'[6]
inclamitans, 'Propere linquite, linquite!'
Quos spectant oculis astra benignius,
paremus. Quid enim pluribus irritum
tempus conterimus? Non asinum lyra
20   nec vis[7] eloquii leniat inscium.
Quo coeptum fuerat prosequimur viae.
Et vix assequimur denique, blandius
orantes veniam noctis et otii
qui primas habitat villicus inclyti
25   horti caupo domos excipit omnia,
nobis laeticiae munera porrigens.
Hic primum tenebras luminibus pigras

: 5 :

Filelfo's journey to Cremona[19]

Finally we left the sad lands of the Milanese which dread deities
are destroying with fleet lightning from a fiery star. While we
travel in a wagon with our sacred Lares[20] and whatever else re-
mains after the long violence of Mars and Ceres' brutal famine,[21] 5
the fever of Apollo[22] already holds all the city's people in its grip.

The Inn on Route to Pavia

With hunger and thirst bearing down on us as we make our
way, a small inn appears at a distance from the road where Pavia 10
would soon receive us. Guided by some evil deity, we turn off to
this place and ask for what we need with our money in hand. In a
fury, the innkeeper orders us to the door: "Go away, go, you
plague-infested beasts," he shouts. "Leave! Leave quickly!" And 15
we—whom the stars look down on with more kindly eyes than
his—obey. But why am I wasting time with more useless words?
Neither the lyre nor eloquent words would soften that ignorant
ass. We continue on the journey we've begun. And scarcely do we 20
arrive at the first house, when finally, after begging politely for
shelter for the night and rest, the innkeeper and caretaker of the
famous garden there hears our whole story and offers us gifts—to 25
our delight.

udis expulimus; pectora laetior
sensus corripuit. Mensa paratior
30   hic apponitur. Hic et Cereris piae,
hic primum placidi copia Liberi
fit nobis. Agimus cantibus altius
pulsantes fidibus sydera personis.
Saltatum choreis cymbala mollibus
35   miscent. Maeror abest et fugit aeminus
omnis cura prior. Nam modice quoque
interdum gravitas exhilarascere
nequaquam dubitat. Sic gravior senex
condiri salibus puberis assolet.
40   Ut Comus tacuit, mox Iocus utitur
dulci colloquio. Post requiem parat
plumis perlevibus lectus honustior.
Dormitur placide. Nox citius ruit
quam par est. Roseo surgit ac aequore
45   Titan arquitenens. Excitor illico
ac me veste parans excito caeteros.
Tendens ad Ticinum quod iacet obvium,
hinc mox perspicuo flumine nobilem
dum namus Ticino—en ingredimur Padum,
50   quo vecti placidum conterimus diem.
Noctu dum requiem praestat et otium
quae ripam tenuit dentibus anchora,
dum somno premimur, mox tonat altius
qui rex omnipotens Iupiter aethera
55   ducit, nec pluviae lentius ingruunt.
Nimbi praecipiti turbine conciti
irrumpunt rapidis amnibus undique.
'O divum genitor, rector et arbiter
rerum quas opifex e nihilo creas[8]
60   quidquid vis geritur: Diluvium,' precor,

Here we first wiped away the awful darkness from our tearful eyes and a happier feeling entered our hearts. Here first a table is laid for us with plenty of holy Ceres and sweet Liber.[23] We sing 30 songs, making the stars ring with the resonant sounds of the lute. Our cymbals mix lively and gentle dances. Sorrow is gone and all 35 our prior care has fled. For sometimes a serious mood is quick to give way to some degree of happiness. Thus a dour old man is often buoyed up by a young man's jokes. When Comus falls silent, soon Iocus turns to sweet discourse.[24] Afterwards a bed heavy 40 with soft feathers brings us rest. We sleep peacefully.

Sailing the Ticino and Po Rivers to Pavia

Night rushes by more swiftly than it should. Bow-bearing[25] Titan rises from the rosy sea, and right then and there I awaken. Af- 45 ter dressing myself I rouse the others. We head for Pavia which lies on our route. From there, soon we are sailing on the bright Ticino river, and behold, we enter now the noble Po, where we spend a peaceful day afloat. While the anchor that holds the bank 50 with its teeth offers rest and calm and while we are buried in sleep, soon the ruler of the heavens, almighty Jove, thunders on high and a driving rain assails us. A cyclone lashes the clouds; they burst 55 over roiling rivers on all sides of us.

"O father of the gods, ruler and lord of the universe," I pray, "maker of things from nothing, creating whatever force exists, hold at bay the flood that overwhelms us." But the god does not 60

'arce quo premimur.' Nil precibus deus
audit, forsitan auri quod inanitas.
Nec summis etiam caelitibus placet.
Nam si vera fatentur Theoleptici,
65   non est quod capiatur precibus deus
ullis, munera quas nulla praeiverint.
Crebris obruimur caelitus imbribus.
Nec prosunt miseris tegmina cymbulae
conductae. Penetrant omnia turbidi
70   nimbi. Sic penitus nos quoque vestibus
frigemus madidis nocte sub horrida.
Dum frigent reliqui, sola voracibus
flamis aestuat Antonia vernula,
nec fallax referat quod patitur malum—
75   forsan ne reliquis iniiceret metum.
Tithoni croceos liquerat excita
uxor iam thalamos, anchora tollitur
et coeptam sequimur remigio viam.
Vix Aethon rapido subdiderat iugo
80   collum, nos excipit grata Placentia
ac dulci miserans hospitio fovet.
Solus dimminuit munficentiam
vectigalia qui Piccolus exigit.
Quo nil invenias rusticius, nihil
85   usquam sordidius. Clamitat improbus:
'Vectigal volumus! Non opus est libris!
Musarum satis est, si satis est opis
in nummis! Faciunt divitiae deos.'
Contra litigo dum principis optimi,
90   quas nuper dederat, me tego litteris.
Quid verbis opus est? Ius valet efferum
nullum, nec pietas flectere Piccolum.
Solus Scaeva malum deterruit virum.

hear our prayers, perhaps because they come with no gold. Nor
does our prayer please the heavenly deities. For if the prophets[26]
speak the truth, the god cannot be charmed by prayers if gifts are   65
not offered first.

We are drenched by unremitting rain from the heavens. Nor
does the protection of the small hired boat help us, so miserable
are we. The thick rains go straight through everything. And so we
freeze in our wet clothing under the bristling night. While the rest   70
of us shiver from the cold, only our servant Antonia burns with
fiery heat, nor would that deceitful girl tell what evil ailed her —
perhaps so as not to frighten us.   75

Arrival in Piacenza

When the wife of Tithonus[27] awakens and leaves her saffron
bed, our anchor is already raised, and we again proceed by boat on
the journey we had begun. Scarcely has Aethon[28] placed his neck
in its yoke when gracious Piacenza receives us and, pitying us, wel-   80
comes us with sweet hospitality. Only Piccolo[29] who collects the
tolls ruins the magnanimity that greets us. For you would find no
one more ignorant nor more crude than he. "The toll is all we   85
want!" this awful man screams at us, "We need no books! As long
as there's plenty of money, who needs the Muses? It's wealth that
makes the gods." I argue back while I shield my body with the
letter[30] that my great prince had given me. Why say more? Nei-   90
ther a sense of justice or duty can move the savage Piccolo. Only
Sceva Curte[31] deters this awful man. After the good Curte hears

Qui postquam didicit Cortis hic optimus
95   impuri solitas insidias viri,
iussit ne stomachum fervere bilicum
demens cogeret. Expalluit audiens
haec vir nequitia nequior ultima,
invitusque sinit solvere cymbulam.
100   Hinc nos Scaeva suis muneribus pius
ut pulchris cumulat, solvimus impigri.
Quod dum postridie per gaudia pulchra Cremonam
    appulimus, pestem iam superasse rati,
dirius in duplicem turbato numine pestem
105   syderis incidimus, incidimusque soli.
Nam vix egressus cymbam, vix urbe receptus,
    dum conduco domum qua residere queam,
vernula quae rerum custos Antonia navi
    sola relicta fuit, morte cadit subita.
110   Tollitur extemplo cunctis ad sydera clamor.
    Vaesanum passim vulgus ad arma ruit.
Moenibus extrudor, tanquam teterrima pestis,
    cum Phoebo et natis mille per obprobria.
Nullane Romulidum plebes vestigia servas
115   dira Cremonensis, quam perimant superi?
Quae te barbaries cepit saevissima more
    immani, gravibus urbs inimica viris?
Quam bene te divus praedae decrevit habendam
    Augustus; superas quae feritate fers.
120   Perfida gens sceleri non uni obnoxia, toto
    flagitiis pariter orbe notanda tuis,
more peregrinos quo tandem pessima cunctos
    odisti, quibus es omnibus ipsa minor?

about the usual traps this man has set, he commands the madman   95
not to rouse his anger. Hearing this, the man, more evil than evil
itself, turns pale and allows, though reluctantly, our little boat to
set sail. And after this, when the good Sceva loads us down with
beautiful gifts, we eagerly weigh anchor.   100

Docking at Cremona

But when we land with great joy at Cremona the next day, now
believing we have escaped the plague, we succumb, yes, we suc-
cumb—since the deity has been angered—to a double pestilence,
one from the stars and one from the land. For scarcely had we left 105
the boat and been welcomed into the city, when, while I am rent-
ing a house where we can lodge, our servant Antonia,[32] who, left
alone at the boat to guard our things, suddenly falls dead. At once
shouting pierces the air.[33] Mad with fear, here and there people   110
rush to arms. I am shoved outside the city walls together with
Apollo and his children,[34] and followed by a thousand curses—as
though I myself were the deadly plague.

An Invective Against the Cremonese[35]

O dread Cremonese plebs, whom the gods would destroy, have   115
you retained no vestiges of the sons of Romulus? What barbarity,
most savage in its monstrous rule, holds you captive, O city hostile
to men of substance? How well did divine Augustus decree that
you should be held for plunder, and whatever you have endured,
your own brutality exceeds.[36] O treacherous people, notoriously
guilty not of one crime alone but equally known throughout the   120
whole world for your outrages, what custom causes you to hate all
travelers to your city, when you, the most iniquitous, are inferior

Dic mihi qua tandem polles virtute, Cremona?
125 Dic mihi quo vitio dedecorosa cares?
Tu sermone mihi tantum blandire doloso,
raetia dum tendas, dum laqueos iacias.
Quos non inducis fallax, non fraude suprema
mittis in insidias, omnis inops meriti?
130 Quid? Quod Marmaricus leo te crudelior ullus
non est? Immitis vipera nulla magis?
Dic, faex Gallorum, quos nutris pectore fastus?
Num quia te Gotti constituere nothis?
Nam genus egregium quod priscis Roma colonis
135 ornarat penitus Attila sustulerat.
Quod siquos forsan servavit saeva colonos
tempestas, siquos nesciit ira probos,
hos tenebris plebs dira suis obscurat, et almam
non sinit in lucem mergere luminibus.
140 Nanque quis ignorat quantis se laudibus effert
Melia progenies, Bartholomaee, tua?
Sola malo gaudes, plebes, inimica poetis
nobilibusque gravis stirpe profecta Gethae.
Hinc immanis amor praedae te saepe anhaelam
145 reddit et infestam, quos alit aura, bonis.
Nam quae te rabies agitat, gens impia, doctos
ut cupias omnis disperiisse viros?
Illustris exosa artes clarumque perosa
ingenium, somnos atque gulas adamas.
150 Ebria gens, laeso penitus quae fracta cerebro
insanis, quae te tristis Erinys alit?
Istic nobilitas non est quae more tueri
se queat ingenuo laudibus et meritis.
Plebs scelerata furit, quae nullo ducta pudore
155 iusque piumque premat, quae malefacta colat.

to all of them? Tell me, may I ask, in what virtue lies your
strength, O Cremona? Tell me, what disgraceful vice do you lack?   125
You flatter me with lying talk only until you can trap me with your
nets and cast nooses. Whom do you not deceitfully entice? Whom
do you, bereft of all virtue yet full of supreme guile, not send into
traps? No Marmarcian lion is more savage than you, no viper   130
more vicious. Tell, O dregs of the Gauls, what pride do you nour-
ish in your heart? Surely not because the Goths established you
for their bastard sons? For Attila completely eradicated the noble
line Rome furnished to their ancient settlers.   135

But even if that fierce storm spared some settlers, if its anger
never touched some good men, still the vile plebs has cast a pall
over these men with its own darkness; nor does it allow them to
return again to the kindly light of day. For who does not know
with what great praises your Melian lineage displays itself, O   140
Bartolomeo?[37] O plebs, hostile to the noble poets and descended
from the stock of the austere Getae,[38] you alone delight in evil.
And so, the savage love of spoils always makes you breathless and
hostile to the good men whom the air nourishes. For what impi-   145
ous rage, O impious nation, drives you so that you would want to
see perish all learned men? Hating the illustrious liberal arts,
loathing a brilliant mind, you love sleep and gluttony. O drunken
nation, you who rage with cracked brain, what baneful Fury nour-   150
ishes you? Here there is no nobility that can defend itself with
glorious deeds and merits in accord with native custom. The ac-
cursed plebs rages. For without the brake of shame, it would de-
stroy both justice and the good; it would cultivate evil. O horren-   155

O genus horrendum, nostrique obprobria saecli,
  non tandem patrii poeniteat sceleris?
Num pestis fortasse faces adveximus ultro?
  Quae nos decepit, ipsa luat facinus.
160 Num si nota latens aegrotae causa fuisset,
  nos tandem longa cymba tulisset aqua?
Humanum crimen, quod culpa insonte carebat,
  humani meruit iudicis officium.
Exactos recipit parvulus hortulus,
165 in quo parva domus cum puteo iacet,
quem ranae celebrant cantibus undique.
Hic nos nemo suis colloquiis, quasi
dirum prodigium et caelitus grave,
dignatur. Manibus nemo pecuniam
170 audet tangere nostram, quasi nummuli
morbum pestiferum contineant quoque.
Hinc nos obsidet infesta Necessitas,
quae potum prohibet, quae prohibet cibum.
Uvae nos recreant, quae nisi turgidae
175 fovissent stomachum, nos sitis et fames
pressissent pariter mortis aculleis.

: 6 :

Crimine suspectum quamquam, Baptista, verebar,
  neglectus tibi me quod nihil obstreperem,
malo tamen siluisse, tibi quam causa fuisse
  criminis, in patriam quo traherere reus.

dous race, O curse of our age, will you never regret your fathers' crime?

But did we carry the torches of the plague of our own free will? Let her who deceived us pay the penalty herself. And if the sick 160 girl's secret plight had been known, may I ask, surely the little boat would not have carried us on such a long journey by water, would it? A human crime which is free even of innocent wrongdoing merits the offices of a humane judge.[39]

Journey's End

Expelled from the city, a little garden welcomes us, where there 165 is a small house with a well and frogs gather all round it with songs. Here no one deems us worthy of conversation — as if we were some dire omen heavy with celestial portents. No one dares touch our money — as if even the little coins contained the mor- 170 bid plague. And so, hostile Necessity dogs us and keeps us from acquiring either food or drink. Grapes, now fat and juicy,[40] restore our spirits, and if they had not soothed our stomachs, thirst and 175 hunger would equally have crushed us with their deadly darts.

: 6 :

To Leon Battista Alberti[41]
On wealth and virtue

Since I've been ignored by you, I was afraid you suspected me of having wronged you because I failed to protest loudly. Still, I would rather have been silent than to have been the cause of a charge that would cause you to be dragged back to your hometown

5   Non fortuna locos eadem servabat eosdem
      quos premit Eridanus, Arnus et ipse rigat.
Mars ferus amborum populos discreverat ira
      multaque fulmineus vulnera miscuerat.
Negligeremne ego te qui sis iucundior omni
10   luce mihi? Dulcis num pateretur amor?
Quid multa? Eadem fuerat mihi causa silendi,
      quae tibi. Neuter habet iure quod insimulet.
Nunc autem postquam populos deus optimus uno
      iunxit amore duos, en tibi pulso fores,
15 scire velim quid agas, quam sit tibi cura Camoenae,
      an penitus nummis deditus invigiles.
Nescioquid Momi sunt, qui te ludere dicant.
      Num mihi quid vitio, num tibi forte datur?
Nam tu divitias forsan studiosior ambis,
20   quas ego, quam par sit, temnere pergo magis.
An nequeas fulvum non dilexisse metallum
      plurima quod vitae commoda ferre valet?
Ast ego quod paucis contentus ducere vitam
      sim solitus, nummi ducor amore minus.
25 Ethioposque senis non est cui littera pectus
      imbuat, at nostri quos iuvet aeris amor.
Ergo dives agis. Paupertas semper habebit
      hunc eadem, iuvenem quaeque secuta fuit.
Dissimili studio simili sub amore probatae,
30   si virtutis honos iunxerit usque duos,
quur fit ut alteruter non sit contentus, utrumque
      ad medium redeat, quidquid uterque colit?
Sic aut divitias nimias contemnere disces
      aut ego pauperiem diffugiam nimiam.
35 Quod si forte nequit neuter praestare, severus
      Momus habet vitio quod det utrique tuus.

to defend yourself. Nor has the same fortune kept the two cities
safe, one hemmed in by the Po,[42] one watered by the Arno. Savage   5
Mars had angrily severed the bond between the peoples of both
cities, inflicting many wounds with fiery speed.[43]

But would I ever neglect you, who are more pleasing than all
life to me? Would sweet Love[44] ever allow it? But why say more? I   10
have the same reason for being silent as you do. But neither of us
has grounds for a fair complaint. But now the almighty god has
joined our two peoples in one love—and look, I'm knocking at
your door. I'd like to know what you're doing, how it goes with
your Muse Camena[45]—or are you devoting all your waking hours   15
to making money? There are some Momuses who say you are
writing satires.[46] Surely you are not by chance being criticized for
the same thing I am? You go after wealth perhaps more eagerly,
while I tend to scorn it more than I should. Is it that you can't   20
keep from loving that tawny metal because it can bring many ad-
vantages to our lives? But perhaps because I'm used to being con-
tented to live my life with little, I'm less beguiled by the love of
money.

Literature affects the heart of no aged Ethiopian[47] as it does   25
ours—yet the love of money pleases us. And so you live as a
wealthy man, Alberti, whereas poverty will always own me, just
as it pursued me when I was a youth. If the glory of virtue has
joined two men with dissimilar interests because of their similar
love of goodness, why would each of them not be content to re-   30
turn to a midpoint between the paths that each has followed?
Thus either you will learn to condemn excess wealth or I will shun
excess poverty.

But if perchance neither one of us can do this, then your severe   35
Momus[48] has the means to find fault with each of us. Is it not

Num temptare libet: liceatne movere quod alto
    robore consenuit invaluitque suo?
Tu mihi ditandi trades praecepta beatur.
40   Qui pauper fias, accipe. Pauca feram.
Semper ego studui, qui me sequerentur euntem
    divitiae ut dominum, quas ego non sequerer.
His mihi nec Venus est, nec amoenus partus amictus,
    illecebrae nullae, deliciaeque minus.
45 Non iocus oscoenus, Cyprii nec copia musti;
    non fomenta sacrae dedecorosa gulae.
Alea nulla meos gaudet didicisse Penates;
    ludus item nullus ridiculosus habet.
Millia nummorum nobis Cyllenius ales
50   attulit et Musae quae periere simul.
Hospitibus nam cum do dignis plurima multis
    munera muneribus, disperiere novis.
Nil mihi servatum est; nec quicquam defuit unquam.
    Sunt mihi cuncta satis, possideoque nihil.
55 Quaque domum subiit nummus virtute paratus,
    hac itidem properat nummus abire foras.
Haec etiam tu mente volens praecepta tueri,
    mox tenuis fias pauperiorque Codro.
Sic cum tradideris mihi tu praecepta quibus sim
60   ditior, adde queam num fieri melior.
Dic inquam pariter num crescere possit in ipsis
    divitiis virtus quae moderata cupit.
Dives erat Crassus nulla virtute decorus;
    ipse Cato pauper laudibus astra petit.
65 Si virtus eadem Croesum tenuisset opesque,
    non tua tempsisset, optime, dicta, Solon.
Dic quem nunc videas decoret quem maxima virtus
    divitiaeque simul, quae superant medium.

pleasing to see whether we can change what has grown old and become powerful through its own deeply entrenched toughness? You'll hand me precepts, O wealthy one, for becoming rich. And I'll tell you briefly how you can become a poor man. I've always 40 been eager for wealth to follow me as its lord, not for me to follow it. What is more, riches have brought me neither a mistress, nor fine clothes, nor enticements or dalliances.[49] I indulge neither in obscene humor, nor in an abundance of Cyprian wine. And I 45 have no disgraceful amounts of food to satisfy a shameless gullet. Gaming and gambling have taken no pleasure in having come to know my home, nor do silly games of chance live there.

The winged Cyllenian[50] has brought me thousands of coins for my Muse, which at the same time have all been lost. For when I 50 give all these things back to my hosts, who are deserving of many gifts in return, then my rewards are completely gone. I have saved nothing, nor do I lack anything. All that I have is enough for me and I own nothing. For when money obtained virtuously enters a house, it hastens to leave the place in the same spirit. If you too 55 would like to observe these precepts, you would soon become poorer and thinner than Codrus.[51] Thus when you give me advice so that I can become richer, consider also whether I would become a better man. Tell me, I ask you, whether virtue, which longs for 60 moderation, can thrive in the midst of wealth? Crassus, who was adorned by no virtue, was a wealthy man, whereas Cato sought the stars with his glorious achievements, though he himself was a pauper. If this same virtue had curbed Croesus and his wealth, he 65 would not have shown contempt for your words, O noble Solon.[52] Tell me this: what man do you now see whom the greatest virtue and exceptional wealth adorn at the same time? I do not think it

Nunquam posse putem fieri, simul inclyta virtus
70   divitiaeque graves in cumulum veniant.
Hae nam corpus avent dulci lenire veneno,
        quo pereat quiquid mens alit alta boni.
At virtus animum sublimia tollit in astra,
        cui parere facit corporeos stimulos.
75   Nosse igitur, Baptista, velim tibi quanta Camoenae
        curat sedet, nummis qui cumules loculos?
Et quod Momus opus rigido sibi sumpserit ore
        mordendum? Gladiis quos petat ipse suis?
Praeterea quantum nos diligis? Illa probati
80   vis an amoris item creverit in cumulum.
Nam te noster amor magis en, Alberthe, profundis
        ignibus exardet, cumque die superat,
qui tamen aequalis vitae si moribus uti
        consuescat, fiet maior et utilior.
85   Nam sibi Pierides me totum et Phoebus Apollo
        adiunxere simul cantibus atque lyra.
Lusimus in satyris; lyricos nunc pectore cantus
        versamus. Curas hisce levare iuvat.
Effera pertulimus longi discrimina Martis,
90   pertulimusque famem pertulimusque sitim.
At nunc Insubrium premit altam saevior urbem
        ira deum laevo sydere cuncta domans.
Pestifer invadens omnes uno ordine morbus,
        millia quoque die corpora mandat humo.
95   Hinc ego vix tandem natisque domoque mihique
        prospiciens cessi loetiferis iaculis.
Nunc me cum totis Laribus nebulosa Cremona
        excipit et Phoebum Castalidumque chorum.
Ille chelyn pulsat. Respondent grata sorores
100   cantibus alternis. Dulcis amice, vale.

would ever be possible for celebrated virtue and substantial wealth
to coincide in the same man. For wealth longs to soften the body   70
with sweet poison so that whatever good is nurtured by our sub-
lime intellect dies. Virtue, however, lifts the mind to the highest
stars; for it forces the body's passions to obey it.

    Therefore, Battista, I would like to know how much care you
devote to Camena, O you who would cram your money-boxes full   75
of coins? And what biting satire will stern-lipped Momus embark
on now, and whom will he seek with his sword? Besides, how
much do you love us? Has the power of virtuous love grown in
you to its full measure? For look, Alberti, my love for you burns   80
with intense fire, and grows each day. Nonetheless, if it can be-
come accustomed to enjoying the habits of a just life, it will be-
come still greater and more useful.

    The Pierian maidens and Phoebus Apollo have joined with me   85
in song and the music of the lyre. We have played at satirical
verses and now we ponder lyric poetry in our hearts. For it is a
pleasing thing to lighten our cares with song. We have endured
the long wars of savage Mars and we have suffered both hunger
and thirst. And now the anger of the gods and an evil star weigh   90
heavily upon the high city of the Milanese, dominating all things.
A deadly plague overwhelms all the people at one sweep, sending
thousands to their doom each day. And so while caring for my
children, my home, and myself, I have hardly given in to its pesti-   95
lent darts. Now cloudy Cremona receives me and Phoebus and the
chorus of Castalian Muses as well, with all my household gods.
Phoebus strums the lyre. The sisters respond, singing pleasing
songs by turns. Farewell, sweet friend.   100

: 7 :

Musis Cremonae nullus est locus sacris,
nullus Minervae, nec deo Maia sato.
Hic sordidae solum vigent artes palam.
Hic turpis urbem quaestus omnem polluit.
5   Lenonibus, scortis et aleae vafris
doctoribus statutus est ingens honos
et publicanis et gulae et veneficis.
Hinc remigandum est; ac retro ad Insubribus
terras propinquas navigandum protinus.
10   Vale, Cremona, manibus diris sacra,
infesta cunctis quos alit virtus viris.
Vale, vale, inquam tertium; et cito cadas
terris favillis concremata funditus;
bene est. Preces tetigere Tartareas canes.
15   Dirae furentis instar adsunt turbinis.
Saevum latrantes igneos morsus parant;
fundunt venenum criminibus; iactant faces.
Ardet Cremona nullius nec syderis
flamis, nec humano igne. Supplicium facit
20   immanis ira pectoris, cunctos bonos
qua tristis odit. En scelus gentem impiam
cruciat suum. Nec sufficit bustis humus.

: 7 :

An invective against the city of Cremona

There's no place for the sacred Muses in Cremona, neither for Minerva nor Maia's son, the god.[53] Here only the vulgar arts thrive openly. Here shameful profiteering pollutes the entire city. Great honor is granted to pimps, whores, and the shrewd scholars of the gaming table, to tax collectors, gluttons, and poisoners.   5

We must row away from here. We must sail away right now, back to the land of the Milanese close by. Goodbye, Cremona, sacred city for the dire shades, hostile to all whom virtue nurtures.   10
Goodbye, I say. And goodbye, for the third time. May you quickly fall to foul ashes, having burned to the ground; that's fine. My prayers have touched the dogs of Hades. Here are the Furies, like an avenging tempest.[54] Barking savagely, they ready their fiery   15
bites; they pour cruel poison from their hair; they hurl their burning brands. Cremona burns with flames that come from no mortal fire or star. She pays the penalty for the anger in her savage breast, which causes the mournful city to hate all good men. Look! Crime   20
torments its own impious folk. Nor has this city enough earth for its tombs.

: 8 :

Aenice, quid facio si forsan, Davale, quaeras,
    vivo quidem, nec me pestis amara tulit.
Carmina multiplici pede ludo — carmina dulci
    tempto lyra. Sumque maius adortus opus.
5   Nam modo res Italas cum mecum mente voluto.
    Phoebus ait: 'Semper tempus inane teris?
Maeonides priscam Graio cum milite classem
    extulit altisonis ille poeta modis.
Aemulus huic noster longo post tempore vates
10   successit tandem Publius ipse Maro,
cui pius Aeneas grates debere fatetur
    ingentis, tantum quem canit ille virum.
At tu nil magna, nil prisca laude, Philelfe,
    temptabis dignum notus utrique solo?
15   Graecia si septem tenuit te nobilis annos
    et docuit quidquid gens habet illa ferax,
si te progenuit quae tot nutrit Itala tellus
    lustra decem decorans artibus ipsa suis,
quid taceas semper? Quid nil sublimius audes
20   quam satyram atque lyram? Fac tuba ad astra sonet
altius!' Hinc igitur saliens nova molior arma,
    quis in se Latium perfurit omne grave,
nec tuus Alphonsus — quin noster — maxima saecli
    gloria praesentis non decoratus erit.
25   Sin forsan rogites quid non promissa fidemque
    servarim, quid non Partenopen ierim,

: 8 :

To Iñigo d'Avalos
On the plague in Milan,
and why his journey to Naples has been delayed

If you ask what I'm doing, Iñigo d'Avalos, I'm definitely alive and the bitter plague hasn't carried me off. I'm writing poems in various meters — trying out the poems to the beat of a sweet-sounding lyre. And I have begun a greater work. For I ponder only Italian things in my mind. Phoebus says: "Why are you always wasting time? That Lydian poet[55] immortalized an ancient fleet and the Greek army in high, resounding rhythms. Our own Publius Maro[56] finally followed long afterwards, and pious Aeneas admits he owes him enormous thanks, since it was that poet who made him great. But will you, Filelfo, who are known in both those poets' lands, attempt nothing worthy of great and epic glory? If noble Greece was your home for seven years and she taught you whatever lore that fertile nation holds, and if the Italian land that nurtured so many also gave birth to you, adorning you for fifty years with her own arts, why would you always be mute? Won't you dare to write something more sublime than satire and lyric poetry? Make your war-trumpet resound to the stars!" And so, I jump up and make an effort to take up new arms, when all grievous Latium rages against itself with arms, and your Alfonso — or rather mine — will be honored as the most glorious man of our century.

But if, however, you ask why I have not kept my promises and my oath, why I have not come to Parthenope[57] — listen to the reasons for the poet's delay and pardon the pious postponement,

accipe quae fuerit cunctantis causa poetae
　　atque ignosce morae, Davale care, piae.
Insubrium terras invaserat undique diris
30　　　pestis atrox facibus, cuncta simul populans.
Hinc me defecit promissi copia nummi,
　　quem labor ingenuus reddere debuerat.
Quaestor et aediles pedibus sibi ferre salutem
　　perrexere omnes. Solus in urbe fui.
35　Quid facerem? Natos num saevae linquere morti
　　fas erat atque mihi consuluisse satis?
Nec facerem, nec erat, qua me subducere fato
　　possem, fulventis copia tanta dei.
Nanque deum censent his tempestatibus aurum
40　　　atque deo maius numen et imperium.
Quae vos vilis humi mortales tanta cupido
　　opprimit immemores numinis et patriae?
Saeva procelloso sulcantes aequora fluctu,
　　hanc terram peregre luctificam colitis.
45　Debetur vobis, si vitam vivitis aequam,
　　in patriam reditus sydera quam decorant.
Illinc ortus enim vester. Deus aetheris alti
　　esse quidem similes vos dedit ille sui.
Vos aurum colitis mira pietate, Lycurgus
50　　　quod metuens patriis expulit e Laribus.
Omnis causa mali, liceat si dicere verum,
　　est aurum. Moechos hoc facit atque dolos.
Omne genus vitii molitur et efficit aurum.
　　Quae vos mortales corripit ergo sitis?
55　Nec tamen in precio est cui desit copia nummi.
　　Non fuit huic virtus qui aeris inops.
Hinc me deridet plebes ignobilis annos
　　quod tot agens nullis prospiciam loculis.

my dear d'Avalos. Everywhere the pitiless plague has invaded the lands of the Milanese, laying waste at the same time to all things with its terrible firebrands. And so, I was not paid the amount of money that was promised me, which the honorable work I did should have earned. The quaestor and the aediles[58] ordered everyone to travel to a safe place. I was the only one left in the city. What was I to do? Was it the right thing to leave my children to a terrible death? Would it have been enough just to have looked to my own interests? I would neither do that, nor was there such an abundance of the tawny god around that I could remove myself from my fate. 30 35

For in these horrendous times people think that gold is a god and that its temporal power and authority are greater than god. O mortal men, what vile lust so obsesses you that you are forgetful of god and your native city? Having plowed seas savage with stormy turbulence, you inhabit this mournful land, a stranger. If you lead a just life, a return to your home — a place the stars adorn — is owed to you, for this is the place you came from. That god in lofty heaven has allowed you to be similar to him. Yet it is gold — though Lycurgus[59] feared it and banished it from his ancestral city and household — that you worship with amazing piety. 40 45 50

If we are allowed to speak the truth, gold is the root of all evil. It creates adulterers and fraud. Gold contrives and causes every kind of crime. Why then does such thirst for it grip you mortals? No value is attributed to the man who is without substantial funds. Virtue is not thought the property of the man who has no money. The ignoble plebs mock me because, after the many years I have lived, I have no prospects for money. By some fate or other I 55

Nescio quo fato mihi fit nunquam ipsa peculi
60   cura fuit. Nec nunc me sitis aeris habet,
divitiis aliis delector Davale nullis,
    quam quibus exultat imperitans animus.
Divitiis animus gaudet quas nulla movere
    vis queat externa. Nam deus ipse sibi est.
65 Sin petis an tandem veniam, ni durior ullus
    inciderit casus, visere vos statuo.
Verum scire velim quam nos sit fronte benigna
    excepturus adhuc rex tuus atque meus.
Num flamis adeo flagrat succensus amoris,
70   ut fortasse deas despiciat comites?
At iuvat aligerum cantus quoque. Saepe Cupido
    cantibus atque lyra corda superba domat.
Si tibi rex ingens fortasse, Lucretia, nolit
    obsequio placidi se tribuisse dei,
75 spero equidem nostris mulcebitur usque Camoenis
    ipsa adeo, ut doleat se tribuisse moram.
Plura quidem dicturus eram. Sed nuncius iste
    obstitit, hinc abiens qui celerabat iter.
Quod reliquum est, istic cum venero dicere pergam.
80   Nunc te cum Musis opto valere piis.

: 9 :

Alphonse, nostri lucidum saecli iubar
decusque regum maximum, si longius
mirationem forsitan silentium

have never cared about money. Neither have I any thirst for cash at this time, d'Avalos, nor have I ever enjoyed any riches other than those in which a commanding mind delights. For the mind enjoys only that wealth which no external force can move: for that is god himself—in and for himself. 60

But if you ask, d'Avalos, whether I'll finally come to you: I am determined to visit, if no harsher misfortune befalls us. But I would like to know how your king and mine, whose demeanor has been kindly up to now, will receive me. Does he burn so intensely with the flames of love that he may perhaps disdain the Pierian goddesses as companions?[60] But poetry also pleases the winged god. Often Cupid rules proud hearts with the lyre and melodious song. If your great king, Lucrezia, does not want to give himself over to the service of the peaceful god,[61] I hope that my lady herself will be so softened by our Muses that she will grieve at having allowed our delay. 65 70 75

I was going to say more but the messenger, who is eager to leave us, forbids it. Whatever else I have, I'll say when I come to you. For now, I and our pious Muses wish you well. 80

: 9 :

To King Alfonso
An exhortation to seek peace

Alfonso, shining light of our century and greatest glory among kings, if my long silence has given you pause, then lend your pious

nostrum tibi dedisset, auribus piis
5   admitte causam nosque dicentes brevi
tantisper audi, dum piae mentis fidem
quaecunque debet esse non dubia tibi
saltem probaris. Nanque de rebus tuum
sit iudicare liberum. Mihi satis
10   dixisse fuerit quod tibi cupio bene
optoque. Nuper fuerat in mentem mihi
ad te ire visendi tui causa — deum
quencunque dulcis pectori inseruit meo
tuarum amor laudum. Ferebam muneris
15   satyras loco centum tuo quas nomini
divo dicavi. Plura nam quamvis velim
de te canendo posteris relinquere,
placuit tamen satyris item in caelum tuum
efferre nomen ob tibi gestas probe
20   res maximas nullis tacendas gentibus.
Id dum voluto, multa solventi pedem
mihi obstitere. Caeteris sed omnibus
iam liberum curis dataeque compotem
factum viae Mars impedit mox ingruens
25   nec me sequi quam coeperam sinit viam.
Sic regredi cogor dolens miseras nimis
aetatis huius quas vices agimus malae.
O temporis teterrimum sydus feri,
quae tanta cepit pestis orbis inclytum
30   Italos genus? Si nos minus pax iuverit,
quidnam iuvet tandem quietis gratia?
Si suscipi bellum solet, quibus licet
frui quiete? Quid movent belli nefas
iniuria nulla lacessiti quidem?
35   Honoris ardor pectus humanum dies
noctesque vexat ac vorax auri fames.

ears to its cause and hear me out while I briefly explain, as long as 5
you esteem the loyalty of a devoted mind, about which you should
have no doubt. For it should be your right to judge a free man[62] in
such matters. For me it is enough to have said I hope and wish
you well. 10

Recently the idea of making a journey to visit you came to me,
for certainly the sweet love of your deeds placed some god or other
in my heart. I have brought you a hundred satires as a gift, which I 15
have dedicated to your divine name. In spite of this, I would like
to leave more works to posterity about you, in lyric meters.[63] Still,
it has been pleasing to extol your name to the heavens in my sat-
ires because of your great deeds, which all peoples on earth will 20
extol. While I ponder this, many things stand in the way of my
departure. Mars, now on the offensive again, impedes me: though
I have a permit to travel and am free from all other cares, he does
not allow me to follow the road on which I had set out. And so I 25
am forced to return, grieving over the miserable events of the evil
times we live in.

O most heinous star of this savage age, what terrible sickness in
the world has seized this famous race, the Italians? If peace does
not please us, why would the love of tranquility give pleasure in 30
the end? If wars are habitually undertaken, for whom is it permit-
ted to enjoy peace? Why do men engage in the infamy of war even
when they are provoked by no wrong? The passion for glory trou-
bles the human heart day and night. This and the insatiable hun- 35

Quo plura possidemus? Ulterius quoque
libido pergit finibus nullis sibi
contenta. Mundus unus uni perparum.
40   Hoc accidit quos nulla ratio temperat,
laxis habaenis quos temeritas impotens
stimulat sui nec iuris esse trux sinit.
Hae sunt mali causae — cupido pervicax
honoris aurique ignis ac nimius furor.
45   Sed te, caput regale, quem probitas virum
ostendit orbi numini deum parem,
Alphonse, regum sydus in omnes plagas
famae coruscum luce, quae ratio ferox
furiis valet nostris et ira dirior
50   iunxisse, principum omnium praestans honos?
Quid polluis manus sacras? Aut quo ruis
praeceps in illos quos ut in primis tuos
debes tueri? Num Philippi forsitan
oblivio te ceperit ducis optimi
55   illius, inquam, principis mitissimi?
Quo vidit uno sol benignius nihil,
nec amantius quicquam tui, qui te ut patrem
veritus, perinde ac filium dilexerat.
Eiusne Blancam filiam castissimam,
60   eius nepotes indolis pulcherrimae
speique maximae furore censeas
tuone dignos? At quibus facias bene:
his si minus facias, quibus es obnoxius?
Philippus ille nihil omiserat tuus
65   quod censuisset splendidis honoribus
aut commodis tibi fore acceptissimum.
Quid dicet omnis gens? Quid aetas longior?
Haud hoc enim contemptui ducas licet.
Qui neglegit quae caeteri de se viri

ger for gold. Why should we possess more? What is more, lust spreads more widely, never contented with any limits for itself. One world is too small for one man. This happens to all those whom reason does not restrain and whom rashness — powerless 40 and uncurbed — goads on and, in its wildness, does not allow to be masters of themselves.

These are the causes of evil — the desire for glory and the madness and passion for gold. But since your virtue, O regal head, shows the world that you are the equal of the divine majesty of the 45 gods, Alfonso, shimmering star of fame among the kings in all regions, what fierce reason and dire wrath can have joined you to our furies, O surpassing glory among all the princes? Why do you 50 pollute your holy hands? To what end do you rush headlong against those men whom you should protect first and foremost as if they were your own? Perhaps you are forgetful of that best Duke Filippo — of that most gentle prince, I say? For the sun has 55 seen no one more kindly or more loving of you than this one man, who revered you as he would a father and loved you as he would a son. Would you believe that his daughter, the most chaste Bianca, and his grandchildren, scions of his greatest and most beautiful hope, would deserve this madness of yours? 60

But if you do not look after those men whom you should look after, to whom are you then indebted? Your Filippo had left nothing undone that he thought you would welcome as honorable and 65 advantageous. What will all the world say? What will the future age say? By no means should you dismiss this as unimportant. People judge a man worthless who pays no attention to what the

70   vel dixerint vel senserint, nequam putant.
Laus gratitudinis, ut aiunt plurimi,
est tanta nulla maior ut dici queat.
Qui caeteris virtutibus cunctos viros
rex antecellis, hacne dicaris minor?
75   Ad haec dei dono vir omnis imperat
et omne regnum caelitus nobis datur.
Humana regna vanitas: quae viribus
nituntur imis, si supernas deserant.
Nam reddit aequa lance pro meritis deus.
80   Sic principes deus bonos auget bonis
malosque rursus afficit gravibus malis.
Qui ius ministrat, iure qui socio utitur
in rebus omnibus, nec ullum dedecus
animos volutat, nec facit sciens probrum,
85   hominibus ac superis probatus omnibus
regnat magisque semper ac magis viget.
Babylon ita tot saeculis in regibus
effloruit iustis. Eandem perdidit
nimis pudendum regis iniusti nefas.
90   Cyrus sibi dum rebus in laetis modum
moetitur, omnis caelites comites habet.
Elatior factus iacet ludibrium
mulieris irae. Rex Alexander puer
probusque prospere gerit quidquid cupit.
95   Mores ubi iam grandis ac vitae decus
mutat, suorum fraudibus cadit miser.
Nam nemo laetatur diu partis bonis
iis usus improbe. Deum probitas iuvat.
Romae quid imperium velim verbis sequi?
100   E regibus primis Numam solum licet
videre iustum, qui mori meruit bene.
At regum postquam iugum populus malum

rest of the world says or thinks about him. The praise for grati- 70
tude, as most men say, is so great that no other praise can be called
greater. Since you who are a king surpassing all men in the rest of
the virtues, would you want to be called less great in this virtue?

What is more, what every man controls is a gift from god and 75
every kingdom is granted to us mortals by heaven. Human king-
doms are empty in themselves: should they ever abandon the sub-
lime powers above, they are dependent on the powers below. For
god renders to each according to his merits, using a just scale.
Thus god increases the store and wellbeing of good princes and he 80
afflicts the bad with heavy evils. The man who administers justice,
who uses the law as his ally in all circumstances and neither pon-
ders shameful acts nor knowingly does evil, rules his kingdom
with the approval of all the gods and men and prospers more and 85
more.

Babylon thus flourished for so many centuries with just kings.
But the crimes and debauchery of an unjust king destroyed that
city.[64] As long as Cyrus maintained moderation in his fortunate
life, all the deities in heaven were his companions. When, though, 90
he became too proud, he fell, the plaything of a woman's anger.[65]
As a boy, King Alexander was upright and accomplished success-
fully whatever he wanted to do. When he sullied his character and
the honor of his now illustrious life, wretched man, he fell victim 95
to the treachery of his own men.[66] For no man is happy for long
when he unjustly uses the goods he has won. Virtue is pleasing
to god.

What can I say? Why talk next about the power of Rome?
Among the early kings, only Numa, who deserved to die well, can 100
be seen as just.[67] Afterward the people brought to an end the evil

solvisset ac se liberum statuit fore.
Dum legibus paret, sibi gentes feras
105   orbemque totum subiugat late imperans.
Sed mox ubi libidini ius cesserat,
civile bellum surgit ac vaecors furor
confundit omnem civium concordiam.
Fit praeda; fit caedes per omne barbari
110   sceleris genus. Servile fert populus iugum,
cuius polos tetigerat arduos prius
sublime nomen, ne Iovi parcens quidem.
Non haec enim mortalium fiunt manu:
sed illius qui solus imperat omnibus,
115   quaecunque mundus altior complectitur
et siquid est inane quod mundum ambiat.
Mortalibus datur exequi nutum dei,
tanquam ministris qui nihil habent proprii.
Sic plurimis item bonis ac maximis
120   te reddit mirabilem populis deus,
Alphonse, cunctis gratia laudis tibi
bonitate partae. Quod sequi pergens diem
ad ultimam, felix eris vel mortuus.
Nam qui mori virtus queat, qua mors perit?
125   Vives in omne saeculum et nomen quidem
gens nulla conticescet excelsum tuum.
Sed quo mihi admirandus appares magis
meliorque caeteris, quibus sese ingerit
fortuna regibus favens, eo magis
130   cupido veri me tenendi concitat.
Quae causa nunc belli tibi? Qui vim intulit?
Qui turbat otium? Quis insidias locat?
Hosti peperceras nimis rebus tuis
gravi ac pudendo proximis conviciis,
135   ut his noceres quos vel invitus colas?

274

yoke of the kings and they decided that they would be free. And
as long as Rome observed the rule of law, she subjugated savage
nations abroad and held the whole world under her dominion. But   105
when law gave way to lust, civil war broke out and mad rage soon
destroyed all harmony among the citizens. There was plunder;
there was slaughter perpetrated through every sort of barbarous
crime. The people, whose lofty name had once reached the far   110
ends of the earth, now bore a servile yoke, injuring even Jove. For
these things are not done by mortal hands but by him who alone
rules all things which the lofty world encompasses and whatever   115
empty space exists that encircles the world. To mortals it is allot-
ted to do god's will, like servants who have nothing of their own.

Thus, Alfonso, because of your many great services, God makes
you wondrous in the eyes of all good and great peoples, thanks to   120
the praise you have acquired by your goodness. If you continue on
this path until the last day, you will be fortunate even when you
are dead. For how can virtue die, at whose hands death itself per-
ishes? You will live for all time and no nation in fact will pass over   125
your glorious name in silence. But the more admirable and the
more noble you appear in comparison to all other kings whom
Fortune favors, the more I am stirred by the desire to uphold the
truth.   130

What is the cause of your war now? Who initiated the vio-
lence? Who now disturbs the peace? Who instigates plots? Were
you too sparing of an enemy who threatened your kingdom and
whose most recent outrages were shameless, so that you have in-
jured those whom you would now court, even if unwillingly? I ask   135

Quaeso: qui arma infesta nunc agitant tua?
Quod ensis iste nudus exposcit latus?
Aliis nocere dum putas, noces tuis.
Florentiae nam quidquid infertur mali,
140   Blancae Philippi filiae illius tui,
Blancaeque natis et nepotibus ducis
infertur eius (quem benignum videras
in te benignitate vix incredibili),
Florentiae te causa nulla reddidit
145   hostem, nisi quod nolit in Venetum trucem
transire mentem, quae nihil sani cupit.
Piene possis quod negat pietas nefas?
Quisquis virum quisquis parentem laedere
molitur unus, num pudicae coniugi,
150   num filiis prodesse iudicabitur?
Accedit ad rem maius et quod maxime
spectes oportet. Si tibi victoriam
casus vel astrorum necessitas ferat,
cui victor adsis? Forsitan putas tibi.
155   Certe tui te cogitatus plurimum,
Alphonse, fallant. Regulum qui pertiment
reddatne tutos omnium rex maximus?
Venetis enim quid deest ut imperio gravi
Italos premant? Quod perfacile fiat quidem
160   sociis tuis armis, cave, sapiens, cave!
Nosti quibus terra marique viribus
pollent, quibusque opibus vigent, concordia
quam diligenti rebus in cunctis solent
uti. Nihil quod commodum ferat sibi,
165   omittit unquam vir Venetus acer, sagax.
Quid si potens qui neminem relinquere
inopem suae consuevit unquam dexterae,
victoriam dabit lacessitis deus?

you this: who is now driving your arms to war? What flank does that unsheathed sword of yours now seek? While you think of harming others, you do harm to your own people. For whatever harmful campaign has been launched against Florence has also been launched against Bianca, the daughter of your own Filippo, 140 and against the children of Bianca and the grandchildren of the duke (that kind soul who, as you saw, showed incredible magnanimity toward you). No cause has made you an enemy of Florence unless it is because that city is unwilling to change her attitude toward the hostile Venetian — and this is an attitude that aims at 145 nothing sound.[68] Could you dutifully do a wrong that duty forbids? Will the man who strives to harm a husband, to harm a parent, be thought to be helping his chaste wife or his children? 150

In addition, there is a more important issue and it is necessary that you consider this above all. If the position of the stars or fate does somehow bring victory to you, for whom would you be the victor? For yourself, you may think. But surely, Alfonso, you would be mistaken in such thoughts. Could the greatest king in 155 the world make those citizens feel safe who fear even the lord of a small principality?[69] But what do the Venetians so lack at home that causes them to threaten the rest of Italy with their oppressive empire? Beware of what could easily happen to your comrades in arms, beware, wise one! You know how great the Venetians' power 160 is on land and on sea and you know what enormous wealth they enjoy. You are also aware what careful agreements they are used to concluding in all their dealings. Typically wily and shrewd, the Venetian never forgets anything that might give him an advantage. 165

What if almighty God, who never leaves anyone bereft of his right arm, should give victory to those who have been attacked?

Praestare certe plurimum rebus tuis
170   laudique iudico tueri quos decet.
Amore si pergas pio et nunquam hostibus
faveas tuis adeo tibi ut obsis volens
sciensque! Nam si posteaquam miseris
revocare spiculum velis, nequeas quidem.
175   Quid pluribus pulso tuas auris monens
ut sus Minervam? Quid fides non audeat?
Vel hinc tibi mox sentiendum censeo
neutram vel in partem gubernaclo rates
tuo iuvandas quae ruinas afferant.
180   Quod siquid hinc forsan timendum cogites,
beneficiis adimendus est omnis metus.
Et antequam pelagus novi flatus ciant,
armanda navis omnibus rudentibus.
Videsne quos minitantur Alpes turbines,
185   quas sint procellas additurae fluctibus
Latii sali? Plaerumque ponto dexteras
qui conserunt dubio. Nocere mutuo
utrique dum cupiunt sibi — Zephyro alteri
Euro alteri fraeti — repente perfurit
190   Arctous axis et feris Aquilonibus
dum cuncta miscet, obruit praeceps fuga
utrosque. Vates opto sim falsus tamen.

Certainly I think it paramount for your own affairs and reputation
to protect those whom it is fitting to protect. If only you would   170
proceed with love for your friends[70] and never show such favor to
your enemy that you willingly and knowingly act against your own
interests! For afterwards, if you should wish to recall your spear
once you have hurled it, you might not be able to. But why should
I hammer away at you with advice, like the proverbial hog and Mi-   175
nerva?[71] What would loyalty not dare?

On the other hand, I think you ought to realize soon that ships
that would bring ruin to neither side must all the same be helped
by your taking the helm. If you think there is anything to be
feared, then all fear should be eradicated with generosity. And be-   180
fore new storms agitate the ocean,[72] your ship must be equipped
with all its ropes. Do you see what whirlwinds are menacing us
from the Alps and what gales they will bring to Latium's sea?   185
They usually engage in battle in dangerous waters. While both
sides strive to harm one another, one relying on Zephyr and the
other on Eurus, suddenly a north wind[73] from the pole rages, and   190
while it confounds all things with icy Aquilonian winds, a panic-
driven flight overwhelms both sides. And yet, I hope I may be a
false prophet still.

Non tibi plures moduli, Thalia,
    dantur. Pone silentium,
dum tamen quicquam referas quod aures
    nostri mulceat Aenici.
5   Hic enim mira pietate regem
        Alphonsum colit optimum.
Solus Alphonsus valet inquietos
    belli frangere turbines.
Portus o nostrae nimium Camoenae,
10   optate Aenice Davale,
lege qui certa regit omne caelum,
    quando sydera turbida
vertet ad nostros pius ille vultus
    ac lucem revehet bonam?
15   Quid ferum Martem dubiamque Pheben,
        quid tristem et gelidum senem
semper horremus? Redeant benigni
    Phoebus, Iupiter ac Cypris.
Dira quid tantum minitantur astra
20   his fulmen regionibus?
Divus Alphonsus trepidas procellas
    non tandem videt Alpium?
Quid iuvat tantos humeris labores
    semper tollere fortibus?
25   Est labor certe subeundus omnis
    et belli rabies feri

: 10 :

To Iñigo d'Avalos
That he should persuade Alfonso to seek peace

No more light little verses are dedicated to you, O Thalia. Make us silent until you can say something that might still soothe the ears of our Iñigo. For he serves the great King Alfonso with extraordinary loyalty.　　　　5

Only Alfonso can curb the restless winds of war. O you, safe harbor for our Camena,[74] most hoped-for Iñigo d'Avalos, when 10 will that righteous god, who rules all heaven with unvarying law, change the stormy stars and bring us good days again? Why should we always tremble before fierce Mars, uncertain Phoebe, and that cold and sorrowful old man?[75] May kindly Apollo, Ju- 15 piter, and Venus return. Why do dire stars threaten these lands with so much lightning? Does not divine Alfonso see the restless 20 storm-winds in the Alps?[76]

What use is it for brave shoulders to take on such great labors? Certainly all the toil and madness of savage war must be undertaken so that the joy of peace may return; for this will bring rest to 25

pacis ut tandem redeat voluptas,
    quae fessos requie iuvet.
Quid iuvat pacis placidam quietem
30   Martis vertere cuspide?
Caelitus nobis ratio tributa
    quid non imperio utitur
et trucis fraeno premit impotenti
    immanes animi feras?
35   Languidae vanis pecudes ferocem
    pastorem superent minis?
Nos nimis terror, nimium cupido
    caecat, quae tenebris tegit.
Nec sinit puras ut amemus auras
40   et lucem aetheris ardui.
Divus Alphonsus quid in arma praeceps
    fertur ceu leo saeviens?
Particeps quare velit esse fati
    ultro quod Venetos premit?
45   Liber ut victor superavit Indos
    urbes condidit inclytas
legibus cunctas decorans verendis
    et quidquid nutrit otium.
Vicit Aeneas Rutulos ut acres,
50   Martis praelia dispulit.
Qui felix unquam fuerit vocandus
    tractans arma peremniter?
Num⁹ deum motu canimus beatum
    qui gaudet requie sua?
55   Bella si gessit memoranda semper
    late gentibus omnibus,
si triumphales titulos ab hostis
    victi rettulit agmine,

the weary. What use is it to overturn the quiet calm of peace with
the lance of Mars? Why does not reason, a gift to us from heaven,   30
exercise its power? Why does it seek to arrest the bestiality of a
hostile mind with feeble reins? Could drowsy cattle, with their fu-
tile bellowing, overcome their bellicose herdsman? Terror and de-   35
sire for power blind men terribly, for they veil us in darkness.

Nor does war allow us to love the pure air and the light of high
heaven. Why is divine Alfonso swept headlong into war like a rag-   40
ing lion? Why would he willingly want to share the fate that bur-
dens the Venetians? When victorious Liber conquered the Indi-
ans, he founded famous cities, adorning them all with venerable   45
laws and whatever nurtures peace. And when Aeneas conquered
the fierce Rutulians, he drove away Mars' battles. Who could ever   50
be happy if called to bear arms year after year? Do we celebrate
a god prosperous in turbulence, who also rejoices in peace? If
Alfonso has always fought memorable wars with all nations far   55
and wide, if he has always returned from the battlefield with tri-

quid sibi Alphonsus cupit? Unde laudis
60   quaerit saemina maximae?
Est satis bello satis et labore
        partum? Plura quid appetit?
Saepe fortunae caput invidenti
        qui subdit dolet ultimum.
65 Finis humanis studiis petendus
        poni debet in omnibus.
Hunc enim noster nisi cogitatus
        spectet, quaerit inaniter.
Bella quem ponant sibi sumpta finem?
70   Pacem? Pace frui licet.
Ergo quid bellum petit? Unde surgit?
        Causam quaero periculi.
Sit satis tantas superasse gentes.
        Non simus reliquis graves.
75 Quisquis iniustis aliena votis
        poscit, numina provocat.
Quae suis reddens inimica rebus,
        sero quod voluit dolet.
Non ego certe Venetos perosus,
80   his te hortatibus alloquor.
Nanque iampridem Venetos amore
        omnis prosequor unice.
Me movet clades Italis futura,
        si ver dimicet alterum.
85 Nonne Francorum celerant catervae
        nostris cladibus inseri?
Quantus, heu, campos cruor et rapina
        stupris caedibus imbuet?
Quis vocat Francos socios furoris?
90   Quisquis bella novaverit,

umphal titles won from his vanquished enemies, what does he
want for himself? Where does he seek the seeds of the greatest
praise? Is glory won in war and through war's toil not enough? 60
Why does Alfonso seek more?

Whoever subjects himself to envious fortune, often grieves in
the end. A limit must be placed on all human efforts. Unless we 65
reflect on this limit, we seek aimlessly. But what end do wars that
are already underway set for themselves? Peace. One can enjoy
peace. Therefore why go to war? From what circumstances does 70
war arise? I search for the cause of our perils. May it be enough to
have conquered so many great nations. May we not be a burden to
those who remain. Whoever demands another's property with un-
just prayers provokes the wrath of the gods. Such a man makes 75
the gods hostile to his cause and grieves too late over the things he
wanted.

Since certainly I do not hate the Venetians, I approach you
with this counsel. For I have long held all the Venetians in special 80
affection. The future calamity facing the Italians moves me, should
another spring bring war. Do not regiments of French soldiers
hurry into the midst of our disasters? Alas, how much murder 85
and pillaging will stain our fields with rape[77] and slaughter? Who
summons the French as our comrades in madness?

Whoever initiates new wars, Alfonso alone can subdue arms; 90

solus Alphonsus valet arma, solus
    irae frangere fulmina.
Nanque si saevum retrahit tridentem,
    fluctus Hadria nesciat.
95   Omne mox caelum redeat serenum
    et Iuno tonitru vacet.
Sume tu iustas Italae querelae
    partes, Aenice Davale.
Non tibi parvas referent Camoenae
100   grates pro meritis tuis.
Ore facundo tumidi reflectens
    Alphonsi cita pectora,
nomen in cunctos tibi comparabis
    annos sole micantius.
105   Corpus extemplo perit omne. Fama
    durat quam bonitas parit.

he alone can break the lightning of wrath. For if he withdraws his savage trident, the Adriatic sea would know no further storm. The whole sky would return to calm and Juno would be free of thun- 95 der.[78] Champion, Iñigo d'Avalos, the just causes of a plaintive Italy and the Muses will bring you no small thanks for your talents. Move the passionate heart of proud Alfonso with your eloquent 100 speech and you will make your name brighter than the sun for all years to come. The entire body dies at once, but fame, to which 105 goodness gives birth, endures.

MELPOMENE
LIBER QUINTUS

: I :

Quem, Melpomene, laudibus unum
ex omnibus ad sydera tollas?
Mortalibus excellere cunctis
quem, Musa, canas voce sonora?
5   Dare nam turpe est terga Thaliae.
Age, dic aliquid carmine dignum.
Aliud convenit alii. Non est
quod idem sit dignum omnibus unum.
Laus militiae ducis est clari,
10   medici si curaverit apte;
gravidos auro loculos facere
est eius qui pelago merces
ac terra vehit undique multas;
at rhetoris ut dicat ab arte
15   idque salutem ut pariat iustis.
Probitatis laudabitur ille
quod turpe pati nolit. At alter
cumulatae virtutis, in enses
quod se intrepide dederit pugnans,
20 captae patriae ductus amore.
Nihil omnino temnimus ullam
bonitatis quod tulerit prae se
vel perexiguam debilis umbram.

MELPOMENE
BOOK FIVE

To Charles VII
Encomium, urging him to liberate Constantinople

Whom, uniquely among all men, would you raise to the stars with
praise, O Melpomene?[1] Whom would you celebrate in sonorous
tones as surpassing all other men? For it is shameful to be routed
by Thalia. Come, say something worthy of song. An encomium   5
for one man does not suit another; if it did, one eulogy would fit
all. Praise belongs to the general renowned in war and the physi-
cian if he cures well. The merchant wins glory if he heaps coffers   10
high with gold when he transports many goods over land and sea.
Orators, however, are praised for speaking artfully and bringing
safety to the just.[2] The righteous man will be lauded for not toler-   15
ating disgrace. Still another—a man of the highest bravery—is
praised because he hurls himself fearlessly into the thick of battle,
impelled by the love of his native city under siege. We condemn   20
nothing wholly if it yields some thin shadow of goodness, however
fragile.

At nunc mera Melpomenen virtus
25   iuvat. Atque merum dicere gaudet
verum dea; nam reprobat ficta.
Si Melpomene ducere veris,
veniat. Veniat Karolus ille,
pia quo gaudet Francia rege.
30   Deus hunc rebus dedit humanis,
fuget ut tenebras, revehat lucem,
puniat sontes, statuat iustus
quaeque meruerint praemia rectis.
Res gessisti, Karole, magnas,
35   quas interitus nesciat ullas,
quas et populi celebrent omnes,
quosque cadens et quos videt oriens
sol, quos Boreas perfltat et Auster.
Tibi trux Anglus cessit, abactus
40   patrio regno tibi surrepto
fraude tuorum, regnaque victus
dedit in meritam sceleris poenam.
Nihil impunitum deus unquam
sinit omni potens, tribuens cuique
45   quod promeruit munus habere.
Deus afflixit durius Anglum,
quoniam quod non decuit voluit.
Sic te, Karole, quoniam fueris
pius, affecit numen honore.
50   Te precor igitur mente volutes
deus ut iustis magna rependit.
Nec enim patitur vincier unquam
meritis, qui nos morte redemit,
patiens quidquid livor et ira
55   potuit dirius impia facere.
Deus ingratos odit eosque

But pure virtue pleases Melpomene. The goddess enjoys speaking the pure truth, for she rejects lying. If Melpomene leads the way to truth, let her come. May Charles also come, in whom pious France rejoices. God has given this man to the world so that a just man may drive out the darkness, restore light, punish the guilty, and grant to the righteous the rewards they deserve. You, Charles, have done great deeds that will be immortal, deeds celebrated by all peoples on whom the rising and sinking sun gazes and whom Boreas and Auster temper with their winds. The hostile Englishman has yielded to you, for he has been expelled from the ancestral kingdom stolen from you through the treachery of your own countrymen. Now defeated, he has given you back your kingdom in just punishment for his crimes. Almighty God never allows any crime to go unpunished, but to each he gives the reward he deserves. He inflicted a harsher punishment upon the Englishman because he wanted what was not fitting.

But since you have been so pious, Charles, the deity has treated you with honor. I beg you therefore to consider how God bestows great rewards upon the just; nor does he who redeemed us from death, having suffered every outrage that impious wrath and spite could inflict, ever allow those who are deserving to be vanquished. God hates those who are ungrateful and he torments them, having weighed their sins on his evenly-balanced scales.[3]

aequa expendens cruciat lance.
Docet id daemon primus, ab alto
solio tenebras fusus in imas.
60   Docet id generis pater humani,
cuius luimus miseri culpam.
Pius es, Karole, semper et idem
memor in primis meriti quo te
deus ornavit. Karole, regum
65   decus o summum, suscipe Christi
signa petentis et irrue fortis
impia properans agmina Turci
loeto tradere. Moenia qui nunc
Thraiciae premit, heu, sacra Romae
70   barbarus audax puer immanis,
Arabis[1] referens omne latronis
scelus et nomen trux Mahometus!
Heu, quam vereor sera futura[2]
tua, Karole rex, arma ruinae
75   quae manet urbem saeva cadentem.
Via nam longa est. Barbarus hostis
premit innumero milite muros.
Geminant ictus. Aerea molis,
quae fulmineo turbine iactant
80   horrisonis[3] tormenta sagittis
sociata tot ut rapiant lucem
oculis hominum Marte sub effero.
Propera, propera, maxime regum
Karole, nostri gloria saecli
85   spesque labantis sola salutis!
Fer opem miserae quae ruit urbi!
Ea si ruerit, quanta piorum[4]
capiet clades nomen et omnes

This the first demon teaches, for he was hurled from his high throne to the depths of the dark abyss. The father of the human race also teaches this, for we wretched men must expiate his sin. 60 Likewise you, Charles, are always mindful, above all, of the favor God has shown you. O Charles, highest glory among kings, take up the standards of the militant Christ, bravely attack the impious 65 legions of the Turks, and hasten to consign them to death. For now, laying siege to the sacred walls of Thracian Rome is, alas, a proud and savage barbarian boy, evoking the name and crimes of 70 the Arab brigand—savage Mahomet.[4] Alas, how I fear, King Charles, that your forces will be too late for the savage ruin that awaits the falling city. For the journey is long. 75

The barbarian enemy and his untold horde lay siege to the walls. They redouble their assaults. The bronze missiles of this mass of men, which they launch with the force of a whirlwind, are 80 so numerous that together with their shrieking arrows they blot out the sun, stealing the very light from men's eyes in this brutal war. O Charles, greatest of kings, glory of our century, and sole hope of our waning safety, hasten! Bring aid to the poor city, 85 which is falling. And if it falls, how great a disaster will befall the

quibus est sancto Christus in ore.
90   Quae cruciatus poena manebit?
Si durum illum viceris hostem
referesque piis signa triumphis
splendida barbaricis, eris unus
quem Melpomene nostra per omnis
95   laudes pergens aequet Olympo.

: 2 :

Quo te, Alfonse, magis mecum, rex, mente voluto,
    te magis admiror, te magis usque colo.
Non est una quidem quae te super aethera virtus
    mira laude ferat; omnibus ipse nites.
5   Hunc decorat pietas: hic est et iuris et aequi,
    laudibus insignis. Praestat at ille fide.
Relligione alius pollet. Fidentius arma
    alter obit tractans bella tremenda manu.
Hic sese humanum gaudet facilemque videri
10   et moderata cupit ordine quaeque gerens.
Hunc delectat honos, quisquis debetur honesto,
    abiectumque nihil nec muliebre sapit
consilium. Multos laudat prudentia rerum
    quos sibi conciliat multus ubique chorus.
15   Alter in eloquii campo spaciatur ovantis,
    qui plus posse putat quam genus omne virum.
Quaerit Olympiacos alius studiosius orbes
    occultasque vias astriferasque vices.

294

name of the devout and all men on whose lips the name of Christ
still lives. What punishment for his torture will await us?   90

But if you conquer the harsh enemy and if you will hoist again
our own flags, resplendent with holy triumphs over the barbarians,
you will be the one whom our Melpomene lifts to lofty Olympus
with all her paeans of praise.   95

: 2 :

To King Alfonso
In praise of love and poetry, not war

The more I think about you, King Alfonso, the more I admire and
cherish you. There is no one virtue that elevates you to the skies
with extraordinary praise; rather, you yourself are resplendent in
all the virtues.

A sense of duty graces one man; another is distinguished by ac-
colades, for he is a man of justice and the law.[5] But another is   5
peerless in loyalty. Still another is powerful in sanctity. One man,
who more boldly takes up arms, engages in fearful wars. Yet an-
other is simply happy to appear humane, cultivated, and good-na-
tured. He loves moderation and does everything in due order. The   10
honor that is owed an honest man delights another, and he em-
braces no task that is undistinguished or womanish. Many are
praised for their prudence in affairs of state, and they are courted
by great crowds everywhere. One man strides onto the stage of
joyous eloquence — for this man thinks he is more capable than   15
any other sort of man. Another is more interested in Olympian
spheres, secret paths, and the movements of the stars. Still others

Quae natura regat, qui rerum firmior usus,
20   cuius ad exemplar prodeat omne genus,
disquirunt alii. Sed tu potes omnia solus,
        nil intemptatum qui facis esse tibi.
Nam cum te noris divina lege creatum,
        qui vel agas semper vel studeas sapere,
25   otia nulla tibi permittis inania, nulli
        desidiae servis. Totus es ipse tibi.
Hinc omnem penitus virtutem amplecteris; omne
        quod facit ut sapias, nocte die sequeris.
Nec tibi do vitio quod, tactus harundine fulva,
30   semper amas. Vires ingenio dat Amor.
Quin si vera loqui liceat nec ficta referre,
        semper amor magnis vult comes esse viris.
Caesar et Augustus flagrasse Cupidinis igni
        fertur. Alexandrum quam sibi iunxit Amor!
35   Nam quid ego memorem sibi quos pietate vetustas
        duxit honorandos, cum Posidone Iovem
et Phoebum et Martem et qui Garamantas et Indos
        stravit et Alciden innumerosque deos?
Francorum domitor regum tutela paterque
40   sentit amoriferas Karolus ipse faces.
Karolus orbe micat inter nomina tanquam
        splendidus astrifero Delius ipse polo.
Hunc si tangit amor, quid non tangaris amore?
        Quod licuit superis, quid tibi non liceat?
45   O me felicem qui te sim nactus amicum;
        nanque pares sola praestat amicicia.
Nec dedigneris mihi quod dicaris amicus,
        pro meritis alium dum bonus alter amat.
Te quasi numen ego veneror. Te prosequor omni
50   officii cultu nec pietate minus.

investigate nature's domain: they ask what a more valid use of things might be and toward what model every genus progresses.[6] 20

But you alone are capable of it all since you leave nothing untried. For since you know you have been created by divine law — indeed you are one who always acts or strives to act with prudence — you allow yourself to spend no time in pointless leisure; nor do you do anything in the service of sloth. You are completely 25 your own lord and master. Therefore you embrace every virtue and all that will increase your wisdom you pursue night and day.

Nor do I reckon as a fault in you that you are always in love, stung by Amor's golden arrow. Love strengthens one's mind and nature.[7] Moreover, if one is permitted to speak the truth and not 30 lie, Love always wants to be the companion of great men. Caesar and Augustus are said to have burned with Love's flames. Think how much Amor enlisted Alexander in his cause! But why should I mention those whom the ancients believed should be honored 35 for their devotion to Love, who laid low Jupiter as well as Poseidon, both Apollo and Mars, the Garamantians and the Indians, Alcides and innumerable other gods? Charles himself — the father and guardian of the French and the conqueror of kings — knows the fiery brands of Love. Charles shines throughout the world 40 among the names of kings, just as Delian Apollo himself glows resplendent in the starry firmament. If Love touches this man, why should you not be touched by Love? Why should what is permitted to the gods not be permitted to you?

Ah, what a happy man I am to have won you as my friend, for 45 friendship alone makes men equals. Nor should you think it unworthy that you should be called my friend, since one good man loves another for his merits. I revere you as a god; I honor you with every service and loyalty. I think that there is nothing in my 50

Te mihi nil vita duco iucundius omni.
　　Tu mihi praesidium, tu mihi magnus honos.
Nam quanti nostrum facias, rex tantus, amorem
　　perspicuum nuper te mihi reddideras.
55　　Non solum affatu modo nos, Alphonse, benigno
　　excipis et pulchris muneribus cumulas;
at geminis etiam reddimus insignibus omnes
　　ut norint rarum nos opus esse tuum;
meque inter proceres numeras quos evehit aula
60　　regia. Quid multis? Me facis esse tuum.
Me fortunatum, me terque quaterque beatum
　　principe te duco. Tu mihi numen ades.
At quid ego meritis pro tantis quibo referre,
　　rex Alphonse, tibi? Quid tibi retribuam?
65　　Non opis est, Alphonse, meae praestare quid, ipse
　　multa movens, animus pectore gratus avet.
Ast illud certe non indignantibus ausim
　　vel diis vel Musis, quod reor usque fore.
Nam te posteritas, quantum mea carmina possint,
70　　per grave virtutis nulla silebit opus.
Haec te sola quidem pulchris cum laudibus unum
　　effert, fortunam quae iubet esse suam.
Haec tibi conciliat quos ulla probatior ornat,
　　vel doctrina potens ingeniumve ferax.
75　　Virtus sola probis te, rex Alphonse, verendum
　　et formidandum te facit una malis.
Hinc omnes adeunt omni te ex orbe diserti
　　ac docti, radiis qui caluere tuis.
Hinc tibi quotidie pulchros ex hoste triumphos
80　　consequeris, dum te stultus ad arma vocat.
Undique bella fremunt; frueris tu munere solus
　　pacis honoratae bella nefanda vetans.

life that pleases me more than you. You are my fortress; you repre-
sent great honor to me. For recently you made clear to me how
important you, so great a king, consider my love for you. For you
not only welcome me with kind words, but you shower me with   55
beautiful gifts. We shall reciprocate, however, with similar gifts so
that all men will know that we are your rare creation. Moreover,
you reckon me among the leading men whom your royal court
hosts. What more should I say? That you make me yours. With   60
you as my prince, I hold myself a fortunate man, a man thrice and
four times blessed. To me, you are a divinity.

But how can I repay your many kindnesses, King Alfonso?
What recompense can I give you in return? It is not in my power
to offer what my grateful heart longs for, though much has been   65
undertaken. But certainly I may venture to say what I think will
happen — if the gods and the Muses are not offended. If my po-
ems are successful, no future generation will be silent about you
because of the weighty impact of your virtue. Virtue alone, who   70
causes Fortune to do her bidding, extols you uniquely with beauti-
ful praises. She wins over to your cause those men whom a quality
more acclaimed than any other embellishes, whether it is fertile
erudition or a powerful mind. Virtue alone makes you, King
Alfonso, venerated by the good and feared by the wicked.   75

And so, all the eloquent and learned men from every region
come to this court of yours, men who are inspired by your bril-
liance. This is why you win beautiful victories over the enemy ev-
ery day, as long as he is foolish enough to challenge you in arms.
Everywhere war roars. Yet you alone, by forbidding impious wars,   80

Iupiter e summa dum terras despicit arce,
    dumque sagax cernit pectora vana virum
85   inconcussa quidem solio vestigia servans
    ipse suo, terrae culmina cuncta movet.
At face fulminea celsas transverberat urbes
    prosternitque solo. Seque docet dominum.
Hactenus haec. Nam plura tibi narrare volentem
90   impediit Xenophon qui celeraret iter.
Hic igitur coram referet tibi filius omnem
    et mentem patris atque animum veniens.
Quare quidquid erit quod nostro nomine natus
    dixerit, id totum manat ab ore patris.

⋮ 3 ⋮

Cum nobis sonipes, Sphortia, muneri
    abs te datur, παῖ φίλτατε,
affers laeticiam Pieridum choris
    et Libero et Φοίβῳ πατρί.
5   Dat fratri citharam Mercurius sacram.
    Parnasus et Ζεὺς τέρπεται.
Te cunctis probitas inclyta gentibus
    clarum facit καὶ τοῖς θεοῖς.
Qui natum patre te magnanimo neget
10   dignum, sui λήθη πονεῖ.
Non est laudibus aedenda benignitas
    vulgaribus σοῦ τοῦ κλυτοῦ.

reap the rewards of honorable peace. While Jupiter looks down
upon the earth from his lofty citadel and discerns in his wisdom
the vain hearts of men, while keeping his feet firmly in his own
domain, he moves all the summits and mountain ridges on earth   85
and strikes the proud cities with his fiery brands, leveling them to
the ground. He teaches that he alone is lord.

But enough of this. For Senofonte,[8] who hastens to be on his
way, prevents me from saying more, though I would be willing.   90
And so, my son will relay his father's thoughts and purpose to
you, face to face, when he arrives. Thus, everything that my son
will report in my name will come from his father's lips.

: 3 :

To Sforza Secondo[9]
Thanks for the gift of a horse

Since you have given me the gift of a horse, O Sforza, dearest boy,
you bring happiness to the Pierian Muses, to father Liber[10] and to
Phoebus Apollo. For when Mercury gave the sacred lyre to his
brother, Parnassus and Zeus also took pleasure. Your celebrated   5
virtue has brought you fame not only among all nations but also
the gods. Whoever would deny that you are a son worthy of your
magnanimous father does so forgetful of himself. But your kind-   10
ness, illustrious one, should not be made known to the world with

Ergo te merito diligo, Sphortia,
    et dignor his τοῖς ἄσμασι
15   vel Graiis cupiens reddere nobilem
    cunctisque nos εὐμνήμονας.

⁞ 4 ⁞

Quam miserae nuper Lydae, Gonzaga, salutem
    abstuleras abiens, hanc tibi mittit amans.
'Heu, heu, quam durus tristi mihi nuncius auris
    perculit attonitas, qui te abiisse tulit.
5   Serta tibi digytis texebam florea caris,
    Karole, quae digytis mox cecidere meis.
Ah, quam crudelem mihi te, mea vita, dedisti,
    qui fugiens Lydam liqueris ecce tuam.
Si melior speranda tibi fortuna dabatur,
10   hanc mihi communem cur fore nolueras?
Sin te praesentis senium, mi Karole fortis,
    ceperat, hoc odio cur digna fui?
Quem mihi nunc animum, dum teque tuasque recordor
    blandicias, ludos, basia, adesse putas?
15   Quo mihi dulcis eras magis et iucundior omni
    luce, magis moveor excruciorque magis.
Hei, mihi dum memini placidos sub nocte susurros,
    terque quaterque suas corpora lassa vices,
quam vellem tecum vel me simul esse vel unam
20   dicier insidiis disperiisse tuis.

ordinary praises. Thus, I rightly esteem you, O Sforza, and I be-
lieve you are deserving of these odes, since I long to make you re-
nowned even among the Greeks and to make myself memorable   15
among all men.

: 4 :

To Carlo Gonzaga
His lover Lyda laments Carlo's absence

As to how you, Gonzaga, recently ruined poor Lyda's life when
you went away, your lover sends you this letter: "How harsh a
message has come, alas, telling me you have gone away. I am
stunned and sad. With loving hands, Carlo, I was weaving gar-
lands of flowers for you, which fell from my hands. Ah, how cru-   5
elly you treated me, my darling. Look, by fleeing you have aban-
doned your own Lyda. If you were given the better chance you
hoped for, why did you not want me to share it? If sadness for   10
your present lot in life had seized you, my good Carlo, why have I
been deserving of this anger? When I think of you, remembering
your sweet words, your games and your kisses, what do you be-
lieve is in my heart now? The more pleasing and the more sweet
you have been to me than all life, the more I am shaken and tor-   15
mented now. Ah, when I recall our soft whisperings in the night,
our bodies three and four times exhausted by their service, how
much I want either to be with you or to have it said that I per-
ished alone because of your treachery. For I remember when you   20

Nam memini cum me nudam complectere nudus,
    dum iungis roseis dulcia labra labris,
dicebas 'Utinam liceat sic usque manere,
    nec nox infesto cedat amica die.'

25 Cum mathutinus Titan spectaret eoum
    iamque suum surgens acceleraret iter,
'Intempestiva quid nos, sol invide (dixti),
    luce premis? Quid nos, invide sol, dirimis?'
Multaque cum molli gemitu suspiria ducens,
30   in sudore tremens totus eras calido;
et dum posticae valvas abiturus iniquae
    pandis, adhuc repetis terque quaterque thorum.
Nec potes avelli quae te complexa tenebam,
    nec sinis avelli quam sub amore foves.

35 At nunc noster amor quo sic evanuit ille,
    qui tibi tum fuerat hortulus, aura, deus?
Quam sumus — oh, stultae! Dementia quanta puellas
    nos rapit! Ah, quantus error in ore sedet!
Tu me dum blandis nudam complecteris ulnis,
40   lumina componens et simulata loquens,
'O mea,' dicebas, 'lux! O mea vita salusque!
    Quam me felicem tu facis una virum!
Lyda, tibi iuro per sacra cupidinis arma,
    perque piam Venerem, perque tuos oculos:
45 optio si detur, te malim nocte dieque
    usque frui dici quam merus orbis herus.'
Haec mihi fingebas vultusque in verba disertus
    indutus similis insidiosus eras.
Nescia nanque doli fraudumque ignara tuarum,
50   me fortunatam rebar amore pari.
Temnebam cunctos qui me, quam despicis olim,
    ardebant. Solus tu mihi numen eras.

were naked and held me, also naked, in your arms, while you
pressed your sweet lips to my rosy mouth, you said: 'How I wish
that I could stay here and that our friend, the night, would not
surrender to her enemy, the day!' When early morning Titan
looked at the dawn and sped away on his journey, as he rose you 25
said: 'O jealous sun, why do you disturb us with this untimely
light? And why, jealous sun, do you separate us?'[11]

"Drawing many a sigh with tender moans, you were trembling
all over, sweating and hot; and even as you spread open the panels 30
of the unfriendly backdoor when you were about to leave, even at
this point, again you returned to the bed—three and four times!
Nor could you be torn away from me who held and embraced you.
Nor did you allow her whom you caressed so lovingly to be torn
away from you. But where has that love of ours gone now, which 35
to you in those days was a garden, a soft breeze, a god? Ah, how
foolish we girls are! What madness seizes us! Ah, how much
wrong the lips can do! With loving arms and eyes closed, you em-
braced me and I was naked; and speaking words you didn't mean,
you said, 'O my light, O my life, and my safe haven! How happy a 40
man you make me—you only! I swear on the sacred shafts of Cu-
pid, on holy Venus, and on your very eyes, Lyda: if I had the
choice, I would rather enjoy you night and day than be called lord 45
of the entire world.'

"These were the lies you told me and the false face you put on:
you spoke skillfully but you were full of treachery. For unaware of
your trickery and not suspecting your deceit, I thought myself for-
tunate in a love between equals. And I, whom you now despise, 50
used to spurn all the men who burned with love for me. You alone

Nec de plebe quidem iuvenes contempsimus, at quos
    et genus et virtus et decorabat honos.
55   Clara pudiciciae titulis tollebar in astra,
    haec me cum fama deseruit celebri.
Te—propter patrem simul et genus omne virumque—
    dum duco nihili, sum quoque facta nihil.
Quid me crudelis, Venetis qua forte puellis
60   obrueris presens, destituis miseram?
Scribe aliquid tandem. Placidis me accerse tabellis.
    Dic veniam. Quod si iusseris, en adero.
Sin te nostra minus Cypris delectat amorque,
    dic saltem. Noli tundere, 'Lyda, vale.'
65   At vos si sapitis, vobis meliora, puellae,
    consulite, o Venetae, quam mihi consului.
Karolus innumeras ardens Gonzaga puellas
    in nullam stabili perflat amore diu.'
Accusat querulis, amice, Lyda
70   te, Gonzaga, modis. Nec audit ullum
    quod possis adhibere sic querenti
    defensor genus acre veritatis.
    Est ingens nimis illa vis amoris,
    quam flama genuit pari voluptas
75   ac caecus puer et Venus proterva.
    Ast ingentior illa rursus et quae
    sit radicibus altius subactis
    ac multo magis omnibus colenda,
    quam virtus peperit. Poeta certe
80   de te iure queratur unus ille,
    quem virtus tibi, qua micas in omnis
    illustris proceres, piis amoris
    vinclis conciliavit atque iunxit.
    Huic et tu pariter, quod esset idem
85   visus non alienus a probatis

were my god. Nor was I contemptuous of young men from the
plebs only; for I dismissed even those whom virtue, noble birth,
and honor graced. Famed for the honors paid to Chastity,[12] I was
exalted to the stars, though she soon deserted me together with   55
my illustrious fame. While for the sake of my father, my husband,
and my whole sex[13] I think of you as nothing, I too have become
nothing. Why, cruel one, have you abandoned me in my misery for
a place where you are now besieged, as it happens, by Venetian
girls?[14] Now finally, write me something! Summon me to you with   60
gentle notes. Tell me I should come. And if you make it a com-
mand, lo and behold, I will be there.

"But if our Cyprian goddess and our love displeases you, at
least speak. Do not bruise me with the words, 'Lyda, goodbye.'
But if you are wise, O Venetian girls, look out for yourselves more
carefully than I have done for myself. Carlo Gonzaga loves many   65
girls. Yet in none does he invest himself for long in a stable love."

Lyda accuses you, Gonzaga, my friend, in plaintive elegies.[15]
Nor does she listen to any bitter sort of truth you could offer in   70
self-defense against her complaints. For too great is the power of
love, which pleasure and the blind boy and reckless Venus have
created with equal fire. But mightier still is that power[16] born of   75
virtue, whose roots have been planted more deeply and which all
men should venerate more highly. Certainly this poet, for one,
could rightly complain about you, since it was your virtue — which 80
causes you to shine brilliantly among all the great princes — that
won him over and allied you to him with the pious chains of love.
And in just the same way, since you certainly thought this man
was no stranger to virtue, you have been a friend sweeter than nec- 85
tar to him.

omnino titulis, eras amicus
suavis nectareo magis liquore.
Ast hunc, Hadriacos ubi recessus
felix incolis et beata regna,
90   oblitus nec amore nec benigno
dignaris, vir amice, quo solebas
affatu. Modo Martis efferati
vis et suspicionis improbatae
formido potuisset impedire
95   scribendi officium — quod ipse nunquam
sane deserui. Nec ullus aestus
ponti, nec rabies Noti, nec ulla
tempestas vetuit mihi decorum.
Qui laudem sequitur meram, nec atrae
100   se culpae socium facit, susurros
vulgi non timet impudentis ullos.
At postquam precibus petita cunctis
pax tandem rediit, nec ullus usquam
impendet metus et vacat nocendi
105   omnis suspicio mihi roganti.
Si Lydam minus audias querentem,
ni responderis ore quo solebas,
excusatio nulla te tuetur.
Dic, sodes, Venetus senatus an te
110   pulchre pro meritis amare pergit?
Verum id non equidem queam vereri.
Nam longe Venetus referre plura
ac maiora solet gravis senatus
quam susceperit. At velim secundo
115   hoc audire loco. Tibine carus
est ut semper erat tuus poeta?
Dicis. Fac videant quod ipse novi:
quam me diligis atque amas benigne.

But now that you are living happily, oblivious of us, in distant Adriatic towns and prosperous realms, my friend, you do not deem me worthy of either love or the kindly words which you cus- 90 tomarily bestowed on me. Only the power of savage Mars and the fear of an unjust accusation could have stood in the way of my duty to write: this duty I have never abandoned. Nor have swell- 95 ing seas, raging winds, or storms of any sort kept me from fulfill-ing my obligation. Whoever pursues only praise and does not make himself a partner in clandestine crime does not fear the whisperings of the ignorant mob. But finally, after all our prayers, 100 long-awaited peace has returned. Fear no longer hangs over our heads, nor can there be any suspicion of my doing harm when I make my request. If you fail to listen to Lyda when she reproaches 105 you, if you do not send word to her as you used to do, no excuse will protect you.

Say, if you will, does the Venetian Senate continue to esteem you so splendidly for your merits? But indeed, about this I can 110 have no fear. For the august Venetian senate usually talks about greater and more generous recompense than it will eventually pro-vide.

But I would like to hear news on another topic. Is your poet as 115 dear to you as he always was? You say that he is. Make sure that they are aware of what I myself know: how much you care for me

Omnes dissimiles tui simulque
120   qui sese similes volunt, ut omnis
laetetur probitas tibique semper
optet quae cupis. At mali gemiscant.

: 5 :

Qui minus summum gregis innocentis
praesulem novit, meritis supremis
quem vocat Quintum pia Nicolaum
    concio Christi,
5   se sciens fallit. Quis enim coruscis
nesciat Phoebum radiis micantem
Gangis a primis populis eoi
    Hesperon usque?
Quintus in terris referens tonantem
10   sol velut splendet. Meritis probatae
mentis et cunctos pietate vincit
    sanctus et acer.
Quis queat laudes patris huius alti
cantibus summas paribus referre?
15   Quem stupent reges, populi verentur,
    orbis adorat?
Unus hic nobis bonitate vera
reddit. Et coram facit esse Christum,
quem sequens cunctis imitatur usque
20   moribus unum.

and how dearly you love me. All men are different from you and yet at the same time they want to be like you, so that all probity 120 will rejoice and hope always for what you want for yourself. But let the evil men lament.

: 5 :

To Pope Nicholas V
Celebrating his election to the papacy and urging a Crusade

Whoever knows little about the highest priest of Christ's innocent flock, a man of supreme virtue crowned Nicholas the Fifth by the Holy Council, knowingly cheats himself. For who of the first peo- 5 ples on earth—all the way from the eastern Ganges to western Hesperus—would not have known Phoebus gleaming with his shimmering rays? Nicholas shines like the sun, while he resembles 10 Jove, the Thunderer, on earth. Both holy and keen-spirited, he surpasses all men in his goodness and the merits of his beautiful mind. Who would be capable of singing the highest praises of this lofty father with appropriate songs? Whom do kings adore and 15 nations revere? Whom does the whole world worship? One man restores truth to us with his goodness. Nicholas renders Christ present to men: him alone he follows and imitates in all his laws and conduct. Hymn this father with worthy praises, my Muse. 20

Hunc refer dignis, mea Musa, patrem
laudibus quantum numeris et ore
quiveris. Vitam gradibus citatis
    perge per omnem.
25   Hic erat Thomas genitus secundis
motibus caeli placido iubente
rege qui mundum moderatur omnem
    lege perenni.
Qui tener postquam docilis vel infans
30   coepit iniectos tenuisse sensus,
sustulit sacrum caput ad supernas
    impiger arces.
Nil inhumana fragilique sorte
esse ducebat precio petendum.
35   Quidquid arceret mare, terra, flamae,
    quidquid et aer,
omne censebat celeri procella
pro dei nutu chaos in profundum
inde cessurum, nihil esse saeclum
40   quod sit in omne.
Nam, quod et tempus recipit, putabat,
temporis legi subici ruentis;
ast id aeternum, moveat quod ipsum
    mobile nunquam.
45   Solus huic mentem superum movebat
rector is, qui de nihilo creavit
quidquid in mundum spatiatur omnem,
    trinus et unus.
Sic ubi saecli didicit fugacis
50   quidquid inquirit studium sciendi
vimque cognovit rationis omnem,
    fertur in altum,

Do as much with words and rhythm as you can: move through his
entire life at a quick pace.

When the serene king who rules the universe with immortal   25
law issued the order and sent favorable omens, this man Tommaso
was born. After he, a tender and quiet child, began to have in-
spired perceptions, he quickly raised his holy head to the sublime   30
citadels above. He considered that nothing should be pursued for
gain in this cruel and fragile life. Whatever ocean, earth, fire, and   35
air enclosed he believed would lapse into deepest chaos with a
swift wind at a nod from God. There is nothing, he thought, that
can exist for all time. For whatever time retains, he thought, is   40
subjected to the law of onrushing time; that alone is eternal which
moves but can never be moved itself.[17]

This man's mind has been moved only by the ruler of the gods,   45
who, being three-fold and unitary,[18] created and expanded the
whole universe from nothing. And so when Thomas had mastered
whatever field of knowledge he pursued in this fleeting era and   50
when he came to know the whole force of reason, he was lifted up

quidquid aeternae stabilisque mentis
splendor illustrat super omne caelum,
55   ac super si quid simulant inane,
        perspicit acer.
Novit in quantis tenebris volutum
errat humanum genus et quod omnis
nostra spe vana trahitur cupido,
60   caeca furensque.
Nam quid in terris humilique mundo
est quod optemus? Perit omne votum
cuius ut compos fueris. Quid ultra
        sis habiturus?
65   Nil diu firmum parat ipsa nobis,
quam vocat vulgus rudis imperita
voce 'Fortunam'; nihil ipsa magnum
        tradere possit.
Quid queat corpus tibi polliceri,
70   cuius infirmum iacet omne robur?
Sola mens mortem fugit; una regem
        novit Olympi.
Mens deum forma simili bonoque
reddit interno. Viget una solum,
75   quaeque si vitam tulit innocentem,
        fit dea caeli.
Hos habens Thomas bene cogitatus,
se sibi totum studium per omne
vindicat.[5] Nec se speculatus extra
80   ducitur aura.
Nil nisi Christum putat esse solum
quod bonum dici queat. Et supremum
quem sibi quisquis statuit, fit alti
        civis Olympi.

on high—to whatever the splendor of his eternal and unwavering mind illuminated throughout the whole of heaven. And if the things he saw took the forms of anything worthless, he quickly 55 perceived it. He knew in what great darkness the human race wanders and that our every desire, blind and mad, is fueled by vain hope. For what can we hope for on earth and in this poor world? 60 Every prayer dies as soon as it has been answered. Why would you hold onto it after this?

She herself, whom the ignorant rabble crudely call "Fortune," 65 provides nothing lasting for us, nor can she can hand down anything of importance. What can the body promise you when all its strength grows feeble? Mind alone escapes death; this one faculty 70 knows the king of Olympus. The mind reflects God form and inner good: it alone thrives alone; and if it has borne a blameless life, it becomes a divinity in heaven.[19] Holding these ideas, Tommaso 75 frees himself completely through all his study. Nor, looking outside himself, is he guided by the favor of fortune. He thinks that 80 nothing except Christ can be called the good. And whoever establishes the lord Christ as the one supreme good for himself becomes a citizen of lofty Olympus.

85 Ergo quis quenquam stupor occupavit,
   si patrem tanta pietate sacri
   in locum coetus statuere Christi
    orbis in arce?

   Nanque qui Thomas fuerat per annos
90 ante tam multos cito Nicolaus
   fit dei iussu veterumque Quinto
    ordine patrum.

   Non id humani posuit voluntas
   nomen erroris, nec amor, nec ullus
95 gratus affectus. Deus ipse iussit
    quod fore norat.

   Vincet hic omnes populos protervi
   barbari, nostrae fidei ruinam
   quisquis extremam minitatur unus
100   teter atroxque.

   Num queant tantas Arabis[6] nefanda
   furta periuri tenebras latronis
   omne per dirum facinus supernae
    fundere luci?

105 Turcus ac omnis Syrus, Afer, Indus,
   omnis Aegyptus, Scytha, Persa, Medus
   fracta submittet patris huius artis
    colla cathaenis.

   Te deus lassis dedit ipse terris,
110 Quinte, qui templi solium supremi
   sanctus et fortis, sapiens piusque
    pace gubernes.

   Pontifex tanta bonitate pollens
   sit diu nobis, pater et sacerdos,
115 pastor et Christi gregis imperator,
    rexque salusque.

Therefore, why should it have surprised anyone that the holy   85
council has elected a father of such great piety as Christ's deputy
in the citadel of the world? For he who had been Tommaso for so
many years quickly became Nicholas V, at the command of God   90
and the venerable fathers. It was neither the velleity of human de-
lusion, or love, or any pleasing affection that established his re-
nown. God himself commanded what he knew would come to be.   95
For Nicholas will be the victor over all the peoples of the violent
barbarian;[20] a man, cruel and hideous, who uniquely threatens the
utter destruction of our religion. Surely now the infamous pillag-   100
ing of the lying Arab thief will no longer be capable of pouring
with every dire villainy so much darkness over such heavenly light?

Every Turk, Syrian, African, Indian, every Egyptian, Scythian,   105
Persian and Mede will submit his neck, bowed and broken, to the
binding chains of this father. But God himself has given you as a
gift, O Nicholas, to weary lands, so that you — who are saintly and   110
brave, pious and wise — may peacefully rule the dominion of this
highest temple on earth. May you who have much goodness live
for a long time as our powerful pope, father and priest, emperor
and shepherd of Christ's flock, our salvation and our king.   115

Hunc deus nobis tueatur unum,
quo nihil Phoebus melius nec omni
gloria toto videt aut videbit
120   dignius orbe.
Quam nimis coetu metuo fideli
ne patrem morbus rapiat subhaerens
artubus talem. Deus O, tuere,
     optime, Quintum.
125 Solus hic possit gravibus mederi
quae modo dirus Mahometus, iste
Turcus immanis tulit, heu, subactae
     vulnera Romae.
Roma quis sese Nova continere,
130 O decus terrae, species Olympi,
possit a maesti lachrymis doloris
     vulnere tanto?
Nunc tui clari proceres in arta
vincla coniecti patiuntur omne—
135 heu—genus probri, meliusque loeto
     nil meditantur.
At puellaris trahitur cathaenis
turba; matronae superos fatigant
flaetibus; nullus vacat impudica
140   Cypride sexus.
Qui scelus tantum prohibere possit
solus est Quintus, pius imperator
et pater regum. Deus, hunc, benigne
     ergo tuere.
145 Principes nulli renuant quod unus
imperet Quintus. Quis enim vereri
Karolum debet fore qui vel ultro
     tendit in hostes?

May God protect this one man for us; for Phoebus sees no one greater, nor will he see anyone worthier of every glory in the entire world. How much do I fear for his faithful council that a disease 120 may attack his limbs and carry off so great a father! O supreme God, protect our Nicholas. For this man alone can heal the griev- 125 ous wounds that the savage Turk, dread Mehmed, has inflicted on conquered Rome. O glory of the earth, O image of Olympus, how 130 can the New Rome[21] keep itself from weeping in grim sorrow over such wounds? Your illustrious nobles — now, alas, tightly bound in fetters — suffer every kind of unspeakable abuse, and they think 135 that nothing is better than death. A crowd of girls is dragged away in chains, married women weary the gods with their tears, and neither sex is safe from shameless rape. 140

Only Nicholas, the pious emperor and the father of kings, can prevent such wrongdoing. Therefore, kindly god, protect this man. May none of the princes refuse what he commands. For who 145 would doubt that Charles should be the one willingly to advance against the enemy? For this one man surpasses all other kings in

Unus is cunctos pietate reges
150 anteit. Alphonsus facilis sequatur,
se nec immunem patiatur alti
    esse triumphi.

Hos ubi Christi reliqui fideles
viderint, omnes alacres capessant
155 arma, qui nullos metuant labores,
    nulla pericla.

Roma mox Quinti Nova Nicolae
signa miretur revocetque passim
laeta maerentis famulosque cives
160   prasule tanto.

O, quibus Musae resonae dederunt
vocis et cantus numeros per omnis
vim, decus, mentem, celebrate Quintum
    carmine, cuncti.

165 Nulla sit nobis super omne saeclum
maior in cunctos populos, nec ulla
celsior, nec quae magis una laudes
    laus ferat omnes.

Quem patrem si vos bene Nicolaum
170 laudibus Quintum super astra summis
tollitis, nihil hoc habet omnis uno
    pulchrius orbis.

piety; Alfonso would gladly follow his lead. Nor would he refuse 150
to share in this glorious triumph. When the others who are faith-
ful to Christ see these men, may all those who would shrink from
neither toil nor danger quickly take up arms. 155

May the New Rome soon marvel at the standards of Nicholas
V and may she, under the protection of this great priest, gladly
bring home her grieving citizens and servants from far and wide.
O hymn our Nicholas, all you to whom the melodious Muses 160
have given the power of voice and song in all the lyric modes, as
well as honor and understanding. May there be no praise greater
for us, for every generation and for all peoples. May there be nei- 165
ther a more glorious encomium nor one that will elevate all his
deeds more than this one. For if you extol father Nicholas V high
above the stars with the loftiest praises, the world will contain 170
nothing more sublime than this one man.

: 6 :

Coepisti tandem sua restituisse parenti
    munera, nate Mari, quae mihi debueras.
Nam nihil optamus voto contingere nostro
    dulcius in natis, quos bene diligimus,
5   quam per virtutis numeros totius ut omnem
    concipiant laudem pectore magnifico.
Non ego divitias vulgus quas ardet ineptum
    admiror. Nec enim sunt bona nec stabiles.
Nil facio magni quidquid brevis auferat hora
10   nec praestare queat vis animi melior.
Sunt ubi Lydorum totus quos horruit orbis
    thesauri? Assyrii qui periere Lares?
Persarum quo gaza ruit Macedumve pyropi
    et quae de tantis Roma tulit populis?
15   Nil est perpetuum; nihil est quod dicere nostrum
    possimus nisi quod ipsa parit bonitas.
Veram sola quidem praestat clarissima virtus,
    nate Mari, laudem, quae fugit interitum.
Hac quod te videam decoratum principis acri
20   iudicio mira gaudeo laeticia.
Quod te magnanimus tanto insignirit honore
    ipse Lodovicus, gloria magna tibi est.
Nam tanto placuisse duci, Sabbaudia cuius
    imperio paret, fert tibi grande decus.
25   Iudicio postquam tibi tanti principis ambit
    laurea pulchra comam Pieridumque nemus,

: 6 :

To Gian Mario Filelfo
That he honor his patrons

Finally, Mario my son, you have begun to return to me, your fa-
ther, what you owed. For we hope for nothing sweeter in our
prayers for our children whom we dearly love than that they 5
should receive with noble hearts every praise for the magnitude of
all their virtues.

I do not admire the wealth which the ignorant rabble are burn-
ing to acquire. Neither is wealth a good in itself nor is it lasting. I
put little stock in something a brief hour may steal away or the
finer power of the mind can surpass. Where are the treasures of 10
the Lydians that the whole world envied? How did the Assyrian
Lares[22] perish? Where has the treasure of the Persians gone and
the gold of the Macedonians? Where are the riches that Rome
took from so many peoples? Nothing lasts forever. There is noth-
ing we can call our own except that which is born of goodness. 15

Illustrious virtue alone is worthy of true praise; for this, my son
Mario, eludes death. I am delighted that it is for this that I see you
honored in the keen judgment of the prince. That our magnani- 20
mous Lodovico himself has singled you out for such honor is a
source of great glory.[23] That you have pleased so great a prince,
whose command Savoy obeys, brings you great honor.

Now, since in the judgment of so great a prince you are a devo- 25
tee of the lovely laurel and the grove of the Pierian Muses, come,

eia, age nocturno, fili, pariterque diurno
    incumbens studio munera digna refer.
Fac dignis totus titulis te sentiat orbis
30   donatum, ne sis dedecori domino.
Fac ut te gratum cuncti memorentque canantque.
    Hac virtute nihil pulchrius esse reor.
Laude Lodovicum facito super aethera tollas,
    qui te tam celsis laudibus extulerit.
35 Nec tibi Martini Lefranci nomen et omne
    excidat officium, quo bene promeruit.
Hunc pariter leges decorant hominumque deumque.
    Hic in Socratico pulvere victor adest.
Hunc Parnassus amat, gemino quo vertice surgens
40   spectat et eoas occiduasque plagas.
Quidquid totus habet terrarum maximus orbis,
    quidquid et oceanus aetheriusque globus,
tu, Lefrance, tenes. Nec in aethera vectus apertum
    ignoras quae[7] sint regna petanda Iovis.
45 Iure igitur tantis cum te virtutibus unum
    audio pollentem promeritumque simul
te, Lefrance, meos primum reor inter amicos
    ducendum; talem te simul esse volo.
Nolim igitur, fili, secus hunc vereare colasque
50   ac patrem, quod te diligit ex animo.
Si virtute mera caperis, si semper honestum
    sectaris, munus solveris omne mihi.

my son, apply yourself to your work both day and night and re-
turn to us worthy gifts. See that the whole world knows you have
been honored with titles, lest you dishonor your lord. See that all   30
men remember your gratitude and sing your praises. I think there
is nothing more beautiful than this virtue. And see that you exalt
Lodovico to the heavens with praise, for he has lavished lofty
praise on you.

Nor should you forget the name of Martin le Franc[24] and all he   35
has done for you, for he is most deserving. The laws of both the
gods and men set this man apart. He is a champion in the So-
cratic arena and he is much loved on Parnassus.[25] Standing on its
twin peaks, he looks down in both directions, east and west. For   40
whatever lands the whole world encompasses and whatever both
the ocean and our starry sphere surround—all this, le Franc, you
possess. And since you have been carried into the open firma-
ment,[26] you know well how the realms of Jove must be sought. Be-
cause I hear rightly that you are superbly endowed with virtues   45
and deserving, I think you should be considered first among my
friends, le Franc. At the same time I want you to think the same
of me. And so, my son, I would like nothing less than that you
should respect and cherish this man as a father, since his esteem
for you comes from the heart.   50

If you are a lover of pure virtue, and if you always pursue
honor, you will reward me in every way.

: 7 :

Βασίνιον τὸν ἐμὸν πολυμήχανον ὄντ' ἀγαθόν τε
Μοῦσα τρέφει καὶ Φοῖβος ἔχων αἰώνιον ὄμμα
μῦθον ἄγει γλυκερόν, Κυλλήνιος ὅν ῥα παρεῖχεν
ἡδυεπὴς δαίμων. γνώμας πόρε Παλλὰς Ἀθήνη.
5 ἡμῶν οὗτος ἐρᾷ, ἡμεῖς δὲ φιλοῦντα φιλοῦμεν.
μέτριος ὤν πάμπαν μὴ τηρεῖ μέτρον ἐπαίνου
Βασίνιος. σεμνοῖσιν ἄρων ὑπὲρ ἄστρα Φιλέλφον
αὐτὰ λόγοις, ἡμῶν πέρι πολλὸν ψεύδεται. ὅσσα,
ὦ φίλε, πλὴν οὕτως σύ γε, ταύτῃ πολλὰ λεγούσῃ
10 θάρρει ὥστε μάλα⁸ τὸ σοφὸν δὴ τοῦτο φυλάξαι,
'μηδὲν ἄγαν.' σοφὸς αἰεὶ γὰρ μέσα πάντα φυλάττει.

: 8 :

Plura quidem faciunt ut te, Simoneta Johannes,
    inter amicorum nomina commemorem.
Prima quidem probitas mihi te facit integra carum.
    Post etiam ingenium, dulcis amice, tuum
5 adde quod una tibi semper stat cura merendi:
    officium semper officio cumulas.

326

: 7 :

To Basinio Basini of Parma,
a fellow poet and friend[27]

The Muse nurtures my Basinio, who is a good man and an inventive one too; and Phoebus Apollo, who keeps a watchful eye on him forever, endows him with the delightful eloquence that the sweet-tongued Cyllenian god[28] supplies, and Pallas Athena gives him judgment. This man loves us and we in turn love him who loves us. Though Basinio is a moderate man, he pays no   5
attention to moderation in his praise. For while he lifts Filelfo to the very stars in his stately speeches, he tells many lies about us. But, since this poem says as many things in the same way, O friend, have the courage to observe this wise maxim: "Nothing in   10
excess." For the sage always takes care to do all things in moderation.

: 8 :

To Giovanni Simonetta[29]
Commemorating their friendship

Several things cause me to count you among my friends, Giovanni Simonetta. The first is your moral integrity, which makes you dear to me. Then after your nature, sweet friend, add your continuous concern to serve well. You perform one service after another, and   5
the fact that you are powerful at oratory and have drunk deeply

Nanque quod eloquio polles Musisque sacratos
　　ebiberis latices fonte sub Aonio
usque adeo miro mihi te coniungit amore
10　　ut nihil ad summum cedere posse rear.
Hae tibi sunt artes, quibus es victurus in omne
　　tempus et extremis notus eris populis.
Sola quidem virtus valet e mortalibus umbris
　　nos immortalis constituisse viros.
15　Nanque nec ad potum, nec ad escam summa deorum
　　nos natura tulit illecebrasque levis.
Ista perinde sibi pecudes communia ducant,
　　ac nobis maius nanque bonum est hominis.
Nullum animal potuit nos praeter nosse decorum.
20　　Illud honestatis vis queat una dare.
Est homini ratio soli data vera superbae
　　munere iusticiae, qua patet omne bonum.
Hac nos ire licet summi ad fastigia caeli
　　atque frui facie colloquioque dei.
25　Omnis enim virtus, quae morum calle paratur,
　　monstrat iter celsum quo petimus solium.
Nec valet ad regem nos perduxisse deorum,[9]
　　qui nos caelesti rore benignus alit.
At mox ingressis offert se splendida nobis
30　　lux ea virtutum, quae pietate viget.
Haec docet una quidem quae sit vis unica veri
　　illius aeterni quod super astra micat.
Hac duce felici nobis licet ore potiri
　　affatuque Iovis et bonitate frui.
35　Quod si sola deo nos virtus reddit amandos
　　caelestisque facit participes patriae,
quid mirum si te virtus mihi pulchra, Iohannes,
　　iungit amiciciae per monumenta piae?

from the waters of the Aonian spring, sacred to the Muses, endears you to me with such extraordinary love that I believe that nothing could reach its summit. These are your arts; with these   10
you will live forever and you will be known to all peoples.[30]

From the mortal shades that we are, virtue alone can make us immortal. For the supreme nature of the gods leads us not to food, drink, or to ephemeral pleasures. Let those common appe-   15
tites bring cattle together. But for us the greater thing is human goodness. No animal except ourselves can recognize moral beauty; that only the power of integrity can confer. The true principle of   20
sublime justice has been given to mankind alone as a gift and it is this that reveals every good. With this guiding principle, we are permitted to travel to the heights of highest heaven and to enjoy the colloquy and the face of God. For every virtue we acquire on the path to moral integrity shows us the road on which we may   25
seek the heavenly throne.

But this principle is not able to lead us to the king of the gods, who nourishes us with celestial dew.[31] However, soon the brilliant light of the virtues, which grows strong with piety, offers itself on our journey. Indeed, this light reveals the sole force of that eternal   30
truth which gleams above the stars.[32] With this auspicious force as our guide, it is permitted to us to come before Jove, to speak with him, and enjoy his goodness.

But if virtue alone renders us beloved to God and makes us   35
participants in his celestial homeland, why should it be surprising if beautiful virtue binds you to me, Giovanni, through the memen-

Quanto igitur, Simoneta, magis te talibus offers
40   laudibus insignem, te magis unus amem.

⁚ 9 ⁚

Dum te nostra, Lodovice, superbius
optat Pieris ad sydera tollere,
nescit principium quod capiat prius.
    Cunctis sic meritis micas.
5   Uno te melior nemo, nec altius
qui te suspiciat digne[10] voluminum
multa congerie. Nanque parentibus
    natus principibus nites.
Hos virtus pariter conspicuos dedit
10   et fortuna potens. Tu quibus aeditus
princeps nec titulis nec specie minor,
    fortunam superas probus.
Te doctrina parem praestitit omnibus
et quos eloquium et quos sapientia
15   illustres facit et tollit in aethera
    fama perpetuos agens.
Indignum reor ullum, melioribus
qui sit deterior, qui inferior suo
sit regno, dominari imperio viris.
20   Quis non paruerit tibi?
Tu quidquid loqueris, sic loqueris bene
ut cunctos superes eloquio viros

tos of a pious friendship? And so, may I alone continue to love you all the more, Simonetta, the more you make yourself renowned through such great deeds.   40

: 9 :

To Ludovico Gonzaga, Francesco Sforza,
and Alfonso of Naples, urging an end to war

While our Pierian Muse, Lodovico,[33] hopes to raise you to the stars more proudly, she does not know what to say first. You shine so brightly in every sphere. No one exceeds you, and no one casts   5
his eyes higher than you, who are worthy of many volumes. For you are the celebrated descendant of princes. Virtue and fertile fortune have distinguished your ancestors equally. You are a prince   10
in no way inferior to your forefathers, either in titles or appearance; a man of probity, you surpass them in fortune. Your learning renders you the equal of all those whom wisdom and eloquence make illustrious and whom fame raises to the heavens, rendering   15
them immortal.

I think that a man who is morally inferior to better men, a man who is beneath the men of his own kingdom in rank, is unworthy to rule with imperial power. But who would not serve you? What-   20
ever you say, you say so well that you will surpass in eloquence all

quos aetas stupet haec. At gravitas tua
   est mirabilis omnibus.
25   Rerum cognitio plurima, caeteris
quae sunt principibus nube reconditae,
est uni tibi. Nam munificentiae
   splendes laudibus inclytae.
Haec virtus homines allicit aurea.
30   Virtus haec superos reddit et inferos
affectos sibi. Nec munificentia
   virtus ulla benignior.
Haec, Gonzaga Lodovice, benignitas,
princeps optime, te principibus facit
35   iis praestare, nutrit quos amor otii
   et qui divitiis student.
Virtus haec eadem te sapientiae
mirandum studiosis facit omnibus,
cantandumque bonis vatibus, ac item
40   quem sumant sibi rhetores.
Nam quod nos reliquos, quos bene plurimos
ipse affeceris et quottidie afficis,
pergamus numero dicere? Quilibet
   se gratum doceat palam!
45   Tu nos innumeris muneribus pius
et pulchris cumulas, nec statuis modum.
Solus Castalidas muneribus foves:
   qui te non igitur colam?
Hinc sit ne liceat ferre silentium,
50   quin coram fatear quam tibi gratiam
magnam pro meritis debeo maximis,
   quae in me contuleris libens.
Quae maiora tibi magnanimo queam
vates quae placeant reddere principi

those whom our age admires. But all men marvel at your gravity. You alone have the greatest knowledge of things that are generally 25 shrouded in fog for other princes. For your light shines brightly from the eulogies of your renowned generosity. This golden virtue entices men. This virtue renders those who dwell in the upper and lower worlds well disposed to it. Nor is there any virtue kinder 30 than generosity. This kindness, O most noble prince, Lodovico Gonzaga, causes you to be superior to those princes whom the love of leisure gratifies and those who strive to amass riches. This 35 same virtue causes you, however, to be admired for your wisdom by all learned men, to be hymned by all good poets, and to be chosen by orators as the subject of their speeches. 40

Should I speak at length about the rest of us, the majority of whose lives you yourself have influenced and influence each day? Let anyone who wishes to do so show his gratitude publicly. You, kind one, have heaped innumerable beautiful gifts upon us; nor do you place limits on your generosity. Since you cherish the 45 Castalian maidens uniquely with gifts, how could I not love you? And so here I cannot be silent, but instead I confess publicly, that 50 I owe you the greatest thanks for the magnificent gifts you have freely showered on me. What greater and more pleasing tribute could I, a mere poet, offer you, a magnanimous prince, than the

55 quam quae te referat gloria nobilem
        digno carmine posteris?
    Hinc nos te numeris prosequimur lyrae;
    hinc te multisonis vocibus impigri,
    quantum possumus, extollimus altius,
60   qui sis praesidio bonis.
    Quid te nostra minus barbitos efferat,
    nervis omnibus in multiplices agens
    ultro se modulos, quem videat viros
        summos vincere[11] laudibus?
65 Ingratus fuero, si meritis tuis
    non respondero vel qua liceat fide.
    Quem virtus lateat nulla micantior,
        qui nobis facias bene!
    Sic et Virgilius cantibus inclytum
70 Augustum decorat. Sic Phrygios duces
    Smyrnaeus Danais carmine subiicit.
        Sic te nos canimus lyra.
    Vobis principibus quid melius potest
    reddi quam meritum gloria praedicans?
75 Nam nunquam moritur quem memorat favens
        late fama peremniter.
    Quid de te loquar excellere pulchrius
    qui totus vigeas nomine fulgido
    quem non una sed omnis decoret viros
80   virtus quae celebres facit?
    Lingua mellifluum Nestora cedere
    dicenti tibi cogas. Referas item
    illum, quem reliquis ingenii bono
        praefert Maeonides, ducem.
85 Tu non Aeaciden non Priamo satum
    horrescas acie. Iusticia quoque

glory of a worthy poem that would render you noble for genera-   55
tions to come?

Therefore, since you are the fortress of the good, we will honor
you with the rhythms of the lyre and we will exalt you diligently
and still more loftily, to the extent that we can, with sonorous mel-
odies. Why should our lyre not celebrate you, sounding spontane-   60
ously on all its strings in many modes, since it sees you surpassing
the most eminent men in renown already? I would be ungrateful if   65
I did not extol your merits with whatever loyalty is permitted.
And may you whom no shining virtue eludes do us good in turn!
Thus Virgil honored renowned Augustus with his songs. Thus
the Smyrnean[34] brought the Trojan leaders under the yoke of the
Greeks in his poem. And thus we hymn you with our lyre. What   70
better gift can be given to you princes than the glory that publicly
proclaims your virtue? For he never dies whom sweet Fame me-
morializes for all time and all the world.   75

In what nobler pursuit should I say you excel, for you are an
emblem of your shining lineage and a man adorned, not by one,
but every virtue that ennobles men? When you speak, you would   80
force honey-tongued Nestor to take second-place to you. Likewise
you resemble the hero whom the Maeonian bard loved above all
the rest because of the goodness of his character.[35] Nor in battle
would you fear Aeacides or Priam's son.[36] Nor would you yield to   85

non cedas nitida Fabricio seni.
    Vincas Attilium fide.
Nam quis te facilem nescit et omnibus
90   humanum? Tua clementia Caesarem
aequat Dardanium magnidecentia
    illum, quem Darius stupet.
Quid me contineo quo minus impiger
percurram brevibus militiam tuam
95   et vitam studeam carmine dispari
    fari magnanimi tui?
Contendant alii ludere tessaras;
certent et socio innectere raetia
quo nummos rapiant fraudibus aleae,
100   dum nos te canimus lyra.
Ecce Lodovicum regis natalis Olympi
    huc tulit. Hunc celebret carmine Melpomene.
Sic inter proceres decorat quos aurea virtus
    hic micat, ut Titan splendet in astra novus.
105   Qui nomen, Gonzaga, tuum non laudibus effert
    rusticus est. Omni nam bonitate viges;
consilio polles; tu fortiter effera Martis
    inter fulmineas arma subis acies.
Hunc cane, Melpomene, quo principe Mantua felix.
110   Felix tempus agit principe fausta pio.
Qui, Gonzaga, tuas virtutes nescit, is omnis
    est virtutis inops flagitiique reus.
Nemo te melior, nec munificentior alter
    est inter proceres quos alit Italia.
115   Solus amas Musas. Tu solus in omnibus artes
    eximias decoras ingeniisque faves.
Hunc unum celebrate, viri, quoscunque superbum
    extulit eloquium, quos et Apollo fovet.

ancient Fabricius in all his shining justice.[37] And in constancy you would surpass Attilius.[38] But who does not know your gentleness and benignity to all men? For your clemency in its majesty equals that of Dardanian Caesar,[39] who caused Darius to marvel. Why should I prevent myself from running briefly through the events of your military career or from striving actively to tell your life story in my poem, though my work is hardly worthy of your noble spirit? Let other men vie with one another at board games and let others try to entrap a fellow player so that they can snatch up coins with the trickery of the dice, while we sing your praises to the strains of the lyre.

But look, the birthday of the king of Olympus[40] brought Lodovico here. May Melpomene hymn this man with song. Thus, like a new Titan amid the stars, he shines among those princes whom golden virtue adorns. That man is ignorant who fails to extol your name, Gonzaga, with praise. For you flourish in every goodness. You are powerful in counsel. You enter the thundering battle-fields and savage fray of Mars courageously. Hymn this man, O Melpomene, for Mantua is fortunate with him as her prince. She lives in a fortunate age, happy in her pious prince. Whoever does not know your virtues, Gonzaga, is devoid of virtue and guilty of great shame. Among all the princes Italy fosters, no one is better than you or more magnanimous. You love the Muses with a unique love. You alone among all men embellish the liberal arts and foster the talents of the great.

O men, whom high eloquence distinguishes and Apollo nurtures, honor this one man. For he satisfies those of you whom ei-

90

95

100

105

110

115

Hic satis est vobis quos aut annalibus altis
120   aut etiam vario carmine cura iuvat.
Hic si vera velim, scribenti porrigat amplam
        materiam rerum, qua mihi surgat opus.
Quippe tener primis qui dum pubesceret annis,
        militiam didicit sub genitore duce
125 et didicit quidquid belli callentior usus
        aut ars ferre queat ingenio docili.
Mox maiora animo secum meditatus ovanti,
        qui bene paruerat, imperitare cupit.
Hadriacos igitur fastus exosus, ut omni est
130   promissae functus munere militiae,
te regumque ducumque decus sublime, Philippe,
        Anguiger O Latii gloria, laetus adit.
Quem tu, cui virtus uni non ficta placeret,
        excipis atque foves patris amore pii.
135 Et quoniam ingenii vidisses luce nitentem
        ingentique animo, praeficis agminibus
Nicoleonque iubes probus ut comitetur, ephebus
        dum petit Ethruscos ut populetur agros.
Hic si cuncta tuis ausis animoque fuissent
140   gesta, Fluentini colla iugo dederant.
Hinc te magnanimus, cui fata deique faverent,
        Sphortia Franciscus poscit adesse sibi.
Ante nec assequitur soceri quam mite Philippi
        pectus, ad id precibus constituisset opus.
145 Multa quidem eventu gessisti praelia fausto
        sub duce Francisco, quae siluisse libet.
Nam si cuncta velim digna memorare Camoena
        ante oriens Titan viderit Antipodas.
Id satis est summae laudi tibi, quin Philippus
150   a genero repetit quo caruisse nequit.

ther lofty annals or lyric meters please. And if I wanted to chroni- 120
cle true events, this man would offer me ample material, so that
the work would take shape in my hands. Indeed, while he was still
young and approaching manhood, he learned in those first years to
be a soldier under his father's tutelage[41] and he learned with a re-
ceptive mind whatever a more skillful strategy or art in war could 125
offer. Soon happily pondering greater things, Lodovico, who had
been commendably obedient, now wanted to command. There-
fore, because of his hatred of Adriatic[42] arrogance, when he had
now fulfilled all his promised military obligations, he gladly ac- 130
companied you, O Filippo Maria, sublime pride of kings and war-
lords and serpent-bearing glory of Latium.[43] And you, to whom
only true virtue would be pleasing, welcomed him and supported
him with the love of a dutiful father. And since you had seen him
shining with his brilliant talent and great heart, you put him in 135
charge of your army and you rightly commanded Niccolò[44] to fol-
low, while the young man pursued the Etruscans[45] in order to
plunder their fields. And if everything had been waged with your
spirit and daring, the Florentines would have offered their necks
to your yoke. And after this, the brave-hearted Francesco Sforza, 140
whom both the fates and the gods hold dear, asked you, Lodovico,
to accompany him. Nor did he win over the kindly heart of his fa-
ther-in-law Filippo until he pleaded for this arrangement to be al-
lowed. And indeed, with Francesco as your captain, you fought
numerous wars that ended happily. 145

But enough said about this. For if I wished to recall all the
pitched battles you fought that were worthy of Camena, the rising
sun would see the Antipodes before I finished. This is sufficient to
pay the highest tribute to you, without adding that Filippo then
asked his son-in-law for the return of the one man he could not do
without. Three and four times Filippo sent letters asking his son- 150
in-law to send you back to him, Lodovico, though he had just re-

Terque quaterque suis generum rogat ille tabellis,
    ut sibi te reddat quem modo cessit ei.
Sphortia quo toto nihil est humanius orbe,
    non audet socero quod rogat abnuere.
155   Te sinit invitus dio parere Mariae,
    quo natura nihil progenuit melius.
Ergo optatus ades, quem tanto admittit amore
    dux pius ut nihil te carius esset ei.
Principe sub tanto virtus tua claruit omnis.
160   Et patuit cunctis quantus in arma fores,
et patuit cunctis quantus probitate fideque,
    consilioque fores quantus et officio.
Ac ni saeva ducem rapuissent fata benignum,
    unus eras illi portus et aura viro.
165   Hoc autem extincto cum iam fortuna deusve
    Insubrium populum fluctibus obrueret
et iam tota salo variis iactata procellis
    publica res triste naufragium peteret,
dum nullus locus esse probis coepisset et omne
170   iam ruerent cives per facinus miseri,
dumque deos hominesque simul discordia demens
    misceret, passim dum furor ingrueret,
secedis, quoniam civilis nollet Erinys
    consilio quicquam nec studio gerere.
175   Otia sed quoniam probitati ferre negatur,
    haud sineris vitam vivere sic vacuam.
Te Florentini Venetique adiere rogantes
    partibus ut nolles non studuisse suis,
teque legunt magnis ut praesis viribus, uno
180   quo duce nil tandem posset obesse sibi.
Dumque petis Tuscos, dum te Florentia rebus
    optat adesse suis, nec Veneti renuunt,

cently released you to Sforza. There being no one kinder in the whole world than Sforza, he did not dare to refuse his father-in-law's request. So, unwillingly, Francesco allowed you to obey the divine Filippo Maria—for nature never engendered a better man than he.   155

Thus, long-awaited, you are here, Lodovico, and the pious duke welcomes you with such love that nothing could be dearer to him than you. Under the auspices of so great a prince, your every virtue has shone. How great a man you are in arms, how great your   160 probity and loyalty, and how great a man of diplomacy, service, and duty you are—all this was here revealed. And if the cruel fates had not seized the kindly duke, you would have been the one refuge, the one favorable wind on his life's voyage. But when Filippo died, suddenly fortune or a god overwhelmed the people of the   165 Milanese in a deluge and the whole republic, now tossed amid variable winds across the sea, headed for sad shipwreck. Now, when there began to be no place for good men and the wretched citizens fell prey to every crime, and when at the same time mind-   170 less discord confounded gods and men and madness assailed men indiscriminately, you then withdrew,[46] since the Fury of this city was unwilling to promote diplomacy or goodwill.

But since honor can be allowed no peace, you, Lodovico, are   175 not allowed to live your life free from war. The Florentines and the Venetians arrive and they ask you not to be unwilling to come to the aid of their states. They choose you to preside over their great forces so that, with you as their leader, nothing can stand in their way. While you, Lodovico, go over to the Tuscans, and while both   180 the Florentines and the Venetians hope you will defend their interests, the mighty warrior Francesco Sforza, having defeated

Sphortia bellipotens oppressa classe Cremonam
   liberat hostili turbine Romulida.
185   Qui Caravaginos ubi cingit milite muros
   et parat obsessis auxilium Venetus,
mox ades, et pugnam Fabii consulta secutus
   detrectas, certa Palladis usus ope.
Non sinit Hadriacus sibi quae consulta ferebas
190   stare loco. Quo fit fusus ut occideret.
Nanque tuo ductu non est res gesta, sed ipsi
   sic placuit Veneto, quem premit ira furens.
Hic igitur tantae percussus vulnere cladis,
   horret et ignorat quam sibi poscat opem.
195   Mille duces capti, flos captus militis omnis.
   Omnis in ambiguo spesque salusque fuit.
Haec tandem melior visa est sententia victis
   ut tecum nollent, Sphortia, ferre manum.
Tunc itaque Alphonsus, qui iam ventura videret,
200   te, Gonzaga, suae quaerit adesse rei.
Qui quoniam nolles ignavam ducere vitam,
   quae tibi condicio digna paratur obis.
Suscipit ingenti res sane pectore magnas
   Alphonsus, nec quas suscipit exequitur.
205   Ergo cum primum licuit tibi, magna volutans
   ac praeclara animo, consulis in medium,
'Quid faciam?' dixti, 'Num tempus inertibus umbris
   semper abire sinam laudis inops meritae?'
Verba dat Alphonsus: 'Venetos non una voluntas
210   continet. Insubrium pectus Erinys habet.
At Florentinus quem longa peritia trivit:
   callentemque facit, Sphortia, te sequitur.
Quae nos tanta tenet mora longior? Astra minantur
   omnibus exitium, qui tibi bella movent.

the Roman fleet, frees Cremona from its hostile vortex.[47] And
when Sforza surrounds the walls of Caravaggio with his army and   185
the Venetians prepare to come to the assistance of the besieged
townspeople, you are soon there. Yet you refuse to go into battle
and following the stratagems of Fabius, you rely instead on the
sure power of Pallas.[48] Nor, Lodovico, do the Venetians follow the
orders you issue. And so they are put to flight and die. For the   190
battle is not waged under your leadership but as it pleases the Ve-
netians themselves, whom mad wrath confounds. Therefore, thun-
derstruck by the wound of so great a disaster, they shudder with
fear and know not what help they should seek for themselves. A
thousand of their leaders are captured, the flower of their entire
army taken. All hope is in abeyance, all safety too. And in the end,   195
it seems wiser to the defeated men to be unwilling to do battle
with you, Sforza.[49]

At this point Alfonso, foreseeing the events to come, asks you,
Gonzaga, to come to the assistance of his state. And since you   200
have no wish to lead a coward's life, you enter into the worthy con-
tract he prepares for you. Now surely Alfonso undertakes great
campaigns with courage, but what he undertakes he does not ac-
complish. Therefore as soon you can, Lodovico, while pondering
great and glorious deeds in your heart, you reflect: "What should   205
I do?" (you say to yourself) "Should I let my life ebb away with
the futile shades, devoid of the praise that is owed?"

Alfonso speaks: "No unified will holds the Venetians together,
and the hearts of the Milanese are held hostage by the Fury. But   210
the Florentines follow you, Sforza—for long experience has honed
their spirits and made them wise. What great delay detains us any
longer? The stars threaten death to all who initiate wars against
you. Should we at last hope for different things from heaven,

215 Num demum sperare licet contraria caelo,
   quod deus imperitat? Quid secus ipse velim?
 Cedamus fatis. Aliud quid fata putemus
   quam quod summa Iovis mens iubet esse ratum?
 Unus hic Italiam superavit saepius omnem.
220   Ingenio viget hic et probitate viget.
 Hunc deus incolumem semper discrimine ab omni
   servat et imperiis auget honorificis.
 Una simul fortuna duos, labor unus habebit.
   Et valeant qui nos quaesierint dirimi.'
225 Haec tu, qui semper studio loquerisque facisque
   cuncta gravi. Nec te poenitet, ecce, rei.
 Solus ades nobis, qui semper in omnia praestes
   te quibus agnoris sorte valere tua.
 Tu virtute tua quantum perfeceris omnes
230   una voce ferunt promeritumque canunt.
 Sphortia, te contra tanti facit inclytus unum
   ut sit nemo quidem quem magis unus amet.
 Iure igitur cuncti celebrent tua nomina vates
   eloquioque graves te super astra ferant.
235 Hic tibi Natalis lucescat sydere dextro,
   quisquis amicorum commoda dexter amas.
 Egi nunc brevibus blanditicias verens.
 Novi nanque, Lodovice, modestiam,
 cuius mirifice nomine duceris.
240   Haec ut sim brevior facit.
 Nunc haec Melpomene. Terpsichore canet
 deinceps plura volenti tibi pluribus
 ferri laudibus in sydera principi
   nostri temporis optimo.

where God is the ruler? Why should I want something else? Let us yield to the fates. Should we believe the fates are something other than what the supreme mind of Jove orders to be established? This one man alone—Francesco Sforza—has conquered all of Italy repeatedly. He flourishes because of his character and his probity. God keeps him safe from every danger always and makes him great with honorable powers. One fortune will hold these two men, Sforza and Gonzaga, at one and the same time. One labor will unite them—forget those who attempted to divide us!"

Thus you spoke, Alfonso—you who always say and do everything with great zeal. But look, do not regret it. You alone are here for us—you who are always superior in all those qualities in which you know that you are powerful because of your destiny. All men unanimously acclaim you and how much you have accomplished because of your virtue, and they hymn your service deservedly. This great man esteems you so highly, Sforza, that there is no one whom he could love more. Therefore let all the poets rightly celebrate your names. Let men of authority lift you to the stars with their eloquence. Let this Christmas shine with a favorable star for you, who are well-disposed toward your friends and take pleasure in their advantages.

Now, I have offered a sweet panegyric, respectfully keeping it brief. For I know you are wonderfully charmed, Lodovico, by the name of modesty. This causes me to be briefer still. So now my Muse Melpomene has sung. Next Terpsichore[50] will sing more songs for you, the best prince of our time, should you be willing to be carried to the stars with praise.

Nunc age, Melpomene, cantu dic nostra supremo,
    quae sunt digna lyra, dic age, Melpomene.
Terpsichore properans numeros et verba canoro
    ore ciet. Noli nectere, diva, moras.
5   Quae pax Italiam multis iam liquerat annis,
    nuper ab aetherio coeperat ire polo.
Huius in adventum ridebant prata coruscis
    floribus et colles germina mille dabant.
Lucebant fontes, sistebant flumina cursum,
10   cedebantque ferae raetibus et laqueis.
Iam nemo insidias; nemo arma infesta timebant.
    Dulcia ludebant otia plena ioci
Aonides. Variis mulcebant cantibus auras:
    Cum cithara Phoebus omne solum streperet,
15   indoluit terras tam dextro sydere Pluton
    laetari dira motus ab invidia
atque ait ergo, 'Nihil possimus? Nostra nec ullum
    sceptra ferant munus? Sic Iovis ira premit?
At Neptunus amat. Neptuni viribus usi,
20   Italiae totas concutiemus opes.'
Hunc igitur Pluton adiens penetralibus imis
    aequoris excitum, talibus alloquitur,
'Non, frater Neptune, vides quanta otia mentes
    en hominum capiunt? Undique bella silent.
25   Nil adamat motum. Torpent iam pace futura
    fulmineae galeae; Martius ensis hebet.

: 10 :

To Malatesta Novello[51]
A dialogue of the gods and a hymn to peace

Come now, Melpomene, hymn events worthy of our lyre, come, hymn them with the highest paeans. Now Terpsichore hastens to initiate the music, the words and rhythms, with her lovely voice. Allow no delay, O goddess. Peace has begun to return from starry heaven, after abandoning Italy for so many years.[52] The meadows 5 smile at its arrival with shimmering flowers and the hills bloom with a thousand buds. The springs glisten, the rivers flow gently, and the savage beasts succumb to traps and snares. Now no one 10 fears ambushes, no one fears enemy arms. The Aonian maidens play at sweet games full of sport and they soothe the breezes with various songs.

While Phoebus made the whole earth resound to the strains of his lyre, Pluto,[53] stung with painful jealousy, grieved that the lands were rejoicing in such good fortune, and he cried, "Have we no 15 power at all? Does our crown and scepter bring us nothing in recompense? Is Jove's anger so omnipotent? But Neptune loves us, and with his help we will shake Italy's wealth to its foundations." 20

And so Pluto went into the depths of the ocean to rouse Neptune and he approached him, saying, "O brother Neptune, do you not see how powerfully peace has taken possession of men's minds? Everywhere wars have ceased. There is no love for war. Now gleaming helmets lie dormant, awaiting the coming peace, 25 and the swords of war grow dull. Does widespread anger please

Te iuvat ira frequens? Tumor horridus? Atra frementi
    turbine tempestas? Me furor ac rabies.
Iam vires excire para tibi. Iure vetusti
30   muneris obstrictum sume deum socium.
Hic memor officii tanto studiosius ibit
    in partes quo te promeruisse tenet.'
Talia dicenti facilem regnator aquarum
    dum parat assensum versus ad arma citus,
35 rursus hebet dubio similem se pectore praestans
    ac secum loquitur consiliumque tegit.
Cui Pluton, 'Quae te dubium sententia versat?
    An te[12] posse neges quod petimus facere?'
'Nil est quod cupiam magis, O germane, petenti
40   quam praestare tibi quod cupis officium.
Omnem equidem Italiam penitus mihi vertere fas sit.
    Et tamen ambiguae me facit unus opis.
Nam Malatestigenum natus de stirpe Novellus
    contemnit vires hic Malatesta meas.
45 Ingenio tantum valet et dulcedine morum
    ut sibi caelicolum conciliarit opem.
Hunc nam Phoebus amat. Felici Iupiter astro
    respicit. Hunc Cypris pectore laeta fovet.
His alacer sese comitem Cyllenius addit.
50   Quo sit ut imperium negligat omnem meum.
Totus est in Musis et Pallados arte Minervae,
    pace nihil pulchra dulcius esse ratus.
Qui facilem si se nostris adiungeret ausis,
    omnia luctifica sterneret ira nece.
55 Est animo ingenti, cui tantum mentis acumen
    iungitis — ac splendor ad probitatis opus —
ut neque blandicias curet, nec iussa, minasve,
    nec monitus ullos. Est satis ipse sibi,

you? Do you enjoy bristling wrath? A dark tempest with roaring
winds? I am delighted by rage and madness. Come now, prepare
to marshal your powers. Take me—a god bound to you by the law
of mutual obligation—as your ally. Mindful of his duty, this god   30
will come all the more eagerly into regions where he knows you
have served him well."

   While the ruler of the seas, roused to arms, prepares to agree
easily to these words, he is slow to speak and shows himself to be
similarly uncertain of heart. He mutters to himself and hides his   35
deliberations, to which Pluto says, "What thoughts are causing
you to waver? Or would you deny that you can do what we ask?"

   "There is nothing that I want more, my brother," Neptune re-
plies, "than to show you the service you want. It may indeed be   40
right for me to bring turmoil to all Italy. Still, one man makes me
hesitant to help. For Malatesta Novello, a scion of the Malatesta
clan, is scornful of my strength. He has such force of mind and
sweetness of character that he has won for himself the protec-   45
tion of the gods. For Phoebus loves him. Jupiter looks upon him
with a felicitous star. Happy Venus cherishes him in her heart.
The swift-moving Cyllenian god[54] makes him a companion to
these gods. Thus it is that he neglects my entire rule. He lives   50
wholly with the Muses and the arts of Pallas Athena, thinking
that nothing is sweeter than beautiful peace. If gentle Novello
were to ally himself with our ventures, his anger could then bring
about wholesale ruin and baleful death. But this is a man endowed
with a great soul, to which you have conjoined—as when luster is
added to a work of probity—such great sharpness of mind that he   55
cares neither for flattery, commands, nor threats or warnings of
any kind. He is sufficient in himself: he rules the proud Flaminian

imperio cuius regitur Caesena superbos
60   inter Flaminios urbs populos celebris,
quae nostrae momenta rei non parva tulisset.
     Sed prohibet dominus bella profana vetans.
Temptemus, germane, tamen quid saeva Tonantis
     fata velint. Nullo munere deero tibi.'
65   Te, Gradive, petens, non tam quid praestitit olim
     officium memorat quam sibi poscit opem:
'O Mars care, mihi si te mea cura piusque
     tangit honos, votis te precor adesse meis.
Temnimur, en placida mortales pace quiescunt.
70   Hoc patruus longe maeret uterque tuus.
Omnia turbemus bellis faeralibus. Omnes
     bella iuvent. Vires eia age pande tuas!'
Cui deus armipotens precibus tam grata petenti
     auxilia haud dubiis annuit obsequiis.
75   Nam memor et raetis quo se Vulcanius astus
     vinxerat et caedis qua puer occubuit,
reddere Neptuno grates pro munere, quo se
     iuverat, instituit atque piare nefas.
Hic et enim, Neptune, tibi ira percitus acri
80   abstulerat natum virginis in facinus.
Sic igitur trucibus passim concurritur armis.
     Littore fit primus motus ab Hadriaco
transiliensque Padum quoque Abdua stringit apricos
     Insubrium campos, concitat omne solum.
85   Una ruina premit cunctos hominesque deosque,
     qua leo terribilis turbine vastat agrum.
Vipera cui longus sopor occupaverat artus,
     mox excita furit virus ab ore vomens.
Nec modo sese audet saevo opposuisse leoni
90   aligero ac fremitus vimque tulisse fera.

people and the celebrated city of Cesena solely with the power he has—and this city could have added great momentum to   60
our cause, but instead its lord prohibits impious wars. Still, my brother, let us make a test of what the savage fates of Jove the Thunderer have in mind. As for me, in no way will I be wanting in my duty to you."

Supplicating you now, O Gradivus,[55] Neptune reminds the god   65
not so much of the service he once performed as of the assistance he now requests for himself: "My dear Mars," he says, "if concern for me and pious honor move you, I beg you to hear my prayers. Look, we are despised: mortals are living in peace. Both your uncles have lamented this situation for a long time. Let us embroil   70
the world in deadly wars. May war please all mortal men. Come, exercise your strength!"

In response to Neptune's prayers, the powerful god of war agrees to supply help gratefully and with immediate compliance. For mindful both of the nets in which Vulcan's cunning had   75
trapped him and of the killing of a boy,[56] Mars decides to thank Neptune for the way he had helped him and to expiate his sin. For Mars, consumed with bitter gall toward you, O Neptune, had slain your son in recompense for the rape of a young girl.[57]   80

Thus commenced the wars between men in arms all across the land. The mobilization of troops begins on the Adriatic coast. Leaping across the Po where the Adda borders the sunny fields of the Milanese, Mars now sows turmoil everywhere throughout he countryside. One catastrophe oppresses gods and men alike, for   85
here the dread lion, like a whirlwind, lays waste the fields.[58] And there the viper, whose body sleep had long possessed, now rages with anger, venom spewing from his mouth.[59] And not only does the savage snake dare to fight the fierce winged lion and stand his ground despite his roaring and his might, but after he has grown   90

Sed magis atque magis postquam flagrasset in iram
 taela per et caedes agmina fundit humi.
Omnia prosternit, turbantur cuncta, ruuntque.
 Pax amota perit. Omnia Marte calent.
95 Pierides cessere loco. Dant terga furori.
 Virtutes nusquam germinat officium.
Est solus Malatesta quidem qui numina curet,
 qui colat eloquium, diligat ingenia.
Huic pax alma placet. Qui ponat praemia laudi
100 solus hic est unus, nec numeres alium.
Dum pugnant alii, dum caedes caedibus urgent,
 artes solus amas tu, Malatesta, bonas.
At postquam summo despexit ab aethere terras
 Iupiter et sensit fratris adesse dolos,
105 indoluit miseras sortes rerumque hominumque.
 Mercuriumque vocans talibus alloquitur,
'I, cito Franciscum verbis hortator amicis
 Sphortiaden revocet victor ut arma celer.
Sic placitum nobis. Satis est ea gloria, fastus
110 quod Veneti solus fregerit imperii.
Plutonique meam postquam narraveris iram,
 consule Neptuno prosit ut ipse sibi.'
Paret Atlandiades. Nil tendit Sphortia contra.
 Mox postliminium pax facit alma suum.
115 At quem pacis amor delectat? Nonne Novellum?
 Nanque aliis alius vivit; at ille sibi.
Ille colit Musas; cultores laudis honorat:
 Est tutela viris praesidiumque bonis.
Ille igitur dignus quem summis laudibus ornet
120 ingenio quisquis pollet et eloquio.
Hunc laudet Sappho paucis et pulcher Adonis.
 Nam nec Melpomenae plura referre licet.

more and more hot with rage, he pours out his regiments on the land amid weapons and slaughter. He levels everything, all things are thrown into disorder and lie in ruins. Peace, long gone, now dies. While Mars rules, the world burns. The Pierian Muses withdraw from this place. They flee, turning their backs to the insanity. No virtues are born of such service. 95

Malatesta alone cares for the gods. It is he who fosters eloquence, who cherishes the things of the mind. Kindly peace pleases this man; he alone and no other would you find who offers rewards for the poetry of praise. While others fight, while 100 slaughter presses upon slaughter, you alone, Malatesta, love the good arts.

But when Jupiter looks down on the lands below from his heavenly summit and sees the treachery of his brother, he grieves over the lives of men and their wretched fates. And calling upon Mer- 105 cury he addresses him as follows, "Go, urge the victor Francesco Sforza with friendly words to withdraw his arms quickly. That is my wish. He has enough glory in that he alone has broken the arrogance of the Venetian empire. After you convey my anger to 110 Pluto, you should advise Neptune to look after his own interests." Mercury obeys. Sforza does not oppose the plan. Kindly peace will soon resume her rightful place.

But whom does the love of peace please? Is it not Novello? For 115 some men live for others. But that man is sufficient in himself. He fosters the Muses. He honors the cultivators of the art of praise. He is the protector and the fortress of all good men. This man — whom anyone who has great talent and eloquence would adorn with his oratory — is therefore worthy of the highest accolades. Let 120 Sappho and beautiful Adonis praise him with a brief hymn. For Melpomene is not permitted to say more.

Patre Pandulpho Malatesta natus,
qui velut sydus proceres in omnis
125   claruit, nulli titulis Novellus
        cedit avitis.
Unus hic dulci fruitur quiete
et suis tutam peperisse pacem
gaudet. Hic nulli gravis est probato,
130   mitis in omnes.
Lumen, aetatis decus et voluptas
summa praesentis simul et futurae,
suavis aspectu, gravis et modestus,
       fortis et ingens.
135 Huius e lingua fluit ille sermo,
qui refert Maia genitum. Nec ore
est minor sensus referens repostum
      mentis acumen.
Omnis hunc virtus decorat suprema,
140 una sed cunctis animosa praefert,
nostra quos aetas habet et veretur
      munera fundens.
Non enim quaerit sibi nec recondit
hic opes tantas quibus altus heros
145 affluit longe, sed eas probatis
      donat amicis.
Quo sit ut tantam sibi compararit
gloriam princeps generosus, omnis
ut sibi miro pietatis igni
150   iungat amantes.
Hunc, pii vates, celebrate vestris
cantibus semper. Modulis lyraque
hunc super cunctos bonitate claros
      ferte Novellum.

The son of father Pandolfo Malatesta, Novello, who shines brilliantly like a star among all the princes, is second to none in his lineage. He alone enjoys sweet tranquility; he alone rejoices that 125 he has brought about a safe peace for his people. This man never comports himself with severity toward a virtuous man; rather, he is merciful towards all men. He is the light, the glory, and the 130 source of the greatest pleasure at the present time and for the ages to come. He is sweet of face; he is serious and prudent, courageous and powerful. His speech flows with eloquence, making one 135 think of Maia's son. And his disposition reveals the keenness of his intellect no less than does his oratory. Every sublime virtue adorns this man. But in the virtue of his soul he is superior to all 140 men of our time whom the present age reveres and honors with gifts. For he does not pursue great wealth for himself nor does he hoard it, though this lofty hero has long been wealthy. But rather he showers it upon his virtuous friends. And so, this great and 145 generous prince has won so much glory for himself that he binds all lovers of virtue to himself with wondrous passion. 150

O hear me, you pious poets, always celebrate this man with your songs. And with your lyric poetry and your lyre lift Novello to the heavens, high above all others famous for their virtue.

Biographical Notes

ᚷᛝᚠ

ALAGNO, LUCREZIA D' (c.1430–1479). Mistress of King Alfonso of Naples. Lucrezia d'Alagno was the daughter of Cola and Covella Toraldo, wealthy Italians residing in Torre del Greco. In 1448 King Alfonso, who was then fifty-four, took the eighteen-year-old Alagno as his mistress. In 1457 Alfonso tried to have Pope Callixtus III annul his marriage to Maria of Castile so that he could marry Alagno, but his request was denied. When Alfonso died in 1458, Alagno's position at court became untenable. After Alfonso's death and the succession of his son Ferrante, Alagno was alleged to have taken as her lover Jacopo Piccinino, the famous *condottiere* and son-in-law of Francesco Sforza who was murdered in 1465 while he was King Ferrante's guest at the Castelnuovo. In 1469 Alagno moved to Rome, where she died in 1479 and was buried in Santa Maria sopra Minerva. She is addressed in Filelfo's *Odes* 2.6, 3.3, and 3.10 as Lucretia.

See Michele Manfredi, "Alagno, Lucrezia d'," in *DBI* 1.554.

ALAMANNI, ANDREA (1421–1473). Leading Florentine humanist, Hellenist, patron and friend of Filelfo. Andrea Alamanni frequented the circles of several influential Florentine Hellenists, including Donato Acciaiuoli, Alamanno Rinuccini, and Niccolò della Luna. He occupied a number of key offices in the Florentine government. In addition to his dedication of *Odes* 3.5 to Alamanni, the some twenty letters Filelfo addressed to his close friend and patron in Florence have been preserved in the 1502 edition of Filelfo's letters. Filelfo's cultivation of his longtime friendship with Alamanni was integral to his project of maintaining his ties to the Florentine humanists after his expulsion from the city in 1434.

For profiles of Alamanni, see Lauro Martines, The *Social World of the Florentine Humanists, 1390–1460* (Princeton: Princeton University Press, 1963), pp. 345–46; Alessandro Perosa, "Alamanni, Andrea," in *DBI* 1.564.

ALBERTI, LEON BATTISTA (1404–1472). Architect, humanist, and "universal man" of the early Renaissance. Born in Genoa during his family's exile from Florence, its native city, Leon Battista Alberti first befriended Filelfo at the University of Padua where both young men were studying law and rhetoric under the influential humanist professor Gasparino Barzizza (1415–1418), who also taught Francesco Barbaro and Antonio Beccadelli (Panormita). Alberti renewed his friendship with Filelfo when he was in Florence (1429–1434), at the University of Bologna (1437–1438), and in Mantua during Pope Pius II's Congress to mount a crusade against the Turks (1459); Alberti was in Mantua that year working on the design of San Sebastiano. From 1434–1472, Alberti spent much of his life in Rome where he served as a secretary in the papal curia. In 1428 he wrote his *De commodis literarum atque incommodis* ("On the Advantages and Disadvantages of Literature") in which he reproaches his contemporaries for their obsession with wealth, he attacks studies in the professions as venal, and praises the pursuit of the liberal arts. When Alberti circulated his prose satire, *Momus* (1443–1450), contemporaries identified the object of Alberti's satire with two popes, Eugenius IV and Nicholas V. Filelfo's *Odes* 4.6, addressed to Alberti, represents a response to the *De commodis* and the *Momus*: Filelfo wonders whom Alberti means to satirize in the *Momus*.

See Anthony Grafton, *Leon Battista Alberti: Master Builder of the Italian Renaissance* (Cambridge: Harvard University Press, 2000); Cecil Grayson, "Alberti, Leon Battista," in *DBI* 1.702–9.

ALFONSO OF ARAGON (1396–1458), King of the Aragonese empire in the Western Mediterranean, including Naples and Sicily. Alfonso was born in Castile, the son of Ferdinando I of Antequera. He received a humanist education in Medina del Campo at the court of Enrico III of Castile, whose daughter Maria he married in 1415. In 1416, on his father's death, he acceded as Alfonso V to the throne of Aragon. In 1420, when Martin V named the Angevin king Louis III as the heir to the Neapolitan crown and enlisted Attendolo Sforza to oust Queen Giovanna II from the throne, the queen called upon Alfonso to come to Italy to defend her, declaring herself ready to adopt Alfonso as her successor. As Alfonso sailed toward Naples in September 1420, Giovanna invested him as Duke of Calabria while she named Braccio da Montone as her *condottiere*. In the face of both the Duke of Milan's (Filippo Maria Visconti) and Pope Martin's support for the Angevin king Louis' succession to the Neapolitan throne, Alfonso and his fleet entered the bay of Naples on July 8, 1421, disembarking at the Castel dell'Ovo. From there he proceeded to the Castelnuovo, where Giovanna and her court received him as her heir. But on September 14 Giovanna stripped Alfonso of the Duchy of Calabria and he returned to Castile. In 1430, when her rule was again threatened by the pope and the Angevin king Louis, Giovanna called for Alfonso to return to Naples as its ruler. Yet when he arrived in Italy, the queen again refused to abdicate. On February 2, 1435 Giovanna died and Alfonso proclaimed himself King of Naples. On route to Naples the Genovese naval captain Biagio Assereto intercepted Alfonso's ships and taking the king, his lord chamberlain Iñigo d'Avalos, and his men prisoner, he brought them to Filippo Maria Visconti. In Milan Visconti welcomed Alfonso to his court, showing him the respect due a king. Alfonso left Visconti's court having signed a secret treaty that bound him to support the duke against all enemies including the pope and Francesco Sforza. But by 1436–37, while the new

Angevin king René readied his army to destroy Alfonso's regiments and to take the Kingdom of Naples for himself, Alfonso persuaded Francesco Sforza, at this time the most powerful general in Italy, to sign a ten-year alliance with him. In 1438/39, Pope Eugenius and others urged the king to make peace with the Angevin King René. In December 1440, the chief of King René's army, Jacopo Caldora, died of a stroke and René was forced to retreat, abandoning Naples to Alfonso. On February 26, 1443, Alfonso at last celebrated his triumph as King Alfonso I of Naples, and wearing the bejeweled crown that signaled his sovereignty, he and his attendants processed through the city. The wars between the great Italian city-states and their *condottieri* went on unabated until 1454, when Milan, Venice, and Florence signed the Peace of Lodi, to which Alfonso became a signatory in 1455. Three years later the king died, on June 27.

In addition to presiding over a brilliant court, famous for its music and vernacular poetry, Alfonso also drew to his circle such luminaries of the humanist movement as Lorenzo Valla, Antonio Beccadelli (Panormita), Giovanni Pontano, Giannozzo Manetti, Bartolomeo Facio, Enea Silvio Piccolomini, Pier Candido Decembrio, and the renowned Greek emigré scholars Theodore Gaza, Gregorio Tiphernas, and George Trebizond. Filelfo's *Odes* reflect his desire to obtain patronage from this pillar of the humanist movement and Alfonso is mentioned in a number of poems, and *Odes* 4.9, 5.2, and 5.9 are addressed directly to the king himself.

Despite his eulogizers' attempts to paint the king as sexually temperate, Alfonso supported a series of mistresses, the best known of whom were the wife of a Barcelona citizen, Gueraldona Carlina, who bore him a son, Ferdinando I (Ferrante I), whom he named his heir to the throne of Naples, and the young Italian heiress Lucrezia d'Alagno (see above).

See Alan Ryder, *Alfonso the Magnanimous. King of Aragon, Naples and Sicily, 1396–1458* (Oxford: Clarendon Press, 1990); Ernesto

Pontieri, *Alfonso il magnanimo, re di Napoli, 1435–1458* (Naples: Edizioni scientifiche italiane, 1975); Ruggero Moscati, "Alfonso V d'Aragona," in *DBI* 2:323–331.

ARCIMBOLDI, NICOLÒ (1404–1459). Parma-born jurist, diplomat, and orator. A longtime friend and advisor of both Filelfo and his arch-enemy Pier Candido Decembrio, Nicolò joined Duke Filippo Maria Visconti's court when Visconti occupied Parma in 1420. After receiving his doctorate in law at Pavia, Arcimboldi was employed as papal orator first under Martin V (1428–1429) and later Eugenius IV (1439). He served three successive regimes as *consigliere* in Milan, under Filippo Maria Visconti (1438–1447); the Ambrosian Republic (1447–1450); and Francesco Sforza (1450–1459). He forged the alliance between Visconti and Francesco Sforza that resulted in the marriage between his daughter Bianca Maria Visconti and Sforza. In 1449 he negotiated an alliance between the Ambrosian Republic and King Alfonso of Naples. After Sforza's accession to the throne in Milan in 1450, Arcimboldi assisted the duke in orchestrating the isolation of Venice from the other Italian powers, principally Florence and Naples. Filelfo addresses his most scathing denunciation of the Ambrosian Republic in *Odes* 1.10 to Arcimboldi, a man whose integrity he regarded as unimpeachable.

See Nicola Raponi, "Arcimboldi, Nicolò," in *DBI* 3.779–81.

AVALOS, IÑIGO D' (c. 1400–1484). Chamberlain to King Alfonso of Naples and Count of Monteodorisio. He was an important patron of the humanist movement. Born of a noble Spanish family, Iñigo d'Avalos came to Naples in the service of King Alfonso of Aragon in 1435. He fought under Alfonso's command in the naval battle at Ponza where the Aragonese fleet was defeated by the Genovese captain Biagio Assereto. D'Avalos and Alfonso were taken prisoner and conveyed to Milan where Duke Filippo Maria

Visconti treated them with every kindness. D'Avalos remained at the Visconti court until 1439 when King Alfonso called him to return to Naples. Filelfo and d'Avalos became close friends in Milan, and their friendship was a key factor in Filelfo's decision to visit the Neapolitan court in 1453. In 1452 Iñigo married Antonella d'Aquino in a union approved by Alfonso, after the king had named d'Avalos his grand chamberlain, conferring the title Count of Monteodorisio on him at the same time. D'Avalos remained faithful to Alfonso's son Ferrante I when he ascended the throne of Naples on his father's death in 1458, despite the revolt of the barons of the realm who supported the pretender Jean d'Anjou against the king. Notwithstanding his advanced age, in 1481 d'Avalos participated in the siege of Otranto; in 1482 and 1484 he fought in the battles Naples waged against the pope, who was allied with the Venetian republic. In June 1484 he led the attack on Gallipoli, then occupied by Venice. He died on September 12, 1484, leaving his wife Antonella, their three daughters, and four sons. Filelfo salutes his friend d'Avalos in verse epistles scattered throughout the *Odes:* 2.6, 3.3, 3.10, 4.8, and 4.10.

See Gaspare De Caro, "Avalos, Iñigo d'," in *DBI* 4.635–36.

BASINIO DA PARMA (Basinio Basini, 1425–1457). Humanist and court poet to the lord of Rimini, Sigismondo Malatesta. Basinio was born into a Mantuan family in Tizzano dal Parma. His father Vincenzo di Basinio was a soldier in the service of Ottone Terzi. Young Basanio studied at the school of the famous humanist schoolmaster Vittorino da Feltre in Mantua and was also a pupil in that school of the Greek émigré scholar Teodoro Gaza. He followed Gaza to Ferrara where he met, and no doubt continued his studies with, Guarino Veronese. He spent the years 1446–1450 in Ferrara hoping to find a permanent post at the court of Leonello d'Este, for whom he composed a Latin poem that was recited on the occasion of the marriage of the daughter of a friend of the duke's. In 1450 Basinio wrote an eclogue dedicated to Pope Nicholas V, whose patronage he also sought. During the same year he wrote three Latin verse epistles to Sigismondo Malatesta, lord of Rimini, in which he offered to celebrate the glory of the Malatesta and their ancestors. He moved to Rimini and soon entered the service of Sigismondo. In 1453 Basinio completed a dynastic epic poem in Latin hexameters for Sigismondo, entitled *Hesperis*. The poem, which imitated Virgil's *Aeneid* and Homer's *Odyssey*, contained thirteen books, including a celebration of Sigismondo's glorious deeds in war and even a Homeric *nekuia*, in which Basinio's prince descends to the Underworld and meets the famous heroes of antiquity. In 1455 he completed his *Astronomica*, a hexameter poem in two books which contains a didactic treatise on the heavens based on Aratus' *Phaenomena*. He also published a polemic in which he argued that the study of Greek was indispensable to scholarship in Latin. Basinio's last work was the *Liber Isottaeus*, an amatory romance in three books, each containing ten Ovidian elegies in epistolary form, with echoes of Ovid's *Heroides*; the *Isottaeus* weaves together fictional tales with the non-fiction story of the romance between Sigismondo and his third wife Isotta degli Atti. Basinio died after a brief illness in Rimini, at the age of thirty-two. Filelfo seems to have stopped in Rimini on his journey to Naples in 1453; it was no doubt to commemorate his visit to Malatesta's court that he wrote *Odes* 3.8 for Sigismondo and *Odes* 5.7, composed in Greek hexameters, for his Hellenist friend Basinio.

See Augusto Campana, "Basinio da Parma," in *DBI* 7.89–98.

BROCARDO, PERSICO (fl. 1440–1465). Milanese humanist and longtime client of the famous condottiere and rival of Francesco Sforza, Jacopo Piccinino. Brocardo became Jacopo Piccinino's chancellor when he served as Visconti's condottiere. When Duke Filippo Maria Visconti died in 1447 and the Ambrosian Republic was formed, Brocardo led the anti-Sforza faction. A probable date for *Odes* 1.7, which is addressed to Brocardo, is 1453, after Jacopo Piccinino had attempted to secure a state for himself. Piccinino had taken up residence in Brescia but in 1453 Sforza captured the city for himself with the help of the Angevin king René. Brocardo had undoubtedly long been a courtier and orator in the Visconti court and also a friend of Filelfo's. Filelfo in *Odes* 1.7 wonders why an educated man like Brocardo would choose to throw in his lot with the likes of Piccinino, whose assassination would be ordered by the condottiere's patron King Ferrante I in Naples in 1465. The learned Brocardo and Filelfo had probably remained friends and perhaps allies over the years despite the continually deteriorating relations between their patrons, Piccinino and Sforza?

CHARLES VII (1403–1461; reigned 1422–1461), King of France. After the death of Charles' father, Charles VI, in 1418, the duke of Burgundy (John the Fearless) and his supporters staged a bloody massacre of the Armagnac supporters of the dauphin Charles VII and the Valois dynasty. In retaliation, Charles and his faction murdered the duke of Burgundy. The duke's son, Philip the Good, then signed a treaty with Henry V, king of England, consigning the dominion of France to England. Charles fought back, leading his troops against both the British and the Burgundians with the brilliant military leadership of Joan of Arc (who was imprisoned and executed by the English in 1431). In 1435, Charles succeeded in negotiating a lasting peace with the Burgundian faction and by 1449 he was able to expel the English from France, effectively bringing to a close the Hundred Years' War between France and England (1337–1453). In 1447, Charles, who was a cousin of Filippo Maria Visconti, was pulled into the anti-Venetian League the duke had formed with Alfonso of Naples and Pope Eugenius IV. In 1452, Charles entered into an alliance with Milan and Florence against King Alfonso of Aragon, an alliance that was effectively neutralized by the Peace of Lodi in 1454.

In an aggressive campaign to obtain either a job offer or an invitation to Charles's court, Filelfo sent numerous letters to Charles's chief counselors, Guillaume Jouvenel des Ursins and his Greek émigré physician Thomas Coronaeus, during the years 1454–1455. At least eighteen of these letters are extant and in print. Filelfo addressed five pieces in his *Carmina* to Charles VII: *Odes* 1.1, 1.4, 2.4, 3.1, 5.1. The rank of their dedicatee ensured that the poems addressed to the French king would be given pride of place; they preface both the first and last books of the collection, thus serving to frame the whole work.

See Malcom Fraham Allan Vale, *Charles VII* (Berkeley: University of California, 1974).

DECEMBRIO, PIER CANDIDO. (1399–1477). Milanese humanist, defender of the Ambrosian Republic, and rival of Filelfo. Pier Candido Decembrio was born in Pavia to the ducal secretary and notary Uberto Decembrio and Caterina Marazzi, the daughter of a distinguished Pavian physician. As a child, Decembrio received his first lessons in Greek from his father and the great Byzantine scholar-teacher and ambassador Emmanuel Chrysoloras, who frequented Uberto's house. The family was forced to remain in exile in Genoa under the protection of the Doge Tommaso Fregosa until they returned to Milan in 1419, when Pier Candido entered into the service of Filippo Maria Visconti as ducal secretary and ambassador, posts he retained until Visconti's death in 1447. In 1424 he married Caterina Bossi, who bore him two sons. On Caterina's death in 1464, Decembrio married the noblewoman Battistina di Battista degli Amedei. Decembrio was commissioned by Visconti to translate into Italian a number of Latin works, including Caesar's *De bello gallico* and *De bello civili* and Leonardo Bruni's *De primo bello punico* he also wrote a *Vita Philippi Mariae Visconti* for his patron. During this time he remained in close touch with the literary luminaries of the period: Antonio da Rho, Gasparino Barzizza, Maffeo Vegio, Guarino Veronese, and Lorenzo Valla among others, although he never relinquished his enmity toward Filelfo, his arch-enemy at the Milanese court.

After Visconti's death, Decembrio supported the newly formed Ambrosian Republic, holding the position of secretary of the citizen's council until the fall of the Republic in February 1450. After Sforza's accession to the duchy in Milan, Decembrio fled from Milan to Rome, serving first Pope Nicholas V and subsequently Pope Calixtus III after Nicholas' death. In 1456 he joined the court of King Alfonso in Naples, where he had been a guest in 1452. After Alfonso's death in 1458, having enjoyed the literary camaraderie of Panormita, Valla, Theodore Gaza, Giannozzo Manetti, Iñigo d'Avalos, and others at the Neapolitan court, he continued to serve Alfonso's son and heir, Ferrante I, until 1459 when civil war broke out in Naples. He then returned to Milan where he lived until 1466, when he was called to join the court of Borso d'Este in Ferrara. During this period he continued to write and circulate many of his works; among these are the *Romanae historiae brevis epitoma* (1450), the *De natura avium et animalium* (1460), the *De origine fidei* (1455), and his *Vita Homeri*. In 1473 he went back to Milan for the last time to face charges that he had slandered the Sforza family. He was successfully defended by one of Filelfo's oldest friends and staunchest supporters, Nicodemo Tranchedini. On November 12, 1477, Decembrio died at his home in Milan after a month-long illness. Filelfo impugns Decembrio as typifying the most corrupt of the leaders of the Ambrosian Republic in *Odes* 3.4.

See Paolo Viti, "Decembrio, Pier Candido," in *DBI* 33.488–98.

GONZAGA, CARLO (1418–1456). Lifelong *condottiere* and second-born son of Gianfrancesco Gonzaga, lord of Mantua, and Paola Malatesta; he was also a poet and humanist educated at the famous school established by Vittorino da Feltre in Mantua. In 1437 Carlo Gonzaga married Lucia di Niccolò (III) d'Este, who died the same year, leaving no children. In 1445 he married Rengarda, daughter of Guido Manfredi, lord of Faenza; they had one son, Ugolotto, and three daughters, Paola, Cecilia, and Gentile. Carlo also had a natural son with his longtime mistress Dionisia, whose surname is unknown. A lifelong friend of Filelfo, Gonzaga changed his loyalties many times to gain advantage for himself. He first served Filippo Maria Visconti, duke of Milan, in 1438–39, against Venetian troops led by Francesco Sforza, who took him prisoner; he then served Pope Eugenius IV in 1444, returning to Milan to serve Visconti again in 1445. With the death of Visconti in 1447, Gonzaga served the newly established Ambrosian Republic in Milan, this time at the side of Francesco Sforza who had left Venice to fight for the Republic. But when Sforza signed the Treaty of Rivoltella with Venice in 1448, abandoning his pledge to defend the Ambrosian Republic, Gonzaga broke with Sforza and was elected Captain of the Ambrosian Republic. His brother Ludovico Gonzaga now having succeeded to the lordship of Mantua, Carlo Gonzaga hoped to become lord of Milan. In August 1449, Sforza offered Gonzaga 12,000 ducats and the city of Alessandria if he would defect to him. On September 11, Carlo signed an agreement with Sforza in which he surrendered Crema and Lodi to Sforza in exchange for Tortona. While Sforza stationed his army outside the gates of Milan, prohibiting all traffic in and out of the city, the Ambrosian Republic desperately tried to solicit assistance from Venice. But on March 26, 1450, Sforza entered Milan, and the city surrendered to him without resistance. In 1451 Carlo Gonzaga defected to Venice; and in 1452/3, as a condottiere for Venice, he attacked his brother Ludovico's army. Ludovico defeated him in 1453, and in 1454 Carlo fled to Ferrara. That year he and Francesco Sforza were discovered plotting against Ludovico to get control of Mantua. In 1455, one year before his death, having been dismissed by the Venetian Republic, Carlo attempted to win a contract as the pope's *condottiere* but his efforts were unsuccessful. He died unexpectedly in Ferrara on December 20, 1456. Filelfo's six poems addressed to Carlo in the collection (*Odes* 1.3, 2.1, 2.5, 3.2, 3.9, and 5.4) span the gamut in terms of tone: the poet ranges from playing Carlo's Ovidian *praeceptor amoris* to expressing his own grief, disappointment, and anger at Carlo.

See Isabella Lazzarini, "Gonzaga, Carlo," in *DBI* 57: 693–96.

GONZAGA, LUDOVICO (1412–1478). Marchese of Mantua after 1444, eldest son of Gianfrancesco Gonzaga, lord of Mantua, and brother of Carlo Gonzaga. Educated by Vittorino da Feltre at his school in Mantua, Ludovico Gonzaga married Barbara of Brandenburg. In the fall of 1447, while the new Ambrosian Republic was regrouping in Milan after Visconti's death and after Francesco Sforza sacked and occupied Piacenza, Ludovico Gonzaga, who had remained loyal to Filippo Maria Visconti for many years, now broke with Sforza and defected to Venice. On September 15, 1448, he fought on the side of the Venetians in the disastrous defeat of their army at Caravaggio. In *Odes* 5.9, the only poem in the collection in which Ludovico Gonzaga plays a role, Filelfo suppresses the marchese's personal break with Sforza during the period of the Milanese Republic, just as the poet makes no explicit mention in the *Odes* of Sforza's sudden defection to Venice. Ludovico Gonzaga is remembered for his urban building projects in Mantua and his patronage of architects and painters in preparation for the pope's international congress held in that city in 1459.

See Lazzarini, "Gonzaga, Carlo." (There is no separate entry for Ludovico Gonzaga in the *DBI*.)

DOMENICO MALATESTA (also known as MALATESTA NOVELLO; 1418–1465). Lord of Cesena and Cervia, brother of Sigismondo Malatesta and natural son of Pandolfo Malatesta and Antonia Barignano. Less powerful than his brother, Malatesta Novello ruled only two cities. Whereas Sigismondo served Sforza, Novello allied himself with Sforza's enemies, Niccolò and Francesco Piccinino. Novello has been judged a weak ruler more interested in the arts and literature than in war and conquest. Under his patronage the Biblioteca Malatestiana in Cesena was founded. Philip Jones characterizes Novello as a "pallid figure, quiet, austere, scholarly, infirm of health, but not incapable of devising policies of his own or resenting the injuries done to him."

P. J. Jones, *The Malatesta of Rimini and the Papal State* (Cambridge: Cambridge University Press, 1974). See also Giovanni Soranzo, "Malatesta, Sigismondo Pandolfo," in the *Enciclopedia Italiana* (Milan: Istituto dell' Enciclopedia Italiana, 1934), pp. 1003–1005.

MALATESTA, SIGISMONDO PANDOLFO (1417–1468), lord of Rimini, Fano, and Senigallia. The brother of Domenico Malatesta and the natural son of Pandolfo Malatesta and Antonia Barignano, Sigismondo Malatesta is generally represented, but most influentially in the *Commentarii* of Pope Pius II, as the quintessential outlaw *condottiere*. Reports (which were never substantiated) claimed that Sigismondo murdered his first two wives, Ginevra d'Este (daughter of Niccolò d'Este) and Polissena Sforza (daughter of Francesco Sforza). Sigismondo and his men are also said to have attacked and raped a Bavarian noblewoman who subsequently died. Upon Polissena's death in 1456, he married his mistress Isotta degli Atti. In the wars between the most powerful Italian states (1433–1463) — Milan, Florence, Venice, Naples, and their client cities — Sigismondo frequently changed allegiances. He served both Francesco Sforza and Eugenius IV as their condottiere; he also fought under the banner of King Alfonso of Naples but defected from him in 1447. At the conclusion of the wars between the great Italian city states at the Peace of Lodi (1455/6), Alfonso of Naples and the other signatories barred him from participation in the treaty. Sigismondo was excommunicated by Pius II in 1459. Always on the lookout for a new patron, Filelfo no doubt addressed his metrical showpiece, *Odes* 3.8, to Sigismondo as a bid for a stipend from Rimini.

Filelfo praises both brothers as protectors and patrons of poetry and the arts in two separate encomia, one for Sigismondo (*Odes* 3.8) and another for Novello (*Odes* 5.10). But he draws a clear distinction between the two siblings, portraying Sigismondo as a war hero, while lionizing Novello as a peacemaker.

See bibliography on preceding entry.

NICHOLAS V (Tommaso Parentucelli de Sarzana, 1397–1455). Pope (1446–1455) and noted humanist scholar. Born at Sarzana near La Spezia of a physician father, Parentucelli studied at the University of Bologna (1413–1416). He became a tutor in the households of Rinaldo degli Albizzi and Palla Strozzi in Florence (1417–1420), and later performed literary tasks for Cosimo de'Medici. He returned to the University of Bologna where he entered the household of Cardinal Niccolò Albergati (1421–1443). In 1444 Eugenius IV appointed Parentucelli bishop of Bologna, elevating him to the cardinalate in 1446. On the death of Eugenius in 1447, Parentucelli was elected to the papacy, taking the name Nicholas V. As ruler of the Papal States, Nicholas acted as a peacemaker, notably in the formulation of the Peace of Lodi (1454–1556). A brilliant classical scholar himself, he made the purchase of ancient Greek and Latin manuscripts and the fostering of humanists and humanism the centerpiece of his papacy. He is credited with founding the Vatican Library. Filelfo had probably first connected with Parentucelli when they were students at Bologna and Padua in 1415–1417; certainly, as his letters show, the two became friends again when Filelfo taught at Bologna in 1428 and 1439. In 1453 Nicholas named Filelfo a papal scriptor and awarded him a yearly stipend. Filelfo dedicated a Greek poem in Sapphic strophes to Nicholas in his *Psychagogia*. Filelfo's *Odes* 5.5 and possibly *Odes* 1.6 also appear to be addressed to Pope Nicholas though the name Nicolò Arcimboldi is written in the margin next to the heading of 1.6.

See Giannozzo Manetti, *De vita ac gestis Nicolai quinti summi pontificis*, ed. Anna Modigliani (Rome: Istituto storico italiano per il Medio Evo, 2005); Joachim W. Stieber, "Nicholas V," in *The Encyclopedia of the Renaissance*, ed. Paul. F. Grendler (New York: Scribners, 1999), 4.316–17; Guillaume Mollat, "Nicolas V," in *Dictionaire de Théologie Catholique* (Paris, 1931), 11.541–48.

SFORZA, FRANCESCO (1401–1466). Duke of Milan, 1450–1466, and Filelfo's principal employer and patron for fifteen years. The *condottiere* son of a famous *condottiere* father, Muzio Attendolo Sforza, Francesco Sforza served Duke Filippo Maria Visconti of Milan in numerous battles against Venice. He married Visconti's daughter Bianca Maria in 1443. In the early 1430s, he gathered around him a large following and amassed significant territorial holdings in Filelfo's homeland, the Marche. His rise to power was marked by shifting alliances. When Visconti entered into an alliance with Alfonso of Naples, Charles VII of France, and Pope Eugenius IV against Venice, he appointed Sforza as the captain-general of the Milanese army; he also backed Sforza's appointment as the commander over the army of the anti-Venetian league. When Visconti died in 1447 and a coalition of nobles and guildsmen assumed control of the duchy of Milan, calling their new regime the Ambrosian Republic, Sforza led the Republic's armed forces to victory over the Venetians at Piacenza (1447), and again at Cassalmaggiore and Caravaggio (1448). Sforza then defected from the Ambrosian Republic, and on October 18, 1448 at Rivoltella, he signed a secret treaty with Venice in which he pledged to retake the former Venetian *terraferma* cities then under Milanese control, in exchange for which the Venetians were to allow Sforza to acquire the lordship of Milan. But on September 24, 1449, the Venetians signed a separate peace treaty with the Ambrosian Republic, excluding Sforza. Sforza then broke with Venice and laid siege to the city of Milan with his own troops. On February 25, 1450, when the captains of the Ambrosian Republic were preparing to surrender Milan to Venice in order to secure Venetian support against Sforza, the Milanese people revolted against their government and forced the leaders of the Ambrosian Republic and their Venetian allies to flee. On February 26, 1450, Sforza entered the city of Milan as its new *signore*. As duke of Milan, Sforza continued to battle the Venetians until, with the support of Cosimo de' Medici and Pope Nicholas V, he instituted the Peace of Lodi in 1454, which, co-signed by Alfonso of Naples in 1455, stabilized Italy. After the Peace he provided modest support to education and the arts in the city: he allocated funding to the university at Pavia and the humanist cause in Milan led by Filelfo, and he commissioned Filarete to design and build the Ospedale Maggiore and to undertake the restoration of the ruined fortress of Porta Giovia in Milan.

Filelfo doles out relatively little praise to Francesco Sforza in the *Odes*. Charles VII, Alfonso of Naples, Iñigo d'Avalos, and Carlo Gonzaga are each the focus of encomia and verse epistles devoted exclusively to them in the *Odes* in ways that Sforza is not. With the exception of the *Praefatio* to the collection, the Duke of Milan is only eulogized in combination with other princes: he is praised with Charles VII (*Odes* 2.4); with Ludovico Gonzaga and Alfonso (*Odes* 5.9), and at the end of a long lamentation for sufferings of the city of Milan (*Odes* 2.3).

See Eugenio Garin, "La cultura milanese nella prima metà del XV secolo" and "L'età Sforzesca dal 1450 al 1500," both in *Storia di Milano* (Milan: Fondazione Treccani degli Alfieri, 1953–66), 6.545–608 and 7.539–97, respectively; A. Menniti Ippolito, "Francesco I. Sforza," in *DBI* 50.1–15; Gregory Lubkin, *A Renaissance Court. Milan under Galeazzo Maria Sforza* (Berkeley and Los Angeles: University of California Press, 1994); Diana Robin, *Filelfo in Milan*; Cecilia M. Ady, *The History of Milan under the Sforza* (London: Methuen, 1907).

SFORZA SECONDO (1433–1492). The count of Borgonuovo and the natural son of Francesco Sforza, born before the duke's marriage to Bianca Maria Visconti. While Secondo grew up alongside his half-brothers and sisters in the family castle at Pavia and the Porta Giovia fortress in Milan, he was not legitimized until 1448. In a marriage arranged by Sforza, Secondo married Antonia dal Verme, the daughter of an eminent condottiere family, the Dal Verme counts of Bobbio. Sforza historian Gregory Lubkin describes Secondo as "politically significant" among the half-brothers and legitimate heirs to the Milanese throne. When the eldest legitimate son of Francesco Sforza, Galeazzo Maria, became duke of Milan on Francesco Sforza's death in 1466, Sforza Secondo defected from Milan, only to be wooed by Galeazzo into returning to the fold. A patron of Filelfo's, Secondo is the dedicatee of three of the *Odes:* 3.6, 3.7, and 5.3.

See Lubkin, *A Renaissance Court;* Caterina Santoro, *Gli Sforza* (Milan: Editori Associati, 1994).

SIMONETTA, FRANCESCO ("CICCO") (1410–1480). Nephew of distinguished Calabrian diplomat Angelo Simonetta. Born in Caccuri, Calabria, Cicco entered Francesco Sforza's service in 1448 when he fought beside him in the battle of Caravaggio against the Venetians. Cicco was subsequently named First Secretary, Presiding Officer of the Privy Chancery, and a member of the Privy Council under Duke Francesco Sforza. King Alfonso conferred on him the honorary title of President of the Camera della Sommaria in the Kingdom of Naples. He became governor of Lodi in 1449, and in 1451 he was named lord of Sartirana. On Francesco Sforza's death in 1466, he became counselor and secretary to Galeazzo Maria Sforza. Filelfo addressed *Odes* 4.2 to Simonetta. In 1480, a year before Filelfo left the city of Milan for good, Cicco was sentenced to death and decapitated by Duke Lodovico (Il Moro) Sforza.

See Lubkin, *A Renaissance Court*; Gary Ianziti, *Humanistic Historiography under the Sforzas: Politics and Propaganda in Sforza Milan* (Oxford: Clarendon Press, 1988).

SIMONETTA, GIOVANNI (d. 1491). Calabrian-born historian, propagandist, and ducal secretary, first to Duke Francesco Sforza and then to his son Galeazzo Maria. Brother of Cicco and nephew of Angelo, Giovanni Simonetta is the addressee of Filelfo's *Odes* 5.8. Commissioned by Francesco Sforza, Simonetta wrote a history of his patron's rise to power, the *Rerum gestarum Francisci Sfortiae commentarii*.

See Ianziti, *Humanistic Historiography*; Lubkin, *A Renaissance Court*.

VIMERCATE, GASPARE DA (?-1468). Milanese statesman and soldier. Born into a noble Milanese family, Vimercate served Filippo Maria Visconti until the duke's death in 1447. When the Ambrosian Repubic was constituted to rule the duchy upon Visconti's death, Vimercate was elected one of the new government's twenty-four captains. He then served in the Milanese armed forces when Francesco Sforza defeated the Venetians at Caravaggio in 1448. In 1450 Vimercate led the citizens' revolt against captains of the Ambrosian Republic. He was subsequently instrumental in paving the way for Francesco Sforza's triumphal entrance into Milan and his accession to the Milanese throne in March 1450. Filelfo's *Odes* 2.10 tells the story of Vimercate's heroism during the final throes of the Ambrosian Republic and his expulsion of its leaders from the city.

See Carlo Guido Mor, "Vimercate, Gaspare da," in *Enciclopedia Italiana* (Rome: Istituto della Enciclopedia Italiana, 1937–45), 35.378.

VISCONTI, BIANCA MARIA (1425–1468). Duchess of Milan and wife of Francesco Sforza. Bianca Maria Visconti was the natural daughter of Filippo Maria Visconti, duke of Milan, and the noblewoman Agnese del Maino, Visconti's mistress. Growing up in a castle in Abbiategrasso where she was given a humanist education in Latin, Tuscan, and Provençal literature, Bianca Maria was betrothed at the age of six to her father's leading condottiere Francesco Sforza, a man twenty-five years her senior. In 1441 Francesco and Bianca were married in Cremona, the city bequeathed to her as part of her dowry by her father. In 1442 Bianca was made regent of the Marche, her husband's native province. Though Bianca and Francesco became estranged from her father after their marriage, Visconti attempted a reconciliation in 1447 when he appointed Sforza captain of his army; but the appointment was soon withdrawn.

Filippo Maria Visconti died unexpectedly on August 13 of that year, and a popular republican government was formed to replace the monarchy. Sforza was appointed the supreme commander of the Milanese army. While he was in the field with his army, Bianca Maria ruled Cremona. She gained renown in 1448 when, dressed in a full suit of armor, she and her Cremonese troops drove the invading Venetian army out of her city. Filelfo celebrated the episode in his poem, the *Sforziad*, where Bianca Maria is portrayed as a female warrior, resembling Virgil's Amazon princess Camilla in the *Aeneid*.

With the expulsion of the leaders of the Republic from Milan in February 1450, Bianca Maria was welcomed back in her native city of Milan. She and her husband Francesco Sforza entered the city in triumph in March 1450, hailed as the new duke and duchess of Milan. In twenty-five years of marriage, Bianca bore eight children who survived into adulthood. She engaged tutors expert in both Greek and Latin grammar and rhetoric to educate them; she arranged royal and noble marriages for all her sons and daughters with the exception of Ascanio, who took orders and rose to the cardinalate. Two of her sons, Galeazzo Maria (assassinated in 1476) and Lodovico ("Il Moro"), acceded to the Milanese throne. Two years after her husband's death, Bianca Maria died at the age of 43. Filelfo, Bianca's court poet who dedicated *Odes* 4.1 to her, was commissioned by Galeazzo Maria to deliver her funeral oration in the Duomo.

See Santoro, *Gli Sforza*; Lubkin, *A Renaissance Court*; Giovanni Benadduci, ed., *Contributo alla bibliografia di Francesco Filelfo*, in *Atti e memorie della R. Deputazione di storia patria per le province delle Marche*, 5 (1901): 1–261; 459–535.

APPENDIX

The Meters of Filelfo's Odes

❦❦❦

The first table below lists the meters used in each of Filelfo's odes in the order in which the odes appear in this volume; the second table lists the various meters used in their order of frequency. Readers interested in a detailed metrical analysis of the various forms of verse may consult the prosody section of any descriptive Latin grammar.

2.3. Sapphic Strophes

2.4. Elegiac Couplets

2.5. Hemiepes and Adonic

2.6. Elegiac Couplets, 1–82; Third Asclepiadean Strophes, 83–137

2.7. Hemiepes and Adonic

2.8. First Asclepiadeans

2.9. Phalaecean Hendecasyllables

2.10. Sapphic Strophes, 1–188; Phalaecean Hendecasyllables, 189–95

3.1. Hexameter

3.2. Third Asclepiadean Strophes

3.3. Elegiac couplets

3.4. Sapphic hendecasyllables, 1–92; Adonic, 93

3.5. Elegiac Couplets, 1–24; Couplets: alternating First Asclepiadeans and Glyconics, 25–30; Sapphic Strophes, 31–66; Iambic Trimeter, 67–98

3.6. Elegiac Couplets

3.7. Couplets: alternating Phalaecean Hendecasyllables and Elegiac Pentameters

3.8. Elegiac Couplets, 1–8; Sapphic Strophes, 9–16; Phalaecean Hendecasyllables, 17–24; Third Asclepiadean Strophes, 25–32; Anapaestic Dimeter, 33–40; Scazons, 41–48; Couplets: alternating Iambic Trimeter and Iambic Dimeter, 49–56; Couplets: alternating Phalaecean Hendecasyllables and Alcaic Decasyllables, 57–64; Iambic Dimeter Catalectic, 65–72; Hemiepes and Fourth Paeon, 73–80; Couplets: alternating Aristophanic and Modified Greater Sapphic, 81–88; Couplets: Anapaestic Trimeter Catalectic and Anapaestic Tripody, 89–96; Hexameter, 97–104

3.9. Elegiac Couplets

3.10. Phalaecean Hendecasyllables

4.1. Alcaic Hendecasyllables, 1–54; Sapphic Strophes, 55–138
4.2. Elegiac Couplets
4.3. Phalaecean Hendecasyllables
4.4. Elegiac Couplets
4.5. First Asclepiadeans, 1–102; 165–77; Elegiac Couplets, 103–64
4.6. Elegiac Couplets
4.7. Iambic Trimeter
4.8. Elegiac Couplets
4.9. Iambic Trimeter
4.10. Couplets: alternating Sapphic Hendecasyllabic and Glyconic lines

5.1. Anapaestic Dimeter
5.2. Elegiac Couplets
5.3. Couplets: alternating First Asclepiadean and Iambic Dimeter verses
5.4. Elegiacs, 3–68; Phalaecean Hendecasyllables, 1–2, 69–122
5.5. Sapphic Strophes
5.6. Elegiac Couplets
5.7. Greek Hexameter
5.8. Elegiac Couplets
5.9. Third Asclepiadean Strophes, 1–100; 237–44; Elegiac Couplets, 101–236
5.10. Elegiac Couplets, 1–122; Sapphic Strophes 123–54

TABLE II

1. Elegiac Couplets: 2.4, 2.6, 3.3, 3.6, 3.8. 3.9, 4.2, 4.4, 4.5, 4.6, 4.8., 5.2, 5.4, 5.6, 5.8, 5.9., 5.10
2. Asclepiadeans: First: 1.5, 2.8, 3.5, 4.5, 5.3; Second: 1.3, 1.9; Third: 2.6. 3.2, 3.8, 5.9

3. Phalaecean Hendecasyllables: 1.4, 1.8, 2.9, 2.10, 3.7, 3.8, 3.10, 4.3, 5.4

4. Sapphic Strophes: 1.1, 1.6, 2.1, 2.3, 2.10, 3.5, 3.8, 4.1, 5.5, 5.10

5. Iambic Trimeter: 1.9, 2.2, 3.5, 3.8, 4.7, 4.9

6. Hexameter: 1.7, 3.1, 3.8, 5.7

7. Sapphic Hendecasyllables: 3.4, 4.10

8. Anapaestic Dimeter: 1.2, 3.8, 5.1

9. Iambic Dimeter: 3.8, 5.3; and Iambic Dimeter Catalectic: 1.9, 3.8

10. Glyconics: 3.5, 4.10

11. Anapaestic Trimeter Catalectic and Anapaestic Tripody Couplets: 3.8

12. Alcmanian Strophes: 1.9

13. Alcaic Hendecasyllables: 4.1

14. Alcaic Decasyllables: 3.8

15. Hemiepes and Adonic: 2.5, 2.7

16. Hemiepes and Fourth Paean: 3.8

17. Pherecrateans: 1.5

18. Scazons: 3.8

19. Alternating Modified Greater Sapphic and Aristophanic: 3.8

Note on the Text

🔊🔊🔊

The five books of Filelfo's *Odae* have been printed only twice since they were first circulated in manuscript in the middle of the fifteenth century. The *editio princeps* is:

Brix   *Odae*. [Brescia]: Angelus Britannicus, 4 July 1497.[1]

A second edition was issued in Paris by Jean Granjon for Thomas Kees, ca. 1511, with brief explanations by Jacques d'Aulnoy (Jacobus de Alneto).[2] A few individual odes have also appeared in modern anthologies and in modern secondary literature.[3] Eight fifteenth-century codices of Filelfo's *Odae* (*Carminum libri quinque*) are known, of which the two that form the basis of this edition are:

F   Florence, Biblioteca Medicea Laurenziana, Plut. 33.34.
P   Paris, Bibliothèque Nationale de France, Lat. 8127

The other six manuscripts are:

Berlin, Staatsbibliothek (Haus Zwei), Hamilton 511
Cesena, Biblioteca Malatestiana, 23.5
Chicago, Newberry Library, 103.8
Florence, Biblioteca Nazionale Centrale, Conv. Soppr. G 2 866
Vatican City, Biblioteca Apostolica Vaticana, Urb. lat. 701
Vatican City, Biblioteca Apostolica Vaticana, Vat. lat. 11518

As far as is known, no autograph manuscripts of the *Odae* survive.[4] However, the Florentine codex *F*, though not copied by Filelfo, contains autograph insertions by the poet: at ff. 111r-v and 120v Filelfo has entered the Greek verses himself with his own interlinear translations in Latin. The most elaborately rubricated of the fifteenth-century manuscripts, *P*, has corrections in Filelfo's hand at ff. 8r, 11v, 30v, 55r, 88r, and 125v, and has Greek verses and Latin translations of them in the author's hand at ff. 109v-110r and 119r. The copyist of *P* has been securely identified as Pagano da Rho, a scribe associated with the Visconti court who copied many manuscripts for Filelfo.[5] The Vatican codex, Urb. lat. 701, previously believed to be an autograph of the *Odae*, despite lacking the poet's additions, is now thought to have been written by Fabrizio Elfiteo, a diplomat for the Sforza and a friend and correspondent of Filelfo.[6] I have examined all eight of the fifteenth-century codices of the *Odae* on microfilm.

In preparing this edition of the *Odae*, I have collated *P, F,* and *Brix.* Only the punctuation and capitalization of the text have been modernized. Otherwise, with the exception of the consonants *i* for *j* and *v* for *u,* I have retained Filelfo's idiosyncratic orthography.[7] Maintaining the original orthography is particularly important in lyric poetry since the quantity of the syllables (long or short) in the Latin words used enforces the complex rhythmic patterns of the *Odes.* Thus Filelfo's reduction of consonant doublets to singlets in such words as *flama* and *Iupiter* (from *flama* and *Iuppiter*) produces short syllables; whereas the doubling of consonants in such words as *millia, relligio, sollemnis,* and *quottidie,* creates long syllables. Filelfo's frequent insertion of diphthongs into words that lack them in standard Latin, however (*baelva* for *belva, caetera* for *cetera, saemen* for *semen, foemineus* for *femineus, loetalis* for *letalis*), does not lengthen syllables since the *e* and hence the syllable in such words is already long. Nonetheless, diphthongization is a signature feature of Filelfo's orthography. In adverbs and conjunctions, *n* is generally used instead of *m* before *q* as in *nanque, nunquam, tanquam;* moreover, in certain nouns and adjectives *y* often replaces *i,* as in *sydus, inclytus, digytus, hyems, lachryma, satyra.* Filelfo characteristically introduces an aspirated *h* non-existent in classical Latin in such words as *Horcus, sepulchrum, trophaeum, cathaena;* moreover, the noun suffix *-tia* is generally replaced by *-cia,* as in *pudicicia, iusticia, avaricia, amicicia, stulticia, laeticia.*

To improve readability and to help readers orient themselves, English titles have been provided for the individual odes.

NOTES

1. Full data on this edition may be found in the British Library's online *Incunabula Short Title Catalogue,* no. ip00606000.

2. *Ode . . . numquam antehac Parrhisijs impressae fuerunt.* Described in the online WorldCat (OCLC), nos. 66433368, 311725681. For the date, see Brigitte Moreau, *Inventaire chronologique des éditions parisiennes du XVIe siècle,* II (Paris: Imprimerie municipale, 1977), p. 77, no. 85.

3. Arnaldi et al., eds., *Poeti Latini del Quattrocento,* contains *Odes* 1.2–4; 1.9; 2.4; 3.3; and 4.2; Alessandro Perosa and John Sparrow, eds., *Renaissance Latin Verse: An Anthology* (Chapel Hill: University of North Carolina Press, 1979), pp. 27–28, contains *Odes* 4.5, lines 1–42 only; and Robin, *Filelfo in Milan,* includes *Odes* 1.10; 2.2; 3.4; 4.5; 4.7.

4. I am indebted to Sylvia Fiaschi, the foremost expert on Filelfo's manuscripts and editorial practice, for having graciously shared with me her opinions on the extant codices of Filelfo's *Odae,* all of which she has examined. She notes that the three manuscripts (*P, F,* and Urb. lat. 701) that were assumed to be Filelfo autographs were each written by a different hand.

5. Filelfo, *Satyrae I,* ed. Fiaschi, pp. LXXI, LXXIX, LXXXI–LXXXII. The information concerning the corrections and additions inserted in Filelfo's own hand in codices *F* and *P* was furnished to me by Silvia Fiaschi.

6. See ibid., pp. LXVIII–LXIX, and A. C. de la Mare, "Script and Manuscripts in Milan under the Sforzas," in *Milano nell' età di Ludovico il Moro. Atti del convegno internazionale, 28 febbraio — 4 marzo 1983,* 2 vols. (Milan, 1983), II, pp. 397–408 at p. 407, note 45.

7. On Filelfo's orthography see Fiaschi's discussion in Filelfo, *Satyrae I,* pp. CXLVII-CLII.

Notes to the Text

ക്ഷേന

PREFACE

1. *Brix. adds* ad Franciscum Sphortiam mediolanensium quartum ducem Inclytum.

2. unius *F* : unus *P*

BOOK I

1. quem *P* : quam *F*

2. nostrae *is my emendation* : nostra *FP Brix*

3. iuvat *Brix*

4. efferi *FP* : efferri *Brix*

5. solus *FP* : solum *Brix*

BOOK II

1. *This line is metrically defective.*

2. *At line 100 the same metrical defect in the Third Asclepiadean strophe (the second choriamb is short a syllable) is found in all the MSS.*

3. Maria *is my emendation* : Marias *FP*

BOOK III

1. genitore tibi *F Brix.* : mihi fratre tibi *P*

2. tuens prima *Brix*

3. Amoratthus *P*

4. foelicibus *Brix*

5. irabar musis et flebam *F*

6. bilis *Newberry, Brix* : biblis *FP*

7. tela *F Brix*

385

8. caedat *Brix*

9. Venus *F Brix* : verus *P*

10. res regestas *F*

11. cunctis *Brix*

12. cum *F*

13. Num fervens *P* : Nunquid se *F Brix*

BOOK IV

1. non *F Brix* : nos *P*

2. vendicat *P*

3. 4.3.69. Timarchum *F* : cinaedum *P*

4. fervor *FP*: furor *Brix*

5. mox Ticinum suscipit *P, Urb. lat. 701* : Pavia mox excipit *F, Brix*

6. *The line is metrically defective; perhaps* cedite *should be read for* discedite, *as suggested by Perosa-Sparrow*

7. vis *FP*: ius *Brix*

8. creas *is my emendation* : creans *FP*

9. num *P* : Non *F*

BOOK V

1. Arabis *is my emendation* : Arabos *FP*

2. futura *is my emendation* : futurum *FP*

3. horrisonis *is my emendation* : horrisonas *FP*

4. priorum *P*

5. vindicat *F* : vendicat *P*

6. Arabis *is my emendation* : Arabos *FP*

7. quae *is my emendation* : qui *FP*

8. λίαν *P*

9. deorum *F* : dorum *P*

10. digne *is my emendation* : digna *FP Brix.*

11. vincere *Brix.* : vinceres *FP*

12. te *F* : quod *P*

Notes to the Translation

ॐ〰ॐ

ABBREVIATIONS

DBI   *Dizionario biografico degli italiani* (Rome: Istituto della Enciclopedia italiana, 1960–).

Epistolae   Francesco Filelfo, *Epistolarum familiarium libri XXXVII* (Venice: ex aedibus Ioannis et Gregorii de Gregoriis, 1502). The full collection in 48 books has never been published.

OLD   *Oxford Latin Dictionary*, ed. P. G. W. Glare (Oxford: Clarendon Press, 1982).

PREFACE

1. Duke of Milan and Filelfo's principal patron: see Biographical Notes.

2. Filelfo's cautionary exempla include Croesus (560–546 B.C.), king of the Lydians, captured by Cyrus, king and founder of the Persian Empire (559–529 B.C.; Herodotus 1.107–28); Marcus Licinius Crassus, First Triumvirate member legendary for his wealth, killed in the Parthian war (53 B.C); the mythical King Midas, whose golden touch brought him ruin; the king of the Medes, Astyages, who was defeated by Cyrus (549 B.C.; see above); and Alexander the Great (356–323 B.C.), who brought down the Persian Empire.

3. The marginalia of F and P identify this "Bias" as Bias of Priene (Herodotus 1.27 and 1.170), one of the Seven Sages of Greece, who brought about peace between Croesus and the Ionian islanders by advising Croesus against also entering into a naval war with the Ionians. See also Cicero *Paradoxa* 1.1.8; Seneca *Ep. 9.18.*

4. In lines 47–50, Filelfo echoes Anchises' counsel to Aeneas: *Romane, memento / — hae tibi erunt artes — pacique imponere morem, / parcere subiectis. . .* (Virgil, *Aen.* 6.851–53).

5. Francesco Sforza's wife, famous for having ridden out on horseback in full martial armor to defend Cremona from the attacking Venetian army: see Biographical Appendix.

6. Both *F* and *P* list in the margin all proper names referred to here and following. Phanes, one of the Orphic gods, is characterized by his radiance and his golden wings. Galeazzo Maria (1444–1476), the eldest son of Bianca Maria and Francesco Sforza, became duke of Milan after his father's death in 1466.

7. Ippolita Maria Sforza (1445–1488), sister of Galeazzo Maria and daughter of Bianca Maria Visconti and Francesco Sforza; Ippolita was destined to figure importantly in the duke's political and diplomatic program. At the age of 10, in 1455 (perhaps the year in which this ode was written), Ippolita was officially betrothed to Alfonso II of Naples, son of Ferrante I and heir to the throne of the kingdom of Naples.

8. The marginalia at line 142 identify the birthday (*natalis*) referred to here as the *natalis Christi* (Christ's birthday).

BOOK ONE

I.I

1. The marginalia identify the thief (*latro*) as "Mahomettus" (Mehmet II), the Turkish ruler of the Ottoman Empire, who sacked and conquered Constantinople in 1453.

2. Peleus's son Achilles drops out of the Trojan war after Homer, *Iliad* 1, and retires to his tent to play lyric poems.

3. The marginalia identify Filelfo's *senem Samium* (old man of the Samians) as Pythagoras, the mathematician and philosopher who was also celebrated in antiquity as a musician. See on this Diogenes Laertius, *Lives of the Philosophers* 8.46, a work Filelfo frequently consulted.

4. See Diogenes Laertius, *Lives of the Philosophers* 8, on the Greek thinker Empedocles, born in Sicily (c. 493–433 B.C.), whose two greatest philosophical works, *On Nature* and the *Purifications*, were in hexameters.

5. Alexander the Great of Macedon (356–323 B.C.), who expanded the Greek empire into Asia, Syria, India, and Egypt, and was famous for his love both of the Homeric poems and lyric poetry.

6. Lines 97–100 refer to two different legends of the founding of Thebes. According to one, Amphion's lyre playing so mobilized the citizens of Thebes that they were able to put away their differences and work together to build the walls that successfully protected the city and presaged its future greatness (Homer, *Od.* 11.262 ff. and Apollodorus 3.43 ff.). In the other foundation myth, the hero Cadmus, son of the king of Tyre, sows a plot of land in Greece with dragon's teeth, which spring from the ground as armed men who will become the forefathers of the Theban nobility.

7. Rhodope is a mountain in Thrace.

8. The Haemus is one of the highest mountains in Thrace. The image of the cypresses shaking their cone-like tops comes from Ovid, *Met.* 10.106.

9. The marginalia identify Saul as the Old Testament king and the prophet as David, the composer of the Psalms.

10. The name "Themistocles" is written in the margins of both manuscripts. The poet jokes here that the ignorant, who do not indulge in lyre playing or in listening to the poets, would confuse the Sicilian tyrant of Syracuse, Gelon (fl. 485 B.C.), with Themistocles, the Greek general (*strategos*) who defeated the Persians at Salamis (c. 480 B.C.).

11. According to Plato's *Phaedo* and Diogenes Laertius' life of Socrates, when the philosopher was in prison, before he took his life, he played the lyre and made a poetic version of Aesop's fables.

12. Tyrtaeus was a seventh-century B.C. Greek elegiac poet from Sparta, whose battle hymns, according to legend, helped the Spartans to conquer Messene.

13. The name "Ismenias," a celebrated Theban flute player, is written in the margins of both manuscripts.

14. Minerva is credited by some as being the inventor of the flute.

15. Apollo's brother Mercury or Hermes, the messenger of the gods, is identified in the marginalia as "Mercurius."

16. The Camenae (Camena, singular) are the Italian woodland goddesses identified with the Greek Muses as deities who inspired poetry and song.

17. The Scythian king Ateas asked the Ismenias to play for him; though others applauded, Ateas pronounced the whinnying of horses sweeter. (Plutarch, *Moralia* 334b).

1.2

18. The marginalia identify him as "Maemo of Siena."

1.3

19. According to some traditions, Homer was born in Smyrna on the coast of Asia Minor: see Cicero, *Att.* 9.9.2.

20. Aeacus in Greek myth was the son of Zeus and the nymph Aegina; he became the father of Telamon and the grandfather of Peleus, father of Achilles. Achilles is regularly referred to in Homer as Aeacides or Aeacus's son.

1.5

21. The Latinized names "Johannes Ossona," "Johannes Aplanus," and "Georgias [*sic*] Bisulcerus" are written in the margin as if the three are members of a ruling triumvirate. Citing contemporary chronicles such as Giovanni Simonetta's *Commentarii*, Francesco Cognasso in *Storia di Milano*, vol. 6, pp. 431–32, notes that the baker Giovanni Ossona and the butcher Giovanni Appiani were elected captains of the Ambrosian Republic in 1449. "Georgias Bisulcerus" is mentioned neither by Cognasso nor his fifteenth-century sources. See 2.2, below.

22. The marginalia identify "Karole" as Carlo Gonzaga. The descriptor *hic . . . orator* is identified as "Philelfus" in the margin.

23. Hercules (known as Alcides since his paternal grandfather was Alcaeus) was the son of Jupiter and Alcmena, who was married to Amphitryon, though she had been impregnated by Jupiter. So Hercules grew up with two fathers like Bisulcero.

24. Milanese jurist and longtime friend of Filelfo: see Biographical Notes.

25. Lines 1–4 and 173–188 seem to be spoken by schismatics adhering to the Council of Basel; see below.

26. The marginalia have placed here the name of Filelfo's addressee in its Latinized form "Nicolaus Arcimboldus" (Nicolò Arcimboldi). But it is more likely that Filelfo is referring at line 17 to the celebrated Peripatetic school philosopher Nicolaos (Nicolaus) of Damascus c. 64 B.C.–4 B.C., the court historian of Herod the Great who wrote a world history in 144 books and a panegyric of the young Augustus and who is mentioned in at least two books Filelfo knew well, Pliny the Elder, *Nat. Hist.* 13 and Athenaeus 14.

27. Lines 16–21: Filelfo refers here to other great sages, philosophers, and icons of wisdom in Greek and middle eastern antiquity — Minerva, the Persian Magi, Babylon, the Pythagoreans, Aegyptus, Indus, Atlas, and Dryades — all of whose names are in the margins of both autograph manuscripts. King Atlas of Mauretania was famed in mythology for his love of astronomy: Cicero, *Tusc.* 5.3.8.; Gallus was often cited as a priest of Cybele (Mart. 3.81; 11.74; Juvenal 8.176).

28. Adam is "that first father" and his name is placed in the margin by the writers of both *F* and *P*.

29. The reference is to Saint Peter.

30. The pallium was the cloak that Greek philosophers habitually wore; it was the badge of their profession. Here it is worn by Saint Paul.

31. Solon (c. 640–561 B.C.) was the famous Athenian statesman who founded the laws that led the way to the city's democratic constitution.

32. Pope Nicholas V (ruled 1446–1455): see Biographical Notes.

33. Probably Pope Eugene IV and the Council of Basel is meant. Eugenius was famous for his austere and monastic mode of life. The Council of Basel later abandoned its allegiance to Eugenius and became schismatic, choosing Felix V as pope in Eugenius' stead. Felix V eventually submitted to Nicholas V in 1449, bring an end to the schism.

34. Filelfo addresses Nicholas V.

35. Cardinal Niccolò Albergati, the saintly archbishop of Bologna, for whom Tommaso Parentucelli, later Pope Nicholas V, worked for twenty years; Parentucelli took the name Nicholas in honor of his patron. Albergati was the Cardinal of Santa Croce in Gerusalemme and his personal arms consisted of a red cross on a white ground; hence the reference to "the title and sign of the Cross."

36. Filelfo again addresses Arcimboldi; "the laws of the citizens and of the holy fathers" are the civil and canon laws, in which Arcimboldi held doctorates. Arcimboldi had been the representative of Filippo Maria Visconti to the Council of Basel; Visconti had favored the schismatic Council against Eugenius during the late 1430s and 1440s.

1.7

37. The name of Filelfo's addressee, "Brocchardus," appears in the marginalia, and just below it is written in the same hand "Franciscus Piccininus" and "Iacobus Piccininus." Persico Brocardo was secretary to the famous *condottiere* Jacopo Piccinino, who married Drusiana Sforza, the natural daughter of his arch-rival Francesco Sforza: see Biographical Notes.

38. For examples in classical literature of the trope of the deceptive appearance of the ocean see Filelfo's influential model, Horace's *Odes* 1.5 and 1.14.

39. Filelfo uses the word *daemon* (Greek *daimōn*), the Latinized term Socrates uses in the *Apology*, to signify the guiding spirit or god who directed his life.

1.8

40. *Podagra*, a rheumatic disease of the feet, legs, and hips, has a substantial pedigree in Roman satirical poetry where a connection between gout, moral depravity and sensual excess is assumed: see Horace *Ep.* 1.2.52, *Sat.* 1.9.32; Catullus 72.1; Juvenal 13.96.

41. On the four shifts in meter in this poem, see the Appendix.

42. Note Filelfo's Ovidian military imagery; more than a mere *miles amoris* (*Ars* 3. 565), Filelfo here has already been a "soldier of the marriage bed," "a warrior of nubile love," twice. He had married the daughter of his Byzantine teacher, Teodora Chrysoloras, in 1425 (d. 1441); his second marriage was to the Milanese noblewoman Orsina Osnaga, c. 1442; and c. 1453 he would marry his third wife, Laura Maggiolini. This seems to date the poem to sometime early in 1453 when our biographical sources state that he began to consider a third marriage; however, at lines 69–70 Venus states that the poet is not yet 52, which would date the poem to around 1450.

43. Venus has been talking (above) about her special power (*vis*) and the power of her sexuality; and here the meaning of *vis* as a primary life force in organisms follows Cicero's use of the word in the *De natura deorum* 2. 24 and *De divinatione* 1.128.

44. Note the conflation here of pointedly marital and martial imagery. *Concordare bene*, to contract a marriage or conclude a peace treaty, is the language commonly used for both kinds of agreements.

45. Neptune, god of the oceans, is also a fertility deity.

46. According to one tradition (Cicero, *De natura deorum* 3.54–55), Vulcan was the son of Nilus, a tutelary god-king of Egypt for whom the Nile river was named.

47. The manuscripts have written in the margins the name "Priapus," the Greek and Roman god of fertility, whose statue, featuring the deity's erect phallus, was often placed in gardens like a scarecrow to ward off birds.

48. This is an allusion to Filelfo's already numerous children by his first and second wives.

I.IO

49. This is a an allusion to the famous characterization of the hero of Virgil's *Aeneid* (1.10) that Filelfo's audience would have immediately recognized.

50. When the popular Ambrosian republic took power in Milan in 1447, a number of Milan's client cities defected to Venice, Piacenza among them. In November of that year Francesco Sforza occupied and sacked the city at terrible cost to its people.

51. The Eridanus is the classical name for the Po river.

52. In the margin next to *infestum virum* is written "Sfortia." Filelfo charges that the Milanese did everything they could to alienate Francesco Sforza.

53. Carlo Gonzaga, on whom see the Biographical Notes.

54. Moguntia is the German city of Mainz. The reference is to German mercenary troops.

55. See note on 1.1.189.

56. *Procul absit vulgus ineptum* (110) is a paraphrase of Horace's famous opening line from *Odes* 3.1, *Odi profanum vulgus et arceo* ("I hate the impious rabble and I keep them at a distance from me").

BOOK TWO

2.1

1. Compare Horace, *Odes* 1.12.1–2.

2. On Bianor, son of the prophetess Manto and the mythical founder of Mantua, see Virgil, *Eclogues* 9.60. According to legend, Manto was the daughter of the famous Greek soothsayer Tiresias; she married a man by the name of Tiberius and gave birth to Bianor.

3. In ascribing Etruscan origins to the founding of Mantua, Filelfo follows a long line of myth-makers from Virgil (*Aen.* 10.198–200; *Ecl.* 9.60) and Servius to Platina and Equicola. What this ode mainly seeks to do is to link Mantua's beginnings, and thus Carlo Gonzaga himself, with the great warrior figures of classical mythology: the first Gonzaga is said to

be a son of Mars; and both Gonzaga and Manto were companions of Hercules.

4. Lake Benacus, now known as Lago di Garda, near Verona, is mentioned by Virgil, *Georgics* 2.160 and *Aeneid* 10.205.

5. See note on 1.1.189.

6. According to Apollodorus 2.5.3, King Eurystheus commanded Hercules to capture a deer with the golden horn that was laying waste the countryside. The goddess Diana, however, caught the hero in the act of harming one of her herd and would have punished him had he not explained to her that he was only following orders.

7. This story appears to be a conflation of the familiar version of Hercules's third labor told in Apollodorus (Hercules's capture of the golden-horned deer and Diana's anger) and the story in Herodotus 4.9 of the Scythians' theft of Heracles's horses while he slept one bitterly cold night and his seduction by an unnamed female sorceress (half-snake, half-woman). The mother and daughter figures, Synesis and Iphis, have not been identified as figures in ancient literature; the Iphis of Ovid's *Metamorphoses* 9 is the daughter of Telethusa.

8. Her name means "wit" or "intelligence" in Greek.

9. *Ducit . . . socium / quem dedit partu Synesi creata / Iphis* (97–99): In this inverted characterization of Iphis's connection to Hercules, Filelfo seems to be aiming for an Ovidian, epic effect in syntactically foregrounding the act (*partu*) over the actors and the crucial role played by a newborn (*Iphis*) over the adult actors.

10. Cirrha is an ancient town near Apollo's shrine at Delphi, for which it is often used as a synonym, connoting the place where prophesies of future events are obtained: see Seneca, *Herc. Oet.* 92; Juvenal 13.79; Statius, *Theb.* 8.331.

11. Mercury was known as the grandson of Atlas; his fame stemmed from his invention of the lyre, a present of which he made to Apollo, rendering him a patron god of music and poetry. Mercury was also the renowned intermediary between the gods, men and the underworld.

12. The thought is reminiscent of Heraclitus, which Filelfo could have known from book 9 of Diogenes Laertius. "All things are in motion" (*cuncta moventur*) may be a translation of Heraclitus' famous dictum *panta rhei*, all things are in flux, known from Simplicius' commentary on Aristotle's *Physics* 1313.11 (Berlin corpus).

2.2

13. Maenalus is a mountain or mountain range in Arcadia, sacred to Pan; hence an image suggesting Arcadia and the tranquility of the countryside as opposed to the savagery of the city; see Virgil, *Eclogues* 8.22; 10.55; *Georgics* 1.17; Ovid, *Met.* 1.216.

14. See Robin, *Filelfo in Milan*, pp. 86–87, and 1.5, above. Between 1447 and the end of 1448 the leaders of the new Ambrosian republic in Milan were members of the aristocracy. But in the elections held in January, May and September of 1449, the popular faction won the majority of seats in the government and the three most powerful captains of the regime were a weaver's son, an artisan, and a notary: Giorgio Bisulcero (or Bizzozero), Giovanni Ossona, and Giovanni Appiani.

15. This concluding section of the poem appears to introduce Francesco Sforza as the savior of the Lombard city, preparing the way for the next poem (*carmen tertium*) which celebrates him as the city's new prince. On Sforza's military career and his rise to power, see Biographical Notes.

2.3

16. *Hadriae vires* (17), "the power of the Adriatic," refers to Venetian Republic and the Venetians.

17. Prior to the fall of the Ambrosian Republic and Francesco Sforza's accession to the lordship of Milan in 1450, the trajectory of Sforza's rise to power is marked by constantly shifting alliances, betrayals and counter-betrayals, on Sforza's own part as well his employers' in Venice and Milan. See Biographical Notes.

18. *Libertas simulata* (69): Note that Filelfo repeatedly refers to the corrupt revolutionary government that took over in Milan after Duke Filippo Maria Visconti's death as sometimes the *republica* and more often

the "false republic" or "false liberty" (*simulata* or *ficta libertas*), so that *libertas* (liberty, freedom) sometimes becomes a pejorative term.

19. Gaspar da Vimercate, soldier and statesman who led the revolt of the citizens against the leaders of the Milanese Republic: see Biographical Notes.

20. A hand in both *P* and *F* writes "Leonardo Venerio" in the margin. Venerio, the Venetian ambassador to the Ambrosian Republic, was murdered by a mob of Milanese citizens on the steps of the Palazzo d'Arengo on 25 February 1450 as he tried stop them from entering the palace. See Robin, *Filelfo in Milan*, pp. 88, 98. Resentment had been festering among the Milanese against Venerio, whom the public identified with the corruption and abuses of the Republic.

21. Liber is the god of wine and revelry; Ceres, the goddess of grain and fertility; Play, Revelry, Jesting and Pleasure are other standard personifications in Roman poetry. It should be noted that Liber, the Roman Bacchus whose name means "free," leads the procession of deities celebrating Francesco Sforza's liberation of Milan from the tyranny of the Ambrosian Republic. Sforza entered the city on 25 February 1450. It was Gaspare da Vimercate, long a Sforza partisan, who formally handed the city over. But his entrance only lasted one hour, after which he returned to Vimercate's camp outside the city. On 22 March Sforza entered the city again but only for a brief ceremonial appearance, this time accompanied by his son Galeazzo Maria and his wife Bianca Maria Visconti. On 24 March 1450 Sforza made final his return to Milan and on 5 June he inaugurated the reconstruction of the Castello (destroyed on the death of Filippo Maria Visconti at the inauguration of the Ambrosian Republic), now known as the Castello Sforzesco.

22. The marginalia identify "this man" (*is*) as "Andreas Biragus." Lubkin, *A Renaissance Court*, p. 325n, notes that Andrea Birago was a Milanese ambassador and principal *cameriere* to Filippo Maria Visconti. Birago is usually thought to have belonged to the pro-Sforza party, but Filelfo appears to be warning Sforza here against a betrayal.

2.4

23. Antiochus III ("the Great"; 223–187 B.C.), the third in a dynasty of Seleucid kings, was chiefly known for his conquest of Parthia, Bactria, Armenia, Syria, Palestine, and parts of India; he was definitively defeated by the Romans in 188. The examples of Pharaoh (from Exodus) and Antiochus suggest a caution against military overreaching or hubris.

24. The marginalia at line 51 identify the "Karolus" here as Charles, king of France ("Karolus rex Franciae"), i.e., Charles VII.

25. The Hundred Years War ended in 1453 and the English withdrew from France.

2.6

26. Count of Monteodorisio, chamberlain of Alfonso V and longtime friend of Filelfo: see Biographical Notes.

27. Alfonso V of Naples: see Biographical Notes.

28. *Consociumque thoro* (2): literally, companion or ally in the marriage or lover's bed. Given the light-hearted, erotic tone of this verse epistle addressed to Alfonso's secretary, the phrase suggests something like "companion in the game of love" or "in affairs of the heart."

29. Francesco Sforza himself had laid siege to Milan, cutting off all supply lines to the city from late 1448 to the city's final surrender to him at the end of February 1450. His blockade resulted in widespread famine which was followed by an outbreak of plague in the city that soon spread outside the city gates to neighboring towns and villages. See Biographical Notes.

30. Parthenope is one of the names by which such Roman writers as Virgil, Petronius, and Ovid, among others, called Naples, since the city was believed to have been built over the tomb of the Siren known by that name.

31. Iñigo must have been around fifty when he finally married. In 1439 Alfonso had unsuccessfully arranged a marriage for him with the noblewoman Enrietta Ruffo; another client of Alfonso's, Antonio Centelles, governor of Calabria, married Ruffo himself. Finally in 1452, with the

consent of Alfonso, Iñigo succeeded in marrying a noblewoman who was, perhaps, more propertied and younger, Antonella d'Aquino (d. 1493), who would bear him seven children and who supported numerous poets and musicians. See Biographical Notes.

32. In 1448, the fifty-four-year-old Alfonso fell in love with the eighteen-year-old Lucrezia d'Alagno (c. 1430–1479). On d'Alagno see the Biographical Notes.

33. *Saxea ne jaceas, sed contra umbone petentem / excipe* (55–56): Neither the OLD or J. N. Adams, *The Latin Sexual Vocabulary* (Baltimore: Johns Hopkins University Press, 1982) cites *umbo, umbonis* (m.) as a metaphor for the female pelvis or genitals, which it clearly signifies both in this passage and again in Filelfo's *Odes* 3.6.11–12.

34. Helios is often identified with Apollo. The Castalian maidens are the Muses.

35. Hesperus is the evening star (the star in the west); "far-away Hesperia" is Spain; "our Hesperia" is the western coast of Italy (see Virgil, *Aen.* 5).

36. Clio is not named in this verse but is identified in the margin.

37. The marginalia at lines 124–5 identify "Anglus . . . dux regum pater optimus" as Filippo Maria Visconti; it is found again at 3.9.40. The name "Anglus" was a toponym derived from the Visconti-ruled county of Anghiera near Lake Como; the Visconti added it to their family name in the thirteenth century.

2.8

38. Gaspar Castaneas does not appear in Filelfo's correspondence and has not been identified in modern studies. In any case, 2.8 appears to be another consolation letter to a Milanese acquaintance written in a vein similar to the preceding letter of condolence.

39. Maeonides is another name for the wandering poet Homer, who is supposed by some to have come from Maeonia; Solon (fl. 600–593 B.C.) was an Athenian statesman, lawmaker, and poet who championed the poor and a broader distribution of power among citizens.

40. Filelfo often consulted Diogenes Laertius's *Lives of the Philosophers* in which, in the life of Diogenes the Cynic philosopher (c. 400–323 B.C.), there are several anecdotes wherein Alexander the Great encounters Diogenes. In the famous one alluded to here, Alexander says that if he were not Alexander he would like to be Diogenes, the man who scorned all wealth and worldly aspirations.

2.9

41. 2.9 is the third in a trio of poems addressed to minor or unknown characters in the *Carmina* to whom Filelfo offers advice. The reference to the god Phanes (lines 8–9; see next note) tips this short verse epistle into an amatory mode.

42. The archaic Orphic god of love Phanes personifies the procreative force in the universe. References to Phanes occur in the Orphic hymns, which were among the Greek codices Filelfo brought to Italy from Constantinople in 1427.

2.10

43. Later in the poem the marginalia identify him as "Gaspar Mercatus": the nobleman Gaspar da Vimercate, who led the Milanese citizens' seizure of the Palazzo d'Arengo and the expulsion of the officers of the Ambrosian republic from the palace on 25 February 1450. On the next day Vimercate gave the order to lower the drawbridge at the Porta Nuova, thus ushering Francesco Sforza and his troops into the city.

44. Phoenix taught Achilles after the centaur Chiron. Whereas Chiron taught him the art of war and music, Phoenix taught him eloquence and accompanied him to Troy.

45. *Hadria* (120), *Hadriaticus* (the Adriatic sea, coast, etc.) are ordinarily synonyms for the Venetians and Venetian power and empire in Filelfo's poetry.

46. The names *Magnes, Phoebus, Jupiter, Aquila* are listed in the margin next to this strophe, suggesting that Filelfo has woven together several mythological stories here. Magnes discovered the magnetic properties of the lodestone by accidentally stepping on one. The *ales* clearly is "the bird

of Jupiter" (*Iovis ales aquila*) in Virgil's *Aen.* 1.394, which swoops down flapping his wings to welcome Aeneas on his triumphal entry into the city of Carthage. Moreover, Aeneas's welcoming *ales* is followed by a long line of birds, just as the birds in Filelfo's ode follow their king (lines 141–44). Lines 139–40 suggest that Jupiter's winged mascot procured the god's lightning from the fire of the sun god, Phoebus Apollo. Finally, the passage alludes to the Roman ritual of withdrawing and reinserting a scepter or sword into a rock at the declaration and conclusion of a war, on which see M. C. Howatson, ed., *The Oxford Companion to Classical Literature* (Oxford and New York: Oxford University Press, 1989), p. 308.

47. At line 141 the marginalia contain the identification *phoenix avis*, indicating that these lines allude to the myth of the resurrection of the phoenix, an Arabian bird that dies and is reborn (*regem renatum*) from its ashes (*post primae positum figurae corpus*) every 500 years (see Herodotus 2.73; Tacitus, *Annals* 6.28; and the Latin poem titled *Phoenix*, very popular in the Renaissance, ascribed to Lactantius). Thus Sforza's triumphal arrival in Milan is compared to Aeneas's in Carthage and the resurrection of the phoenix, which Lactantius treats as an allegory for the resurrection of Christ.

48. *Hic* (185) obviously refers to Gaspar and pulls him back into the poem from the above passage.

BOOK THREE

3.1.

1. Euterpe, the Muse of Music, the inventor of the flute and the guardian of all wind instruments, was usually said to be the daughter of Mnemosyne (Memory) and Jupiter, though Filelfo makes Apollo the father of the Muses (1.9.105 and elsewhere). The Gorgon is associated with the Muses through Pegasus, the winged horse and mascot of the Muses, who was born from Gorgon's blood when Perseus decapitated her. Pegasus is also associated with the Muses' spring, Hippocrene, whose fertile waters he was the first to discover on Mt. Helicon.

2. Charles VI (1368–1422) was king of France 1380–1422; when he died his son Charles VII (1403–1461) came to the throne, ruling France from 1422 to 1461. See Biographical Notes on Charles VII.

3. Cyprus is the mythological birthplace of Venus.

4. For the legend of the Trojan founding of France, see M. J. Heath, "Renaissance Scholars and the Origins of the Turks," *Bibliothèque d'Humanisme et Renaissance*, 41 (1979): 453–71, and R. E. Asher. *National Myths in Renaissance France: Francus, Samothes and the Druids* (Edinburgh: Edinburgh University Press, 1993).

5. "Dardanians" are Trojans. Filelfo's learned readers would be familiar with the epithet from the *Aeneid* if not the *Iliad*.

6. Virgil, *Aen.* 1.242–49: here Venus tells Jupiter of the Trojan leader Antenor's founding of Padua (*ille urbem Patavi sedesque locavit/ Teucrorum . . .*).

7. Another name for the lands near Lavinium, the city Aeneas was destined to found in Italy after his arrival from Troy, according to Virgil.

8. This passage recalls one of Filelfo's most frequently repeated themes, that the corrupt Ambrosian republic (the "rabid tyrants," as he calls them) had failed to commemorate Duke Filippo Maria Visconti's death with a period of public mourning and proper burial services and that this wrong would not be rectified until Francesco Sforza (supported in part by Charles VII) came to power. See Charles VII in the Biographical Notes.

9. René d'Anjou (1409–1480), duke of Anjou and brother of Charles VII, who long laid claim to the throne of Naples, challenging Alfonso of Aragon's right to the Kingdom; René was thus Sforza's ally against Alfonso before the Peace of Lodi (1454).

10. When the Turks sacked Constantinople in 1453, humanists all over Europe responded to the destruction and occupation of the Greek city that was regarded as the last bastion of Greco-Roman culture in the east; see James Hankins, "Renaissance Crusaders: Humanist Crusade Literature in the Age of Mehmed II," in idem, *Humanism and Platonism in the Italian Renaissance*, 2 vols. (Rome: Edizioni di Storia e Letteratura, 2003–

2004), 1: 293–424. The "French disaster" is probably the fall of Acre in 1291, which led to the final expulsion of the French from the Holy Land and the end of the Crusader Kingdom of Jerusalem.

11. Sigismund (1368–1437) was the king of Hungary and later Holy Roman Emperor (1410–1437). He was defeated by the Turkish sultan Bayezid I at the battle of Nicopolis in 1396, when leading a Christian crusading force that was attempting in vain to relieve the Turkish siege of Constantinople.

12. Saladin (1138–1192, the first sultan of Egypt) was a Muslim hero and leader in the Third Crusade. Having captured Jerusalem in 1187, he defeated the German emperor Frederick I, King Richard I (the Lionhearted) of England, and King Philip II of France in the third crusade. For the Latin title *amyras* or *amuras*, signifying sultan, king, or general, see Du Cange's *Glossarium mediae et infimae Latinitas* (1681 and many later editions).

13. Guy of Lusignan (d. 1194), a French knight who became king of the crusader kingdom of Jerusalem. He was decisively defeated by Saladin in the Battle of Hattin (1187).

14. John Hunyadi (1400–1456), Voivode of Transylvania, later regent of the Kingdom of Hungary, father of Mattyas Corvinus, won some brilliant victories against the Ottomans in the early 1440s.

15. Sultan Murad II (1404–1451).

16. See Horace, *Odes* 3.30.

17. *Tanti pietatis amore*: like all Filelfo's heroes, Charles resembles Virgil's Aeneas, "a man distinguished by his loyalty and sense of duty to family and state" (Virgil, *Aen.* 1.10: *insigne pietate virum*).

3.2

18. This eulogy which Filelfo dedicated to Carlo Gonzaga may have been later revised for use as his funeral elegy (he died unexpectedly in Ferrara on 20 December 1456): see Biographical Notes.

19. Manto is an Italian nymph, prophetess, and mother of Ocnus, who founded the city of Mantua. Ocnus's father was the Tuscan river Tiber.

20. A recurrent theme in Filelfo's *Odes* is the corruption of the city and the newly founded Ambrosian republic. Gonzaga defected to Venice in 1451, when the city of Milan, which lay in ruins at the end of the civil war, was seized by Francesco Sforza; he thus chose to disassociate himself from the Republic and what he may have viewed as the new tyrannical regime of Sforza.

3.3

21. *Vitrea bilis*: literally, glassy bile. Filelfo is clearly alluding to Persius 3.8: *turgescit vitrea bilis*. Horace uses a similar image in *Satires* 2.3.141 with a similar meaning. The *OLD* notes that *bilis* (bile) — whether characterized as *atra bilis* (Plautus, *Am.* 727; Cicero, *Tusc.* 3.11), *splendida bilis* (Horace, as cited), *luridae bilis* (Seneca the Younger, *Ep.* 95.16), or *vitrea bilis* — is generally used in Latin literature to suggest the causes or effects of madness, melancholy, anger or depression.

22. Lucrezia d'Alagno, noblewoman and mistress of King Alfonso: see Biographical Notes.

23. Filelfo left Milan for Naples ("Parthenope": see on 2.6.24) in July 1453. Having arrived in Rome on 18 July, he was lavishly entertained by Pope Nicholas V. He finally arrived in Naples on 1 August 1453, where he was received by Alfonso's chief secretary Iñigo d'Avalos. He brought with him a copy of his *Satyrae* and perhaps drafts of his *Odes* and his *Sforziad*. There King Alfonso made him a knight of the Order of the *Stola d'Oro* and crowned him Poet Laureate. While he was in Naples Filelfo attempted to effect a reconciliation between Francesco Sforza and Alfonso. Filelfo departed from Naples on the 24 August. All this took place against the background of the fall of Constantinople to the Turks on 29 May 1453. After Naples, Filelfo traveled to Rome, where he received an appointment as papal secretary, and then to Tolentino, where he assisted in finalizing a peace treaty between his native city and San Severo. He departed for Milan again on 21 September 1453.

24. The reference to Agnes with her fiery arrows and her domination of the King of the French alludes to Charles VII's long relationship with his mistress Agnès Sorel (1422–1450), a noblewoman born at Fromenteau,

France, who was probably the most influential of Charles's friends and advisors. She died suddenly — of poison, it has been conjectured.

25. The marginalia include the name "Iole," Hercules' last mistress, whom he brought home to his wife Deianira at Trachis. But Filelfo's reference sounds more like the story of Omphale, Queen of Lydia (Maeonia), to whom Hercules was given to serve as a slave. She dressed him in women's clothing to hide his presence in the household from her husband, according to some versions of the myth.

26. Filelfo alludes to the story of Mercury's grandfather Cronus's castration of his father Uranus with a jagged-edged sickle which his mother Gaia puts in his hands; see Hesiod, *Theogony* 173–180. We would expect Filelfo to allude to the grandfather of Mercury with Mercury in the genitive; but here the grandfather Cronus is conflated with the archetypal thief, liar, and trickster Mercury — certainly a god identified with various tools, instruments, and mechanical devices.

27. Priapus, whose name is written in the margin of one of the manuscripts, was the god of fertility and the deity most worshipped by the women of Lampsacus on the Hellespont, where he was born. According to Greek myth, Priapus was the son of Venus and Bacchus (some say Mercury or Adonis) whom the goddess bore at Lampsacus; he was so ugly that the goddess abandoned him at birth, but he was rescued by local shepherds. In Italy, statues of Priapus were placed in gardens to ward off birds: he is always depicted as a small, deformed character with an enormous erect phallus.

28. Some of the characterizations of married women, such as this one, come straight out of Juvenal, *Satires* 6.

29. In Filelfo's explanation here of what a woman wants, the legal language of marriage alliance (*foedere iungere*) is analogous to that of treaty-making in war,.

3.4

30. Filelfo may be addressing in this ode Ambrogio Trivulzio, who was a military captain of the Milanese state and also, briefly, of the Ambrosian

Republic; or he may be addressing here the city's patron saint, Ambrose. Note that in the margin "Ambrosius" is written with no surname.

31. Dis, another name for Pluto.

32. The Triones constellation: also known as the Bears.

33. The humanist scholar Pier Candido Decembrio (1399–1477), formerly Filelfo's rival at the court of Filippo Maria Visconti, was the chancellor of the Ambrosian Republic: see Biographical Notes.

34. *Cinaedus*, catamite, the passive partner in homosexual congress, more generally in invectives connotes effeminacy in a man, a type representing the antithesis of the ideal of Roman manhood.

35. Phalaris (c. 570–549 B.C.) was tyrant of Akragas, famous for the tortures to which he subjected his victims, among which was a bronze bull in which he roasted his captives alive.

36. Hannibal's eight-month siege and ultimate capture in 219 B.C. of Saguntum, a city in Spain allied with Rome, was considered the triggering incident of the Second Punic War.

37. The poem ends with the formulaic and yet ambiguous ablative phrase *sorte secunda*, which can be read as "if" or "since our lot (fortune or destiny) is favorable."

3.5

38. Florentine humanist and Hellenist friend of Filelfo: see Biographical Notes.

39. The reference is to Pythagoras (whose name appears in the margin), born in Samos c. 531 B.C., who according to legend instructed his disciples to maintain silence for years of meditation before they were permitted to address the master.

3.6

40. Count of Borgonuovo and natural son of Francesco Sforza: see Biographical Notes.

41. For *umbo* (lit. "shield") as a metaphor for the female pelvis or genitalia, see note on 2.6.55. *Decus* (12) refers perhaps both to Sforza's bride's womb and her virginity.

3.7

42. This short hortatory lyric poem is a companion piece to 3.6. As with 3.6, "Sphortia Secundus" is written in the margin to identify the addressee.

43. The Euripus is a channel between Boeotia and Euboea.

3.8

44. Lord of Rimini and famous *condottiere*; married to Francesco Sforza's natural daughter Polissena: see Biographical Notes.

45. *Variis . . . modulis* (4); *vario . . . carmine* (6): Note the poet's repetition (twice in this short prologue) of his plan to provide metrical variety in this most rhythmically diverse of all the *Odes*. Poem 3.8 is like a dance number with constantly shifting rhythms—a metrical tour de force containing thirteen meter changes.

46. From sunrise to sunset, from the Ganges to the Ebro (Iberus) river in Spain: i.e., it would take all day to recite Sigismondo's praises.

47. Polissena Sforza (1428–1449), Francesco Sforza's illegitimate daughter by Giovanna d'Aquapendente, married Sigismondo Malatesta in 1442; when Polissena died suddenly in 1449, Malatesta was accused of her murder.

48. I.e., Fortuna.

49. As opposed to goods of the body like health and goods of the soul, in Aristotle's famous division of goods.

50. Again, Fortuna.

3.9

51. In this letter Filelfo rebukes Gonzaga for his multiple betrayals: of his court poet (Filelfo); of Lyda, his lover; and of Milan, his adopted city and employer.

52. See note on 1.1.189.

53. Fictional character allegedly modeled on a longtime mistress of Carlo Gonzaga known as Dionisia: see Biographical Notes.

54. Carlo Gonzaga served Venice as its military captain from February 1452 through June 1453, when he was defeated by his brother Ludovico in the Mantuan territories Castelbelforte, Castel Bonfisso and Bigarello; see Biographical Notes.

3.10

55. Datable to June 1451. Plague hit Milan hard and peaked in the early summer and fall of 1451. Desperate to leave the city, Filelfo wrote Iñigo d'Avalos in Naples and other friends describing the conditions in the city and asking for help.

56. The son of Phoebus Apollo referred to here is Aesculapius (the name written in the margin by the author), the god of healing and the inventor of medicine, who is said to have expelled the plague from Rome in 462 B.C. by appearing in the form of a serpent and to have thereby saved the population from devastation. The story Filelfo refers to of Aesculapius's rescue of Rome *flatu* ("with a breeze," or possibly "with a breath") has not been identified.

57. The names of Oedipus and Jocasta appear in the margin to clarify the reference.

58. A reference to the famous opening of the *Iliad* 1, where Apollo, to punish Agamemnon, sent a devastating plague on the Greeks (Graiugenas) who were encamped outside Troy at the opening of the Trojan War.

59. In the margin are written *Thebae, Jocasta, Oedipus, Apollo*, and *Athenae* to specify that Filelfo is following Aeschylus' and Sophocles' versions of the Oedipus myth. Lines 23–25 allude to the opening scene of the *Eumenides* where an ailing Orestes has gone to the temple of Apollo at Delphi to pray for release from the Furies (carriers of plague, pestilence, and madness), who have afflicted him as the result of his matricide. Apollo instructs Orestes to go to Athens as a suppliant (*rogans*) and to ask the gods, Athena in particular, to help him.

60. The same formulation (*rapax milvus*, rapacious kite or ravening hawk) is also found in Martial 9.54.10, probably Filelfo's source.

61. Penates: a Roman family's household gods; thus hospitality, house or household.

62. "Father Paean" is Apollo.

63. Celsus, *De medicina* 3. 21, a Roman medical writer Filelfo would have known, defines dropsy as a disease in which the patient retains excess water, usually on the surface of the body, under the skin; the only cure according to Celsus is abstinence from all drink.

64. In the margin of F, Codrus is identified as Karolus Codrus Arretinus. Silvia Fiaschi has identified Filelfo's Karolus Codrus as Carlo Marsuppini, his rival and successor at the Studio Fiorentino (University of Florence), occupying the Chair of Greek after Filelfo. Marsuppini (1399–1453) was born in Arezzo; he was later a papal secretary and a Chancellor of Florence. In the Renaissance, Codrus is frequently alluded to as the contemporary of Virgil who criticized him (Virgil, *Eclogues* 5.11; 22; see also Juvenal 3.203) as an inferior poet, but who himself has nothing and is given nothing.

BOOK FOUR

4.1

1. Duchess of Milan and wife of Francesco Sforza: see Biographical Notes.

4.2

2. Francesco ("Cicco") Simonetta, humanist historian and chief secretary-treasurer of Francesco Sforza: see Biographical Notes.

4.3

3. The marginalia for this poem contain the name Lydus with no further identification. Lydus seems to be a fictional appellation for a character who personifies greed and moral corruption.

4. Enceladus, son of Titan and Terra, was in mythology the most powerful of the hideous Giants. They rose against the gods but were defeated by Jupiter. According to Virgil, *Aeneid* 4.179, Terra (Ge, Gaia, or Mother Earth) in anger against the gods gave birth to Fama (Rumor or Fame) as sister to Enceladus (*Terra parens . . . Enceladoque sororem progenuit*).

5. On gay culture in fifteenth-century Florence, see Michael Rocke, *Forbidden Friendships: Homosexuality and Male Culture in Renaissance Florence* (Oxford: Oxford University Press, 1996).

6. In 1426/7, when Filelfo returned to Italy from Constantinople, he brought back with him a twelfth-century codex containing Hesiod's *Works and Days* (now in the Biblioteca Laurenziana in Florence: Plut. 31.39). This was among the first manuscripts of Hesiod known in western Europe. According to the poet's advice to his brother Perses, there are three types of men: the first and best who decides for himself what is right and just; the second, who listens to a good adviser; and the third, who neither thinks for himself nor seeks prudent advice.

7. In his notorious diatribe *Against Timarchus* (345 B.C.), the Greek orator Aeschines ridiculed Demosthenes' political ally, Timarchus, as an effete sexual abuser of boys. Aeschines' speech in effect made the name of its target synonymous in antiquity with degeneracy. This would have been a recondite reference indeed, since Aeschines' orations were completely unknown until Filelfo brought them to Italy in a cache of Greek codices he bought in Constantinople in 1427 (see Introduction, at note 4); but note that manuscript *P* has *cinaedum* (catamite) for *Timarchum*.

8. *Fide Pelasga* (76): literally, a Pelasgian pledge, an epithet for the Greek people, who in Roman rhetoric were proverbially untrustworthy. See Virgil, *Aeneid* 2.106: *ignari scelerum tantorum artisque Pelasgae*.

9. Filelfo alludes to a complicated genealogy of tricksters and thieves united by ties of blood and marriage: Autoclus, father-in-law of Sisyphus, who according to some traditions was grandfather to Sinon, who (some say) was Ulysses' step-brother. Filelfo's sources include, certainly, Virgil, *Aeneid* 2 and, probably, Hyginus, *Fab.* 95.2, among others.

10. Traitors, like the Palamedes of Sinon's story in *Aeneid* 2.81–85, were always put to death.

11. According to Hesiod, *Theogony* 820–60, Typhon was a hundred-headed monster who terrorized the gods until Zeus destroyed him, sending him down to Tartarus for eternity.

4.4

12. Alessandro Sforza (1409–1473; lord of Pesaro, 1447–1473), was the younger brother of Duke Francesco Sforza. He served Francesco's eldest son Galeazzo Maria who became duke on his father's death. Alessandro was an avid book collector and humanist scholar, as was his wife Costanza da Varano.

13. *Ales* (winged one): Mercury is written in the margin.

14. Titus Manlius Imperiosus Torquatus (fl. 360 B.C.), a famous Roman hero who exemplified Roman *pietas* (duty to country and clan). When his son killed a Latin champion, Manlius Torquatus signed a warrant for his son's death. The example of Manlius and the exempla that follow are briefly recounted in Valerius Maximus 5.6.1–5.

15. Lucius Junius Brutus, consul in Rome in 509 B.C. Avenged Tarquinius Superbus's rape of Lucretia, wife of his fellow consul, by obtaining the exile of the Tarquin family. He had his two sons put to death for trying to restore the rule of the Tarquins in Rome.

16. Around 300 B.C., according to Roman legend, Marcus Curtius saved the Roman republic by leaping, in obedience to an oracle, into a huge pit which had suddenly opened in the forum, the so-called *Lacus Curtius*. Curtius plunged into the chasm on horseback and it closed over him, thereby saving the meeting place of the senate and Roman people.

17. The Decii, the father (Publius Decius Mus, c. 340–300 B.C.) and later his son of the same name, sacrificed themselves for the Roman republic by charging into enemy ranks and certain death. Both are legendary exempla of Roman *pietas*. Codrus, the legendary eleventh-century B.C. Athenian king, is said to have immolated himself in the same way after hearing that the Delphic oracle had prophesied that the Spartans would be victorious in their war with the Athenians if Codrus's life were spared.

18. Filelfo refers here to Giacomuzzo (Muzio) Attendolo Sforza, count of Cotignola (1369–1424). He was the father of Francesco Sforza, duke of Milan, and of Francesco's younger brother Alessandro Sforza, lord of Pesaro. Other than the Sforza dukes of Milan, Alessandro was the only member of the lineage to rule a state.

4.5

19. The narrative of this ode is an imitation of Horace's *Satires* 1.5, which describes the comical ups and downs of the two-week journey that the poet and his patron Maecenas made to Tarentum when they left civil war-torn Rome in 37 B.C. But whereas Horace's travel poem is in hexameters, Filelfo's is in the first Asclepiadean meter, as is Horace, *Odes* 1.1.

20. Lares: originally Roman farmland gods, later household deities similar to the Roman Penates.

21. Compare Horace, *Odes* 3.24.1–13, where Horace uses the phrase *dira Necessitas* (savage Need) and tells of the Scythians' escape from it in a *plaustrum* (wagon), a rather rare word in the sophisticated, urbane milieu of Augustan poetry. Compare also Horace *Odes* 1.35.17: here the exact words Filelfo uses in *Odes* 4.5, *saeva Necessitas*, are found in one manuscript tradition of Horace's *Odes*. In both these odes Horace personifies hunger, as does Filelfo.

22. *Fervor Apollinis*: the plague that raged between 1450 and 1452 in which some thirty thousand died in Milan.

23. Ceres and Liber, the goddess of bread and grains and the god of wine.

24. Comus and Iocus are gods of revelry.

25. *Arquitenens* (or *arcitenens*): a mock epic epithet usually applied to the Titan-like sun god Apollo; see Ovid, *Met.* 1.441; Virgil, *Aeneid* 3.75.

26. Filelfo uses the Greek word *theoleptici* here, designating prophets, soothsayers, or others divinely inspired.

27. Tithonus is the husband of Aurora, the goddess of dawn. The allusion, full of foreboding, is to Virgil, *Aeneid* 4.585: where the line *Tithoni*

414

croceum linquens Aurora cubile ("Aurora leaving the saffron bed of Tithonus") introduces the scene of Dido's self-immolation.

28. Aethon is one of the sun-god Apollo's horses.

29. The tax collector is identified in the margin as Johannes Piccolus (Giovanni Piccolo).

30. In this graphic description Filelfo depicts himself unrolling or unfolding the duke's huge vellum letter of safe passage and using it as a shield to protect his body while he argues with the tax collector.

31. Identified as Scaeva Cortis (Sceva Curte) in the margin.

32. Identified as Antonia Alipranda in the margin. Alipranda was the subject of the only letter in Filelfo's published Latin letters about his journey to Cremona in September 1451, addressed to Giammario Filelfo: see *Epistolae*, ff. 66v-67.

33. These lines echo Virgil, *Aeneid* 4.665–66, depicting the shouting, panic and grief that break out in the city after Dido is found dead.

34. Phoebus Apollo is, among other attributes, the god of medicine and healing. His "children" (*natis*, 113), here as elsewhere in the *Odes*, are the Muses: the spirit and inspiration for poetry and song without which Filelfo cannot work.

35. The major themes of humanist invective are all represented here in Filelfo's formal rant against the Cremonese: drunkenness, brutality, excessive anger, hostility to learning and the arts, avarice for material possessions. Filelfo here aligns himself with aristocratic culture (*omnia bona*: the humanities, virtue, honor, cultivation of the arts and learning) against plebeian inhumanity (*omnia mala*: savagery, gluttony, greed, envy and rage).

36. Cremona suffered from a succession of Roman colonizations and land confiscations from the end of the third century B.C. onward. Its land was confiscated for a new colony of Roman veterans in c. 41 B.C. (Virgil, *Eclogues* 9.28).

37. Possibly a reference to the famous humanist Bartolomeo Sacchi, called Platina (1421–1481), born in the village of Piadena near Cremona.

38. The Getae were a Thracian tribe who settled c. 300 B.C. on the lower Danube; later writers erroneously confused them with the Goths.

39. This formulation is illustrative of one of Filelfo's major thematic concerns in the *Odes*, i.e., the connection between sin and responsibility, on the one hand, and the meting out of punishment and rewards (judgment), on the other, leading to a broader consideration of the role of free will vs. fate.

40. The Filelfo family would have arrived in the countryside outside Cremona at the height of the harvest season.

4.6

41. "Baptista Alberthus" is written in the margin. Leon Battista Alberti was a writer, architect, satirist, papal official, and friend of Filelfo since their student days at the University of Padua: see Biographical Notes.

42. Filelfo uses the ancient name for the Po: Eridanus. Pavia, the ancient capital of Lombardy and the ceremonial capital of the Renaissance duchy of Milan, is on the Po.

43. Filelfo refers here to the long wars between the Visconti and Florence that lasted with various intermissions from the 1390s to the 1440s. The long hostility between Milan and Florence came to an end in 1451, when Cosimo de'Medici and Francesco Sforza formed an alliance between the two cities that lasted until 1494.

44. *Amor* (referred to alternately by Filelfo as *Cupido* and *Amor*) is here personified.

45. See note on 1.1.189.

46. Momus, the god of criticism, reproach, and satire, is as old as Hesiod (*Theogony* 214) and is a character in Lucian (*Jupp. Trag.* 19 ff.). In 1450 Alberti published his prose satirical fable, *Momus*, indebted to Lucian's dialogues; see Alberti, *Momus*, ed. Sarah Knight and Virginia Brown (Cambridge, Mass.: Harvard University Press, 2003), in this I Tatti series. Some contemporaries identified Alberti's architect-god Zeus with Pope Eugenius IV.

47. For the connotations of "Ethiopian" (*Aethiops* or *Aethiopicus*) see Juvenal 2.23, and parallel usages in Catullus, Cicero, Virgil, Ovid, and Petronius. In Latin literature *Aethiops* or *Aethiopicus* is metonymic for the illiterate, the uncultivated, the non-Italian, or the cultural other.

48. Lucian's Momus exemplifies the voice satirizing conventional moral philosophy (the various popularizations of Stoicism), while he mocks his fellow gods.

49. *Illecebrae nullae, deliciae minus:* Filelfo's imagery again suggests pleasures specifically sexual: see Cicero, *Pro Caelio* 12; Catullus 2.1.

50. An epithet for the winged god Mercury, god of money-making, trade, cunning, trickery, and oratory.

51. This Codrus is the legendary pauper Juvenal describes in *Satires* 3.203–11, who had nothing and therefore could lose nothing.

52. Herodotus 1.30–35 reports that when Solon (Athenian archon, reformer and poet, fl. 593 B.C.), who was renowned for his wisdom, visited Croesus, the king of Lydia (who was as renowned as Solon, not for wisdom but for his great wealth; fl. 540 B.C.), Croesus asked the wise Athenian whom he thought was the happiest man on earth, fully anticipating that he would name the king. Instead, telling stories that illustrated the instability of fortune, Solon's answer to Croesus was that no man could be counted happy until he was dead, since any man, no matter how rich, prosperous, or happy, might suffer a reversal of his good fortune at some point in his life, as indeed happened to Croesus at the end of his.

4.7

53. Mercury.

54. Compare Virgil, *Aeneid* 4.470–73. The passage suggests an analogy between Orestes' guilt and Cremona's.

4.8

55. Filelfo uses the Latin place-epithet "Maeonides" (the Lydian) for Homer; this toponym is also used by Ovid, *Amores* 1.15.9; Persius 6.11; Statius, *Silvae* 5.3.130; and Martial 5.10.8. In the margin "Homerus

Maeonides" is written. The themes in this poem bear a strong resemblance to those in 3.10.

56. I.e., Virgil.

57. See note on 2.6.24.

58. Filelfo uses the ancient Roman terms for the ducal secretaries and officers of the treasury.

59. Lycurgus (c. 775 B.C.), according to legend the founder of the Spartan constitution, among other reforms banned gold coinage and other metal currencies.

60. Filelfo presses his usual antithesis between the Muses and literature, on the one hand, and sexual love and the carnal passions on the other. He has already written about Alfonso's passion for his mistress, the noblewoman Lucrezia d'Alagno, earlier in Odes 3.3 and 3.10.

61. Filelfo clearly alludes here to Apollo, though the only name supplied in the margin is "Lucretia." Placidi, here translated "peaceful," can be translated a number of different ways, including "kindly," "indulgent," and "favorable," but "peaceful" seems most appropriate in light of Filelfo's ubiquitous use of Apollo in the Odes as the god in every way opposed to his antithesis Mars.

4.9

62. Since the whole opening passage sets the stage for the patron-client relationship Filelfo wants to establish for his visit to Alfonso's court, liberum is here rendered "free" or "independent," i.e., not subject of Francesco Sforza's rule.

63. By his use of canendo Filelfo seems to be referring to his current lyric work, the Odes, as opposed to the one hundred satires he has already finished writing.

64. The king is identified in the margin as "Sardanapolos," the last king of Assyria and ancestor of later rulers of Babylon, who was a legendary figure for his effeminacy, transvestitism, cruelty, excess and debauchery. He is said to have burned down his own palace (Cicero, Tusc. 5).

65. According to a gruesome story in Herodotus 1.205–215, Cyrus, king of Persia (fl. 547 B.C.), as a result of his own arrogance, was defeated in battle by Tomyris, the queen of the Massagetae, who then drank Cyrus's blood.

66. Alexander the Great (356–323 B.C.) died at the age of thirty-two after surviving a momentous mutiny of his own men the previous year. He is believed to have died of natural causes; but the second century A.D. Greek historian Arrian in his *Anabasis* (7.27) reports a number of variant accounts of Alexander's death, alleging that he was assassinated by his own men. Arrian's works were among the 300 previously unknown Greek codices that Filelfo's friend Giovanni Aurispa brought to Italy from Constantinople in 1423: see *Carteggio di Giovanni Aurispa*, ed. Remigio Sabbadini (Rome: Tipografia del Senato, 1931), pp. 10–15.

67. On Numa Pompilius (c.715–673 B.C.), the legendary second king of Rome who may have been an historical figure, see Livy 1.18–22. Noted for having championed and maintained peace rather than war, Numa is also credited with having established Roman religious practice.

68. On April 9, 1454, Sforza, Venice, and Florence signed a mutual defense treaty, the Peace of Lodi, excluding Naples. This was an act that gave deep offence to Alfonso, in particular because Venice had been at war with Naples since 1449, inflicting repeated damage on Alfonso on land and at sea. In January 1455, Alfonso finally became party to the Peace of Lodi. As noted in the Introduction, Filelfo was in the process of collecting the odes between the end of 1453 and the end of 1455 or the beginning of 1456.

69. The word Filelfo uses here is *regulus* (156), meaning a little king or ruler, not to be confused with the second-century B.C. republican hero Regulus. Note that in Filelfo's manuscripts names and places are always highlighted by being reproduced in the marginalia, which is not the case with this lower-case noun.

70. "Pious love" in Virgilian terms means loyalty and fidelity to one's family, friends, and allies.

71. *Sus Minervam [docet]* is proverbial in Latin for a situation in which the person giving advice knows far less than the one being advised: see Erasmus, *Adagia* I.i.40.

72. Invoking Horace's famous "Ship of State" ode (1.14) and its imagery, Filelfo here warns Alfonso, who had recently waged war with Florence, Venice, René d'Anjou, and Francesco Sforza, against the gathering winds of yet another futile war.

73. The adjective *Arctous* (from the proper noun Arctos, the northernmost constellations, the Big Bear and the Little Bear) can be translated as "northern" or "arctic."

4.10

74. See note on 1.1.189.

75. Phoebe, the goddess of the moon associated with darkness and the Roman goddess Diana, is named at line 15 and also in the margin. The marginalia also identify the obscure reference in the line that follows, to an unnamed *tristem et gelidum senem* (16), as Saturn, the Roman god (Kronos in Greek mythology) and early king of Latium in Roman myth; he is associated with "sowing" (*satus*) and also with blight.

76. In the years 1435–1443, René d'Anjou, the Angevin claimant to the Neapolitan crown, descended with his army into the Kingdom of Naples, attempting repeatedly to seize Alfonso's throne. Filelfo paints an accurate picture of Alfonso under siege from all sides.

77. *Stuprum* (rape, line 88) is a particular concern of Filelfo's. Book 2 of his *Sforziad* narrates the widespread incidence of rape and sexual abuse of women and children on the part of soldiers of the occupying army during Francesco Sforza's sack of Piacenza in 1447.

78. Juno, goddess of marriage: that is, marriage alliances could be concluded in time of peace without the threat of war being the driving force behind such arrangements.

BOOK FIVE

5.1

1. The Muse of tragedy.

2. This classical prooemium recalls Horace, *Odes* 1.1.

3. See Virgil, *Aeneid* 12.725 for a like passage on Jupiter and his scales.

4. The marginalia indicate that the poet refers here to two different enemies of the Italians: "Mahometus Arabs" and "Mahometus Turcus." The first is the founder of the Muslim religion, the latter Mehmed II, who in the first half of 1453, the probable date of this poem, was threatening "Thracian Rome," i.e., Constantinople.

5.2

5. What follows at lines 5–21 is a standard feature of classical rhetoric, the priamel (*hic . . . ille, alter . . . alter, sed tu. . . .*: one man does this, another that. . ., but you, etc.). Filelfo's model is Horace, *Odes* 1.1.

6. Here is the stock medieval metaphysical doctrine (*primum in aliquo genere*) that every genus models itself on some best example of the genus; see A. C. Lloyd, "Primum in genere: The Philosophical Background," *Diotima* 4 (1976): 32–36.

7. *Ingenium* (mind, intellect, talent, genius, one's particular nature), a complex notion difficult to translate in one word.

8. Senofonte, Filelfo's son, accompanied him on his journey to Naples in 1453.

5.3

9. Sforza Secondo (1433–1492), the count of Borgonuovo and illegitimate son of Francesco Sforza; see Biographical Notes.

10. Liber, the Italian god of wine, often appears with the epithet *pater*.

5.4

11. In these words attributed to Gonzaga, Filelfo adapts the Provençal genre of the *aubade*, a poem by a lover greeting the sun, to Latin elegy.

12. Filelfo here personifies *Pudicitia* (Chastity), a Roman cult figure with a shrine erected to her as early as 296 B.C.

13. Lyda uses here the expression *omne genus* to mark her status as not only a wife and daughter but a member of the female sex. See numerous examples in the OLD for *genus muliebre*, *genus mulierum*; and Seneca, *Phaed*. 564 where *genus* occurs by itself.

14. In 1451 Carlo Gonzaga defected from Milan and Francesco Sforza to serve as captain of the Venetian army; he remained in Venice until he defected to Ferrara in 1453; see Biographical Notes. So the original composition of this poem, like many of Filelfo's *Carmina*, can probably be dated c. 1451–1453.

15. The phrase *querulis modis* immediately suggests Roman and especially Ovidian elegiac verse, in which Lyda's letter to Carlo is set. Compare Ovid, *Pont*. 4.9.21; *Tr*. 5.1.60; *H*. 205; *Ep*. 5.73.

16. Neither Filelfo nor the marginalia name the divinity or divine quality (*illa*) that is called the progeny of *virtus*. It seems likely that he means *iustitia* or *probitas* (goodness, righteousness or probity), a favorite idea of his, to which he returns at the conclusion of this poem (line 121). *Illa* in these lines, however, recalls more significantly Filelfo's *Odes* 1.10.23–24: *Celsa quidem probitas firmis radicibus haerens, / vim monstrare suam*. . . .

5.5

17. Filelfo alludes to the Christian Platonic doctrines that creation is ontologically dependent on God and that time is the moving image of eternity.

18. *Trinus et unus* (48): the Christian god—the one—is comprised of a trinity of father, son, and holy ghost. *Trinitas* has been written in the margin.

19. Filelfo alludes vaguely to the well-known Augustinian doctrines that intellect and will are both involved in the return to God. See Robert J. O'Connell, *St. Augustine's Confessions: The Odyssey of Soul* (Cambridge, Mass., 1969).

20. "Mahometus" (i.e. Mehmed II, the conqueror of Constantinople) is written in the margins of the manuscripts next to these lines. In September 1453, after the fall of Constantinople to the Turks, Nicholas tried unsuccessfully to launch a crusade to take back the city from the Ottoman ruler.

21. Constantinople was often called "the new Rome."

5.6

22. The Lares are the Roman household gods; they are understood as ghosts of family members and as cult figures for clans and families.

23. Ludovico I of Savoy (1413–1465), Duke of Savoy from 1440 to 1465, Prince of Piedmont. Ludovico attempted to conquer Milan during the period of the Ambrosian Republic.

24. Martin le Franc (c. 1410–1461) was a famous French poet who worked in the court of Ludovico I of Savoy in 1451 and held the office of papal protonotary under Nicholas V. His most famous work was *Le Champion des dames* (1440/41), a work praising the deeds of women throughout history.

25. I.e., he had been trained in philosophy at Paris and was a poet.

26. *In aethera vectus apertum* (43): see *Aeneid* 1.155 and 1.587 where almost the exact phrase occurs in the same metrical position.

5.7

27. Basinio Basini of Parma (1425–1457), a prolific humanist poet at the court of Sigismondo Malatesta in Rimini. See Biographical Notes.

28. *Cyllenios* (3): an epithet for Mercury or Hermes, referring to his birth on Mt. Cyllene in Arcadia.

5.8

29. Humanist biographer of Francesco Sforza and brother of Cicco: see Biographical Notes.

30. Compare Virgil, *Aeneid* 6.852 ff., in which Anchises reveals to his son Aeneas his destiny and that of his descendants.

31. I.e., God's grace, not just virtue, is needed for salvation.

32. Filelfo invokes the well-known principle of mystical theology that purification precedes illumination.

5.9

33. Lodovico Gonzaga, lord of Mantua, brother of Carlo Gonzaga and longtime patron of Filelfo: see Biographical Notes.

34. The reference is to Homer's *Iliad*; Smyrna was one of the legendary birthplaces of Homer.

35. *Maeonides* (84): another term for Homer, Maeonia being yet another city where the poet, according to legend, was born. The hero Homer preferred to all others is identified as "Ulysses" in the margin.

36. Aeacides, the son of Aeacus, here specifically his grandson, Achilles, whose name has been written in the margin, along with the name Hector, son of Priam.

37. Gaius Fabricius Luscinus (fl. 282–272 B.C.), a hero of the Romans' war with Pyrrhus and a standard exemplar of virtue in later Latin literature, representing a bygone era in republican Rome when justice, frugality, and self-sacrifice prevailed. See Cicero, *Off.* 3.87; Horace, *Carm.* 1.12.40; Martial 11.2.2.

38. Attilius is identified in the margin as Marcus Attilius Regulus. Regulus (consul 267 B.C.) is another iconic figure from early republican Rome; his heroism and sacrifice are exemplified in Cicero, Horace, Livy, and Valerius Maximus. He defeated the Carthaginians, capturing Tunis in the first Punic war, but died a horrible death under torture in Carthage after he was captured in the Second Punic War c. 251.

39. Identified in the margin as Alexander the Great (356–323 B.C.). Alexander defeated the army of Darius, king of Persia, at Persepolis.

40. Christmas: the phrase "birthday of the king of Olympus" illustrates a typical humanist conflation of classical and Christian figures and holidays.

41. Lodovico's father, as noted in the marginalia, was Gianfrancesco Gonzaga (1395–1444), the first marchese of Mantua. He was known for

his military successes, his library of Greek and Latin codices, and his patronage of perhaps the most renowned of the early humanist teachers, Vittorino da Feltre.

42. Adriatic is regularly an epithet for the Venetians.

43. "Philippus dux" is written in the margin to identify this *anguiger* or snake-bearer as Filippo Maria Visconti, the deceased duke of Milan (d. 1447); the Visconti arms show a snake consuming a child.

44. Identified in the margin as "Nicolaus Picininus." The famous *condottiere* Niccolò Piccinino (1386–1444), a rival of Francesco Sforza, first served the Medici in Florence as the captain of their armed forces; he soon defected to serve Filippo Maria Visconti. As captain of the Venetian army, Sforza defeated Piccinino in the battle of Monteloro in 1443.

45. *Ethruscos* (138): Filelfo uses the archaic name for the Tuscans or Florentines.

46. Filelfo in *Odes* 5.9 all but suppresses Lodovico Gonzaga's sudden betrayal of his longtime colleague in arms, Francesco Sforza. See Biographical Notes.

47. In 183–4, Filelfo suddenly shifts into the highly stylized epic diction of Ennius and Virgil (*bellipotens; hostili turbine Romulida*). Sforza acquired the lordship of Cremona for the Visconti after the battle of Soncino on 16 March 1431. Cremona was given by Visconti to his daughter Bianca Maria as part of her dowry when she married Sforza.

48. Filelfo characterizes Lodovico here following two different classical traditions: that of Pallas Athena, the Greek goddess of wisdom (who also has associations both with war and the arts), and that of the Roman general Quintus Fabius Maximus Verrucosus Cunctator (consul 233 B.C.), who is famous for avoiding pitched battles, pursuing instead a strategy of waiting until his opponent exhausted himself.

49. In fact, after the battle of Caravaggio the "defeated men" persuaded Sforza to defect to Venice, and on 18 October 1448 he signed the treaty of Rivoltella, in which he contracted to lead the armed forces of the Republic of Venice; see Biographical Notes.

50. Terpsichore is the Muse of dancing and joyous poetry in contrast to Melpomene, the Muse of tragic poetry.

5.10

51. On the condottieri Malatesta Novello (lord of Cesena, 1418–1465) and his more famous brother Sigismondo Pandolfo Malatesta (lord of Rimini, 1417–1468) see Biographical Notes. Both Malatesta brothers (Sigismondo more so) were embroiled in the power struggles among Visconti, Sforza, the Gonzaga, and the King of Naples from the 1430s through the '50s.

52. A reference to the Peace of Lodi, signed April 9, 1454. The poem seems to have been written just before the peace was signed, in the last throes of the war between Milan and Venice.

53. Pluto, king of the Underworld, god of death and brother of Jupiter and Neptune. Here Pluto stands for war, and Neptune represents the Naples of Alfonso of Aragon, a great naval power, which did not embrace the peace of Lodi until 1455.

54. Mercury, the messenger of the gods, god of communication, trade and business, and the deity who conducts spirits to the Underworld after death. He is also the god of eloquence and elsewhere in the poem stands for diplomacy.

55. Gradivus, a surname for Mars: he who marches out.

56. The allusion to "Vulcanian cunning" refers to the mythological tale of Vulcan's catching of his wife Venus and her lover Mars with a net; the death could refer to Mars' murder of Neptune's son. According to the mythographers it was Neptune who had to persuade the gods to free Mars and Venus from Vulcan's trap.

57. Here "Alcippe Martis filia" (Alcippe, daughter of Mars) is written in the margin to identify the unnamed *virgo*. According to Apollodorus (3.14.2), Mars's daughter Alcippe was raped by Neptune's son Halirrhotius, whom Mars killed to expiate the offense committed against his daughter.

58. "Leo Venetus," the lion being the symbol of the Venetian government and Venetian power, is written in the margin at line 86.

59. "Vipera Sphortiana" is written in the margin at line 87. Francesco Sforza, Venice's former leading condottiere, now Duke of Milan, repeatedly engaged Venice in a series of battles for hegemony over the region (1452–55/6). After marrying Bianca Maria Visconti, Sforza quartered the Visconti serpent with his own arms, hence the "Sforzian viper."

Bibliography

Adam, Rudolf Georg. "Francesco Filelfo at the Court of Milan: A Contribution to the Study of Humanism in Northern Italy (1439–1481)." Ph. D. Dissertation, Oxford University, 1974.

Ady, Cecilia M. *The History of Milan under the Sforza.* London: Methuen 1907.

Albanese, Gabriella. "Le raccolte poetiche latine di Francesco Filelfo." In *Francesco Filelfo nel V Centenario della morte,* pp. 389–458.

Bentley, Jerry H. *Politics and Culture in Renaissance Naples.* Princeton: Princeton University Press, 1987.

Benadduci, Giovanni. "Prose e poesie volgari di Francesco Filelfo" and "Contributo alla bibliografia di Francesco Filelfo," both in *Atti e memorie della R. Deputazione di storia patria per le provincie delle Marche,* 5 (1901): 1–261 and 459–535, respectively.

Bianca, Concetta. "Alla corte di Napoli: Alfonso, libri e umanisti." In *Il Libro a corte.* Edited by Amadeo Quondam. Rome: Bulzoni, 1994, pp. 177–201.

Cognasso, Francesco. "Il Ducato visconteo e la Reppublica Ambrosiana." In *Storia di Milano,* vol. 6, pp. 3–448. Milan: Fondazione Treccani degli Alfieri, 1955.

Fiaschi, Silvia. "Prima e dopo la raccolta: diffusione e circolazione delle *Satyrae* di Francesco Filelfo." *Medioevo e Rinascimento,* 14 (2000): 147–65.

Filelfo, Francesco. *Epistolarum familiarum libri xxxvii.* Venice: Gregorii de Gregoriis, 1502.

———. *Satyrae I. Decadi I-V.* Edited with an introduction and notes by Silvia Fiaschi. Rome: Edizioni di Storia e Letteratura, 2005.

Francesco Filelfo nel V Centenario della morte, Atti del XVII convegno di studi maceratesi Tolentino, 27–30 settembre 1981. Padua: Antenore, 1986.

Garin, Eugenio. "La cultura milanese nella prima metà del XV secolo." In *Storia di Milano,* vol. 6, pp. 545–608.

Gualdo Rosa, Lucia. "Il Filelfo e i Turchi." *Annali della Facoltà di lettere e filosofia, Università di Napoli*, 11 (1964–1968): 109–65.

Hankins, James. "Renaissance Crusaders: Humanist Crusade Literature in the Age of Mehmed II." In *Humanism and Platonism in the Italian Renaissance*, 2: 293–425. 2 vols. Rome: Edizioni di Storia e letteratura, 2003–2004.

Lubkin, Gregory. *A Renaissance Court. Milan under Galeazzo Maria Sforza.* Berkeley—Los Angeles—London: University of California Press, 1994.

Luzio, Alessandro and Rodolfo Renier. "I Filelfo e l'umanesimo alla corte dei Gonzaga." *Giornale storico della letteratura italiana*, 16 (1890): 119–217.

Martines, Lauro. *Power and Imagination: City-States in Renaissance Italy.* New York: Alfred A. Knopf, 1979.

Poeti latini del Quattrocento. Edited by Francesco Arnaldi, Lucia Gualdo Rosa, Liliana Monti Sabia. Milan-Naples: Ricciardi, 1964.

Robin, Diana. *Filelfo in Milan: Writings, 1451–1477.* Princeton: Princeton University Press, 1991.

——. "Humanist Politics or Vergilian Poetics?" *Rinascimento* 25 (1985): 101–25.

——. "Reassessment of the Character of Francesco Filelfo." *Renaissance Quarterly* 36 (1983): 202–24.

——. "Unknown Greek Poems of Francesco Filelfo." *Renaissance Quarterly* 37 (1984): 173–206.

Rosmini, Carlo de'. *Vita di Francesco Filelfo da Tolentino.* 3 vols. Milan: Luigi Mussi, 1808.

Ryder, Alan. *The Kingdom of Naples under Alfonso the Magnanimous: the Making of a Modern State.* Oxford: Clarendon Press, 1976.

Santoro, Caterina. *Gli Sforza.* Milan: Dall'Oglio, 1968.

Welch, Evelyn S. *Art and Authority in Renaissance Milan.* New Haven: Yale University Press, 1995.

Index

❧❧❧

Lower-case roman numerals refer to pages in the Introduction; multipart arabic numbers refer to book, poem, and line of the English translation of the *Odes*. Notes are referenced by the book, poem, and line number to which the note number refers (e.g., 1.3.29n20).

Jocasta, 3.10.19n57
Jocus, 2.3.126
John VIII Paleologus, Emperor, ix
Jouvenel des Ursins, Guillaume,
xiii
Jove, 3.3.44, 4.9.110, 5.5.11, 5.6.43,
5.9.217
Julia family, 3.3.93
Julius Caesar, 1.10.82, 2.6.31,
3.1.45, 5.2.31
Juno, 1.9.97, 4.9.95n78, 4.10.95
Jupiter, 2.1.130, 3.1.12n1, 3.1.23,
3.3.30, 4.1.20, 4.10.15, 5.2.36,
5.2.81, 5.10.14n53, 5.10.46,
5.10.103–111; poem dedicated to,
2.2. *See also* Zeus
Juvenal, *Satires 2*, 4.6.25n47; *Satires
3*, 3.10.100n64, 4.6.57n51; *Satires
6*, 3.3.70n28; *Satires 8*,
1.6.20n27; *Satires 13*, 1.8.1n40,
2.1.105n10

Lactantius (attrib.), *Phoenix*,
2.10.144n47
Lacus Curtius (Rome), 4.4.25n16
Ladislaus, King of Poland, ix
Lampsacus, 3.3.50n27
Landino, Cristoforo, xx
Lares, 4.5.4, 4.5.4n20, 5.6.12,
5.6.12n22; of Gauls, 3.1.79
Latium, 2.3.44, 3.2.13, 3.8.25,
4.1.99, 4.9.185, 5.9.132
Laurentine fields, 3.1.91
Lavinium, 3.1.91n7
Le Franc, Martin, 5.6.34n24,
5.6.34–50
Lethe river, 1.10.84

Liber, 2.3.125, 2.3.126n21, 3.1.43,
4.5.30, 4.5.30n23, 4.10.44,
5.3.2, 5.3.2n10. *See also* Bacchus
liberal arts, consolation of, 1.2
Libya, 3.9.6
lion, 3.1.54–57; Marmarcian,
4.5.130; Venetian, 3.9.59,
5.10.86n58
Livy, *Books 1–5*, 4.9.101n67
Love, 4.6.10
love and marriage, xvii–xviii; ad-
vice on, 3.3; praise of, 5.2; re-
marriage, 1.9
Lucian, *Jupiter Tragoedus 19ff*,
4.6.17n46
Lucullus, 1.7.94
Ludovico I of Savoy, 5.6.21,
5.6.22n23, 5.6.33, 5.6.34n24
Ludus, 2.3.126
Lycurgus, 4.8.52, 4.8.52n59
Lyda, 3.9.51, 3.9.73–97, 5.4
Lydian mode, 1.1.161
Lydians, 5.6.11
Lydus, invective against, 4.2n3, 4.3
lyre, invention of, 2.1.153n11
lyric meters, 1.1.74
Lysias, ix

Macedonians, 5.6.13
Maecenas, 1.10.78
Maemo of Siena, 1.2.2n18; poem
dedicated to, 1.2
Maenalus, Mount, 2.2.26,
2.2.26n13
Maeonia, 5.9.69n34
Maeonides, 2.8.16
Maggiolini, Laura, xxii n5, 1.9.7n42

Publication of this volume has been made possible by

The Myron and Sheila Gilmore Publication Fund at I Tatti
The Robert Lehman Endowment Fund
The Jean-François Malle Scholarly Programs and Publications Fund
The Andrew W. Mellon Scholarly Publications Fund
The Craig and Barbara Smyth Fund
for Scholarly Programs and Publications
The Lila Wallace–Reader's Digest Endowment Fund
The Malcolm Wiener Fund for Scholarly Programs and Publications